NO HIDING PLACE

The New York Times

Inside Report on the Hostage Crisis

NO HIDING PLACE

ROBERT D. McFADDEN, JOSEPH B. TREASTER and MAURICE CARROLL

WITH

Lawrence K. Altman, M.D., John Kifner, Drew Middleton, Terence Smith, & Steven R. Weisman

Introduction by A.M. ROSENTHAL

Times BOOKS

Published by TIMES BOOKS, a division of
Quadrangle/The New York Times Book Co., Inc.
Three Park Avenue, New York, N.Y. 10016

Published simultaneously in Canada by
Fitzhenry & Whiteside, Ltd., Toronto

Library of Congress Cataloging in Publication Data
Main entry under title:

No hiding place.

   Includes index.
   1. Iran Hostage Crisis, 1979-1981 — Personal narratives. 2. Iran Hostage Crisis, 1979-1981 — Addresses, essays, lectures. I. McFadden, Robert D. II. Treaster Joseph B. III. Carroll, Maurice
E183.8.I55N55   1981   955'.054   81-14527
ISBN: 0-8129-0980-1   AACR2

Manufactured in the United States of America
10 9 8 7 6 5 4 3 2

PREFACE

No Hiding Place is the story of the American hostage crisis in Iran. It is based on hundreds of interviews with hostages and members of their families, government officials, diplomats, military officers and others who played roles in the unfolding drama.

Part I, drawn from personal narratives of the hostages themselves, is the "inside" story of what happened in Iran: the takeover of the United States Embassy in Teheran on November 4, 1979, and the experiences of the hostages in the ensuing 14½ months of captivity in Iran. It is the product of detailed interviews by *The New York Times* with 20 of the hostages, information from four others at news conferences and accounts provided by 14 hostages to other news organizations.

Part II is the "outside" story of the crisis, a series of articles illuminating key decisions and turning points. These include the United States decision to admit the Shah of Iran for medical treatment; the story of that medical treatment; the decision to preserve the hostages' lives, even at the expense of the national honor; interviews with and accounts of the Iranian captors and stories of the raid that failed to free the hostages and of the negotiations that finally succeeded.

The term "Persian" rather than "Farsi" is used throughout the text in referring to the language of the Iranian people. Debate over this usage continues, with legitimate points made on both sides. Some Iranians regard "Persian" as having colonial overtones, but it is the preferred expression in English, "Farsi" being the Iranian term for the native tongue.

Contributions to the story of the American hostages were made by the following staff members of *The New York Times*:

B. Drummond Ayres, Josh Barbanel, James Barron, Francis X. Clines, John II. Crewdson, Karen DeWitt, Clyde Haberman, Robin Herman, Donald Janson, Robert Lindsey, Iver Peterson, Timothy H. Phelps, William M. Robbins, Lynn Rosellini, Nathaniel Sheppard Jr., William K. Stevens, A.O. Sulzberger Jr., Philip Taubman, Matthew L. Wald, Carolyn Weaver

Editing: Roger Jellinek, Howard Angione, Irv Horowitz, Carolyn Lee
Research: Cary Kenney, Linda Amster
Chronology: David Karpook

We would also like to express our gratitude to Sam Summerlin, who conceived of this book project and provided invaluable guidance in its production.

The Authors

CONTENTS

Part III — The People

Introduction

Somehow, the country did not want to ask many questions. The home-coming seemed enough — the joy of the return, the sense of relief, the pride in the conduct of 52 Americans, perhaps the expiation (well, we couldn't get you out but see how happy we are to get you back), certainly the very act of touching hands in celebration, the national sense of com-munity — all that seemed quite enough. And there was a reluctance to let go, even when the yellow ribbons began to look a little dreary in the wintertime.

The new President had a message for the hostages — that's how they'll always be known, even in freedom. Your jobs are waiting for you, he said; turn the page. That's what the country wanted, too, to get on with it.

There were a few questions here and there, more like musings, touches of embarrassment, asked mostly to get them off the chest rather than in expectation of any real answer.

You mean that's all there is to it, the Iranians are going to get away with it? And what happens if somebody grabs another embassy some-place? And what about the boys who came back from Vietnam — where were their parades and yellow ribbons? And what about the boys who didn't? And the eight who died in the raid?

It was rather strange that there were so few questions when it ended. For 444 days the country had been moved, angry, frustrated and *quite* full of questions about what happened, what went wrong, what was going on. The taking of the hostages had become not only a nagging part of everyday life but had helped bring about the defeat of one President and the installation of another with a very different view of society and government.

All during those days, the people of the country struggled with the meaning. Some thought it was a national humiliation. Others thought it was about time we found out we were weak and did something about it. There were some who had said, during the captivity, that it showed we were powerless in a new world and others who had insisted that the problem was not lack of power but a lack of guts in the White House.

Nobody knew exactly what it all meant. But Americans told each other just to wait until it was all over, then we'd find out why the helicopters crashed in the desert, why we went in and failed or why we didn't go in earlier or why we went in at all, why our friends didn't do more, who was to blame. There were plenty of questions, but people seemed to agree that we couldn't talk about it much until the hostages were freed — then we would demand and get answers.

But when it was over, in a country where words like "full-scale inquiry," "smoking pistol," "cover-up" had become part of the national vocabulary, there were few questions raised and no answers volunteered.

Almost nobody examined the points of decision or even asked what they were, although they were plain enough to see. In the pages that follow, these points of decision will be explored.

The decision to support, over decades, a man who turned out to be detested by his people. The decision to let him into the United States — compassion or stupidity? The decision, when the embassy was taken, that the lives of the hostages were more important than anything else, a decision that would have been taken by few countries. The decision to try to negotiate with kidnappers, rather than use force. Then the decision to use force, but timidly, almost fearfully, with a built-in military timetable for aborting, a timetable for failure.

Then the decision not to talk about it much for months, followed by the decision to make it very much a part of the political campaign and to talk about it a lot, at moments of political choice.

There were some rather desultory hearings, but neither the Congressmen who asked questions nor the Carter Administration diplomats who answered them seemed interested in probing deeply. The whole attitude seemed to be the same as President Reagan's: Turn the page.

There were reasons, of course, why so few penetrating questions were raised, why there was so little inclination to look backward.

To start with, there seemed to be little to gain. For a full-scale, deeply prepared and tough-minded inquiry to take place, there has to be a strong political motivation or strong public pressure.

The Democrats certainly did not want that. The Reagan Administration wanted to focus American attention on itself, not on an Administration that had lived briefly, failed and died.

All that Congressional and television and press scrutiny would have taken away from the President and focused on the past at the very moment he was trying to lead the country down new roads.

What's more, any major inquiry would have forced the Reagan Administration and the Republicans to come up with some pretty good answers as to what they would have done differently.

Maybe they had some ideas. If so, those were some of the best-kept secrets in American history. But even if they did, what point in surfacing them?

If there were other revolutionaries having thoughts about seizing American embassies, let them wonder what the new American Government would do, what it meant by its statement that there would be punishment, not negotiations.

There is another kind of inquiry, the never-ending inquiry of self-examination, which is the most important kind. It can come out of a sense of desperation. *Why* must we be prisoner to foreign oil and where is our independence going?

Or, even more painfully, it can come out of self-loathing — the questions that will never end about Vietnam, why we fought as we did and did not fight as we might, and why, having done what was done, we turned against our own American victims, the Vietnam veterans.

While it is the task of journalists to continue to probe and push, there is no fire in the American belly or misery in the mind for an official inquiry into the hostage crisis.

There are those who talk about guilt in the national psyche, who feel that because we were stupid enough and insensitive enough and callous enough to support a despotic Shah that we are responsible for the crimes against us of an equally despotic Ayatollah.

It won't work. The Shah was our mad fool and the Ayatollah is theirs, and both are destined for equally glorious places in world history.

But, having put investigation and guilt aside, there remains perhaps the most fascinating question. It is not what this tells of the Ayatollah and the Shah and Iranian terrorists but of ourselves.

We are not simply what we appear to be. But what we appear to be is indeed a large part of what we really are.

I read that somewhere a couple of years ago and it stayed with me. It means so many things, some of them rather frightening.

It means that there really is no hiding place, that the mask becomes the face. You may protest and say, "No, it is not I," but it is, or in large enough truth to matter. You can fool all of yourself some of the time; but if you fool all of yourself all of the time, you are smashing mirrors.

It is a frightening thought, if you are miserable with yourself as an individual or as a nation. It is exhilarating if you feel there's a little hope left. It means that others do matter, that decency is quite as important and real as meanness, that neatness counts and there is always one more choice to be made. As we are, so we acted during the hostage episode, and as we acted, so we are.

For instance, quite level-headed and dignified, fairly reticent. We were different, in our emotional response, from our national caricature — a caricature is not what we appear to be, but what we are falsely made out to be — of a country full of bluster and elbow, of overweaning ego and loud noises.

Our emotions were deep, but we muted them publicly because we felt it was in the best interests of the hostages to do so — and anyway we weren't quite sure what we would do if we had our choice.

The fact is that there is remarkably little stomp and bluster in American international posture, given our strength. Perhaps Vietnam did that for us, perhaps we were less overbearing than we thought. Compared with the Russians, we are modest; compared with the French, positively demure.

The United States is a nation that sees itself as believing in law and order, and that is how we behaved. There were "Nuke Iran" bumper stickers, but they were not on the cars of the judges who ruled that Iranians had exactly the same rights in this country as anybody else.

Americans put a lot of store in the individual and we acted that way during the hostage crisis. That may be less a question of virtue than of good fortune.

If you are born in India and live in a society where millions have died of starvation or religious warfare or typhoon and where a man's labor is less valuable than that of a good ox, it takes more strength to believe in the value of the individual.

The hostages were individuals to Americans, and it was the realization that they were indeed individuals — each one by each one — that was the base of American policy for months, and its weakness. What if your child were there, would you go in and bomb Teheran or storm the embassy?

Some other characteristics also showed up that were not quite as attractive as dignity, faith in the law and belief in the individual. We like to think of ourselves as independent-minded, but we often seem to be follow-the-leader. And if we seem to be, we probably are, in some measure.

During the days of captivity, when we were told that saving the lives of the hostages was the paramount value, we accepted that without much question or discussion.

Then when Mr. Carter decided to send in the helicopters, which probably would have resulted in the death of many of the hostages, the only real fault we found was that the mission failed.

We were told that the capture of the hostages was one of the most important issues in the world. But we were agreeable when the government said or did little for months because it lacked the wit or the strength to do anything much.

We agreed that it all must be taken out of politics. But it was obvious during the campaign that the Carter Administration regarded the entire hostage affair as make or break, politically — and millions of Americans voted against Jimmy Carter because they believed it really was part of politics of the most essential sort, the politics of leadership.

And for all our sentimentality we are often seen as being quite unknowing and uncaring about the sentiments and needs of others. During the hostage crisis we showed that, too — plainly.

It was one thing for us to refuse to "apologize" to a mad dictator for our support of his predecessor. It was another to fail to understand that the Iranian passion was not based simply on the Ayatollah's rhetoric but on a deep hatred for a Shah we had supported and whose police, with the United States saying not a word, had tortured and killed thousands of Iranians.

We simply could never understand that 52 Iranians were as important to other Iranians as 52 Americans were to other Americans, and that a lot more than 52 Iranians had been killed by our own client, the Shah.

We still don't seem to get that point, not as a matter of guilt or excusing the hostage taking. But it is important to comprehend it in order to understand what took place.

Why was it all so important to us? More people die in fires or in automobile accidents or in plane crashes — many, many times more. Why the anger, the sense of mourning for those 52, who after all were government servants and expected to take risks when they served abroad?

Partly because of compassion, certainly, and partly because of embarrassment — here were these crazy, wild-eyed Iranians making the United States look like a clown.

But mostly, I believe, we mourned because there was a feeling in this country until the 444th day that it was not just the 52 but all Americans and, worse still, our very government that had been taken captive and held hostage in that embassy.

No amount of reticence, logic, patience, or understanding could assuage that sensation, ever.

There are countries and civilizations that treat victims with contempt and hatred. Stalin shot Soviet prisoners of war or put them in labor camps. In primitive societies the wounded were left in the open to die. The victim is often seen as unclean.

INTRODUCTION

The hostages, as we all knew, were honorable and faithful men and women who had done their duty, but they were essentially victims. And this country greeted them with love.

That was part of the American character revealed: compassion for the victim.

But that compassion could not extend to the leader taken prisoner.

That is why Mr. Carter had to go. He had been taken and could not free himself.

At least, it is to be hoped that the kidnappers of the world are aware of the fact that all future leaders of the United States will closely study the fate of the captured President.

A.M. Rosenthal

PART I

Inside

1

November 4, 1979

The first streaks of pearl daylight crept out of the great Iranian Salt Desert, brushing the slopes of the Alborz Mountains and racing down into the nearly deserted streets and narrow alleyways of Teheran. It was not cold for midautumn. Temperatures hovered in the low 50's and a gentle wind scythed over the silent city. But decks of clouds stretched to the horizon and dawn came bleak and unpromising to the Iranian capital. "It was a gray, drizzly, overcast day," Richard Queen, an American consular official, recalled. It was Sunday, November 4, 1979, and for dozens of Americans it was a day from which there would be no hiding.

On the broad avenue of Takht-E-Jamshid, a downtown thoroughfare that had been renamed Taleghani Avenue after a revered cleric of the Islamic revolution, a throng of 450 angry young demonstrators appeared outside the United States Embassy compound, as it had for days, at about 7:30 A.M. and took up its chant:

"Death to the Shah!"

"Death to Carter!"

"Death to America!"

The admission of the overthrown Shah of Iran, Mohammed Riza Pahlevi, to the United States for cancer treatment two weeks earlier, on October 22, had been generating increasingly hostile daily protests outside the yellow-brick walls of the parklike embassy compound.

American flags had been burned. Clubs had appeared. The protesters' curses had grown louder and more vile. Now, the crowd's rage had reached a fever pitch. Many members of the embassy staff were openly uneasy.

Moorhead C. Kennedy Jr., a Harvard-educated economics specialist and one of the mission's highest-ranking diplomats, was in his office on the second floor of the chancery, the main embassy building, as the seething crowd shrieked outside.

"I remember standing in a window and looking down on all the noise and anti-American anger," he said. "And I wondered to myself what it would be like to die."

Three hours later, a Marine guard burst into Kennedy's office and shouted: "Everybody downstairs! There's a break-in!"

Screaming protesters had breached the great wrought-iron main gates and were pouring over the walls at various points. Some waved clubs and sticks and a few carried pistols. Huge posters of the Ayatollah Ruhollah Khomeini bobbed on poles as the crowd went wild.

"I looked out again as we left," Kennedy said, "and saw this sea of fanatical faces and heard these voices. They were like — they were lowing for death."

It was the opening cry of an organized assault that was to become the most flagrant violation of diplomatic standards in modern history, the seizure of an embassy and a 444-day siege that would scar the lives of scores of American hostages and their families, transform the United States and Iran into warlike enemies and rally Americans together in a sense of outrage and national purpose that had not been seen in years.

The story of the embassy takeover and of the hostages' life in captivity is an account of men and women who explored the limits of their endurance in an ordeal that led to several attempted escapes and at least two attempted suicides.

It is, in many respects, an ugly story. No hostage reported being subjected to systematic torture, mutilation or sexual abuse. But all were mentally or physically maltreated and many came home with bitter feelings for their Iranian captors. Some also have spoken ill of the clergymen who visited them in captivity, of the Carter Administration, the

Iranian revolution and, reflecting the tensions of their ordeal, of one another.

Some were subjected to beatings, mock executions and episodes of Russian roulette. Others were put through daily indignities and cruel humiliations. All were blindfolded and bound or handcuffed to chairs for weeks at a time. A few endured the agonies of months of solitary confinement in dank, windowless dungeons and dark closets. Most suffered deprivation, in which conversation, fresh air, exercise, news, mail and showers were forbidden.

Many evolved the kinds of resourcefulness well known to prisoners: the use of toilet paper and wastebaskets as secret communication links; nicknames and words of contempt for captors in codes and languages the Iranians did not understand; a Marine's morale-boosting cartoon drawings; arm-wrestling matches between one hostage and a guard, and hours spent teaching English and other subjects to captors.

For most, however, there were endless days of boredom, loneliness and doubt, of bad food, filthy living conditions and numbing routine relieved only by books, playing cards, solitary thoughts and occasional conversations with, or outbursts of defiance against, their captors.

Slowly they learned to cope with captivity. Some cooperated with their captors, others resisted. Most fell somewhere in between. Hard feelings between those at the extremes appear, in retrospect, to have been inevitable in the climate of fear and uncertainty that prevailed.

From the standpoint of the hostages, the captors, too, evolved. Their early masks of rage and cruelty gradually softened into faces of men and women with goals, desires, faults and opinions from politics and revolution to cookery and culture, and with personalities that ranged from brutal to friendly and, at times, even compassionate.

The hostages' story is, finally, a tale of enormous complexity, a tortuous odyssey of 52 to 66 Americans held for up to 14½ months by hundreds of Iranians in dozens of places in addition to the embassy, including apartments, homes and jails in Teheran, Tabriz, Qum, Isfahan and other cities, villages and rural areas. Some of them were moved as many as 24 times.

It is clear also that the story is not complete. Some hostages have declined to discuss particular experiences; some have refused to talk at all about their life in captivity.

NO HIDING PLACE

Because the captivity unfolded over so many months, the hostages — deprived of watches, calendars, nearly all news and all but brief and occasional glimpses of the outside world — recollect their experiences less in day-to-day events than in personal dramas of suffering and crushed hopes: days of unforgettable terror, unannounced moves to new places of imprisonment, melancholy holidays and, in the last months, taunting mirages of freedom.

But for all, the day of the embassy takeover will be etched in memory for years to come.

The United States Embassy in Teheran is an imposing setting, even by the luxurious standards of the diplomatic world. It is a sprawling, 27-acre compound of trees, lawns and some 25 buildings crisscrossed by paths and driveways and surrounded by 8-to-12-foot walls secured by a number of metal gates. The compound is roughly a rectangle with a chunk shaped like an upside-down "L" missing on the northwest corner.

It is set amid elegance and ugliness in a city of more than four million people dating to ninth-century Persia, where civilization flourished when Europe was barbarian. To the north of the compound, broad avenues lined with tall trees stretch away into successively wealthier communities, with the richest in the northern suburbs surrounding the Niavaran Palace, once the Shah's principal residence. The peaks of the Alborz Mountains shimmer in the northern background.

Immediately south of the embassy rises Teheran's dazzling downtown skyline of palaces, monuments and skyscrapers, where the exquisite swirls and blues of ancient Persian buildings contrast sharply with the dull geometric shapes of modern glass and steel office towers. Bars, cabarets and movie houses that once dotted the downtown area are gone, swept away by the Islamic revolution. Posters of Ayatollah Khomeini frown from the walls. There is a somber air on the boulevards where fashionable Western dress and elegant shops once lent Teheran a European flavor. Now, the fashionable shops are gone or converted to more practical purposes. Men in turbans and green revolutionary fatigues are common in the crowded business district. And the faces of Iranian women are once again shrouded under traditional chadors, the long, dark, hooded garments dictated by the morality of Islamic culture.

Farther to the south, beyond the downtown area, lie Teheran's fes-

6

tering slums, a vast panorama of tin-roofed shanties and mud-walled huts, where hundreds of thousands of poor people live amid open sewers, crowded alleys and teeming bazaars. Plumes of yellowish smoke rise from nearby factories, casting a pall over the area.

In the center of the city, the United States Embassy is one of dozens of foreign legations, but it is by far the most impressive in Teheran. It is, in fact, one of the biggest and best appointed diplomatic missions in the world. Where embassies in other capitals sometimes occupy a large building, or even a whole block, the American compound in Teheran covers the rough equivalent of 25 city blocks. Its sheer size, let alone the array of electronic equipment it once held, is a reflection both of the great favor the United States enjoyed in prerevolutionary Iran and of the enormous strategic importance the United States attached to its once-secure anchor of military bases and listening posts in the Persian Gulf and along the southern rim of the Soviet Union.

The main buildings in the compound are the chancery, the embassy's principal office structure, which is a 90-room, two-story brick bastion near the center of the south wall near the main gate; the consulate, another two-story building, on the western perimeter; the mansionlike residences of the ambassador and his deputy, both set amid rolling and wooded lawns on the eastern side of the compound; a 10-story apartment building for embassy visitors, at the northern wall; and, just to the south of the apartment building, a warehouse whose windowless basement was known among staff members as the "Mushroom Inn." Barracks, guardhouses, a commissary, a radio tower, staff offices and several utility buildings dot the grounds.

By the autumn of 1979, the size of the staff had been cut drastically from the days when the Shah was in power, from hundreds of officers, attachés and lower-level personnel to only about 65 Americans, including a handful of security people to keep up a shadow of appearances.

Like most embassies, the compound was a militarily indefensible position anyway. But now, just 13 Marine guards with light arms and a few civilians were responsible for the security of an area the size of a small town, surrounded by a mile-long wall.

Sundays are working days in the Islamic world, and November 4 began as had many earlier days, both inside and outside the compound. The skies were glowering, but the customary smog that hangs over Te-

The Seizure:

When the invasion of the United States Embassy began on the morning of Nov. 4, 1979, not all of those who were soon to be held hostage were in the compound. Kathryn L. Koob and William B. Royer Jr. were at the Iran-America Society and L. Bruce Laingen, Victor L. Tomseth and Michael Howland were at the Iranian Foreign Ministry.

1: A crowd began gathering outside of the main gate at 7:30 A.M. The invasion of the grounds began between 10:15 and 10:30 A.M. **2:** Perhaps as many as 45 Americans were in the embassy's main building, the chancery, at this time. **3:** At least 14 other members of the staff were in the consulate. **4:**

Four others were in an apartment building at the north end of the complex. **5:** As the gravity of the situation became evident, a group of about 10 Americans locked themselves behind steel doors in the east wing of the chancery and began shredding documents and smashing electronic equipment. **6:** At the consulate, orders had been received to evacuate the building. Several groups left the area in the rear of the embassy grounds, encountering no resistance at first. One band of about six, including Richard I. Queen, was soon captured but five other consular officials found successive havens first in private homes and then at the Canadian Embassy. They escaped from Iran in January 1980.

7: In the first days and weeks of captivi[ty] nearly all of the hostages were housed in [the] ambassador's residence, where they we[re] bound to chairs or handcuffed and blindfol[ded] 24 hours a day. **8:** Toward the end of Nove[m]ber, several of the Americans were moved t[o a] warehouse basement that had been convert[ed] before the seizure into a barracks. The[se] quarters were dubbed the Mushroom Inn. Other hostages were kept in several small st[aff] houses on the grounds, as well as in the ch[an]cery and several other buildings scatter[ed] over the 27-acre site.

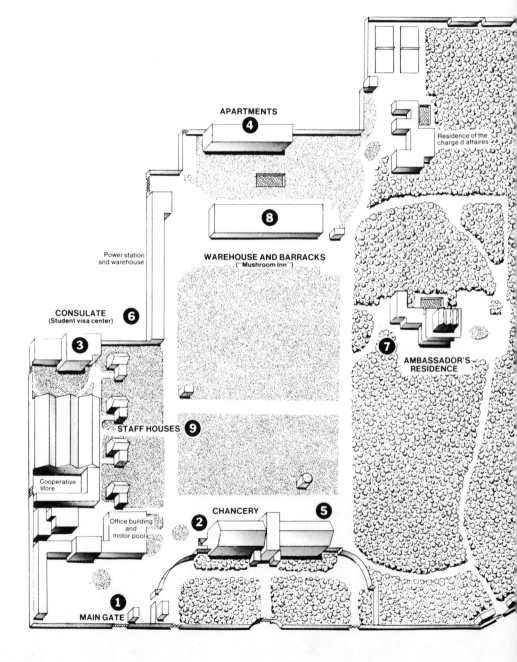

the chancery,

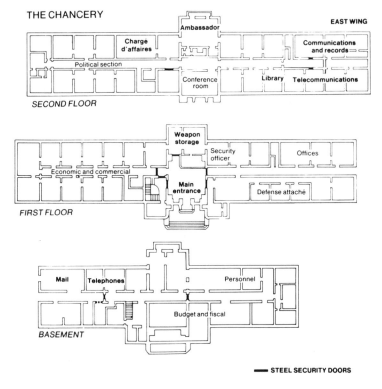

THE CHANCERY

Ambassador

EAST WING

Chargé d'affaires

Communications and records

Political section

Conference room

Library

Telecommunications

SECOND FLOOR

Weapon storage

Security officer

Offices

Economic and commercial

Main entrance

Defense attaché

FIRST FLOOR

Mail

Telephones

Personnel

Budget and fiscal

BASEMENT

▬▬ STEEL SECURITY DOORS

heavy front doors at the main en-
ce on the first floor were bolted
by marines. Cpl. Westley Wil-
s and several other marines
an prying open a case of rifles,
guns and pistols kept on the first
r. The work of destroying secret
sensitive data went on behind
l doors in the east wing of the
ond floor.

e Iranians finally got inside the
ncery by ripping out the bars on
ement windows with a truck.
e time before noon, they began
our into the basement. Corporal
ams and Sgt. John D. McKeel Jr.
the invaders on a staircase and
tear gas. They backed upstairs,
bbing more weapons from the
e and joined the other Ameri-
s on the second floor.

hile most of the embassy's per-
el faced imminent surrender, 10
bers of the staff continued
dding material in the top-secret
room in the communications
records section. Somewhere be-
n 3 and 3:30 P.M., an Iranian
er, realizing that some Ameri-
s were still in the vault, held a
to the throat of one of his hos-
s and threatened to kill him un-
those in the safe room.surren-
The chancery had fallen.

0 miles 200

Caspian Sea

SOVIET UNION

Tabriz

Teheran

Meshed

Qum

IRAN

Tabas

AFGHAN.

Isfahan

Ahwaz

Abadan

Kerman

IRAQ

KUWAIT

KERMAN

Persian Gulf

SAUDI ARABIA

PAK

Gulf of Oman

heran had been swept away by early morning breezes as the embassy personnel arrived for work, many from apartments elsewhere in the city. They were joined by dozens of Iranians who served in clerical posts and as translators and guards.

Relations between the United States and Iran had badly deteriorated in the previous year, and one result was that the top-ranking officials of the embassy were not present on the day of the takeover. A new United States Ambassador, Walter L. Cutler, had been named the previous April to succeed William H. Sullivan, but his selection had been rejected by a new Iranian Government anxious to register its displeasure with Washington. Cutler had never taken up his post.

The embassy was under the direction of a chargé d'affaires, L. Bruce Laingen, a 57-year-old career Foreign Service officer. But on the morning of the takeover, he and Victor L. Tomseth, the senior political officer and the embassy's second-ranking diplomat, had driven with Michael H. Howland, a security officer, to the Iranian Foreign Ministry on Foroughi Avenue, little more than a mile to the south, to discuss continuing diplomatic problems and the status of some American military officers at the embassy.

That left a group of six section heads — the third tier of the administrative hierarchy — nominally in charge. The six were Moorhead Kennedy, the acting economic counselor; Richard H. Morefield, the consul general; Air Force Col. Thomas E. Schaefer, the defense and air attaché; Army Col. Charles W. Scott, chief of the defense liaison office; Bert C. Moore, the administrative counselor, and John E. Graves, the public affairs counselor.

With so many people nominally in charge, there was, in fact, no clear chain of command and no one was actually in charge of the embassy. Security was in the hands of Col. Leland Holland, an Army officer who held the title of chief of embassy security, a relatively low rank on the staff's table of organization.

Kennedy, a 49-year-old veteran of nearly two decades of diplomatic service, had been posted to Teheran only two months earlier, but had witnessed an alarming deterioration in American-Iranian relations in his short tenure. In recent days, high Iranian officials had told him that the militant students who were staging the daily demonstrations outside the embassy could no longer be controlled.

NOVEMBER 4, 1979

The embassy had repeatedly warned the State Department, after the former Shah was hospitalized in the United States, that the situation was getting out of hand and that Iran could not be relied upon to protect the embassy in case of attack, Kennedy said. The warning was ignored. Indeed, instead of reducing the embassy staff in the face of the mounting danger, Kennedy said, the State Department kept adding to the staff. More and more newly posted members were arriving in Teheran each week. "One of our people went into captivity suffering from jet-lag," Kennedy said.

Of the State Department's refusal to confront the warning signals, Kennedy said, "That was a fundamental mistake." Allowing the Shah into the United States had given the militants the excuse they were seeking, he noted. "We threw a burning branch into a bucket full of kerosene."

As Sunday morning wore on, the menace from the demonstrators outside the walls seemed to grow, and staff workers inside watched with mounting concern. Some were ordered to lock their safes and office doors.

But it was too late. The invasion began between 10:15 and 10:30 A.M.

"To put it bluntly," said Sgt. James M. Lopez, a 21-year-old Marine guard, "all hell broke loose and we couldn't stop it."

Dozens of Americans — perhaps as many as 45, but in any case most of the embassy's personnel — were trapped in the chancery when the mob, armed with sticks, lead-pipe clubs and a few pistols, rushed into the compound.

Elsewhere on the grounds, at least 14 members of the embassy staff were in the consulate; four others were in the apartment building inside the north wall and three were in the warehouse. A few Americans were outside the embassy compound. To many, it was unclear what was happening or what the Iranian demonstrators intended to do.

"We did expect the possibility that they would come over the wall and burn some buildings, but it was low on the list of possibilities," said Duane L. Gillette, a 24-year-old Navy petty officer involved in low-level intelligence work. "The fact that it happened just showed that we were unprepared."

At the chancery, the heavy front doors were bolted shut by Marines

9

who retreated from the main gatehouse and got inside just as the crowds rushed up the steps and began pounding to get in. As he fell back, Cpl. Westley Williams, 22, pulled out his walkie-talkie and radioed a warning to all security personnel in the compound.

Embassy personnel trapped inside the chancery, meanwhile, were ordered to high-security areas behind heavy steel doors on the top floor of the two-story building.

Several of the trapped Americans should not even have been there. Elizabeth Ann Swift, a political officer, was supposed to have been on vacation but had cut short a visit with friends on a farm in Iran and had returned only the night before. That morning, she had intended to accompany Bruce Laingen and Victor Tomseth to the Foreign Ministry, but she had called Tomseth at the last minute and had begged off.

William F. Keough, the 49-year-old head of the American School in Islamabad, Pakistan, was visiting the embassy. He had run an American school in Teheran before the fall of the Shah and had come back to pick up some books he had left behind. "It was just a fluke," he said.

Donald R. Hohman, an Army medic, said that mere chance accounted for his presence, too. "I nearly never got captured at all," he said. "The day it happened, I'd just finished hiring a Pakistani nurse for a job in the dispensary at the compound. Another guy there, also a nurse, asked me to come over to his apartment in town. I considered doing that, but then decided that I had a little more work to do. I remember telling the guy, 'I'll just stay here.' I'll never forget saying that. So I stuck around the embassy and just a couple of minutes later all hell broke loose. They busted right in on us."

Looking out windows from the second floor, some of the Americans saw a bedsheet banner with a message in English suggesting that the demonstrators wanted access to the building only to stage a sit-in.

Meanwhile, several Marines, including Corporal Williams, who had put on flak jackets and helmets, began prying open a case of rifles, shotguns and pistols on the ground floor of the chancery. They also carried tear gas grenades.

Alan B. Golacinski, the embassy's regional security officer, reached Bruce Laingen by radio just as the chargé d'affaires was leaving the Iranian Foreign Ministry. Laingen decided to stay at the Foreign Ministry rather than return to the besieged embassy. "It was clear at that point," he said, "that I could not ever have gotten there physically."

To minimize bloodshed, Laingen ordered that no guns be fired at Iranians. Later, when it became apparent that the invaders intended to seize the compound, he ordered the destruction of secret documents. No shots were fired and only tear gas was used in what proved to be a delaying action to give the document-shredders time to work. Corporal Williams recalled that Golacinski had asked Laingen's permission to go outside to try to persuade the demonstrators to disperse. The corporal thought it was a harebrained idea, but Golacinski went out and, moments later, apparently became one of the first hostages.

Soon afterward, Moorhead Kennedy looked out a second-floor window and saw Golacinski being led around outside with his hands tied behind him. "Golacinski was outside yelling in to us to surrender, that resistance wouldn't work in the long run," Kennedy said. "We were delaying. We didn't know there was a pistol at his head."

In the east wing of the chancery's 30-room second floor, activity by American and Iranian employees was feverish. This wing — consisting of the political and communications sections and, in an inner sanctum at one end, the vault and safes containing top-secret documents — was sealed off by steel security doors *(at position "A" on diagram for second floor of chancery)*.

A group of about 10 persons, following contingency plans, opened the 6-inch-thick steel doors of the high security vault *(at "B" on diagram for second floor of chancery)*, unlocked the safes and began shredding papers. At this point, they were destroying material that was something below the level of top-secret. "That's standard for anywhere, once you realize that something's going to happen and something might be compromised," said one worker who had been in the vault. Later, after Laingen gave the order, they began shredding top-secret documents, smashing electronic equipment and feeding codebooks and other secret data into grinders, the worker said.

They worked calmly. "These are older people you're talking about, with a lot of good heads on their shoulders," he added.

Others in the sealed-off outer offices manned radios and telephones, calling Washington to report what was happening and Iranian Government officials to try to get help. Iranian officials were either unreachable or unresponsive, but before the lines went dead some calls got through to the State Department. "Washington asked how long we could hold out and I replied, 'Until hell freezes over,' " said Charles Jones Jr., a communications specialist. "At the time, I thought we could."

John W. Limbert Jr., a political officer, got a line through to the office of Prime Minister Mehdi Bazargan. "I kept saying to the man on the phone, 'What are you going to do?' And they kept saying that help is on the way — sort of like, 'The check is in the mail.' And I kept saying 'But what are you going to do? They're coming through the windows.' "

The Iranians, in fact, were coming through the windows. They got into the chancery by rolling up a truck, attaching chains to the bars of basement windows and ripping them away. Sometime before noon, the invaders began pouring into the basement.

"There were between 300 and 500 of them and they came in like water over a dam," Jones said. The embassy personnel, he said, "kept moving to higher floors, like people trying to escape a sinking ship."

Corporal Williams and another Marine, Sgt. John D. McKeel Jr., under orders not to fire, met the invaders on a stairway, leveled their shotguns and started backing up. Two tear gas grenades were set off and the Marines donned masks as gas began billowing through the area. Sergeant McKeel sprayed one attacker in the face with chemical Mace.

Remembering the crated weapons on the first floor, the Marines ran upstairs and grabbed armfuls of rifles and shotguns and fled toward the second floor as the shouting invaders moved up from the basement.

Donald Hohman found himself cut off as the Iranians rushed onto the chancery's main floor. "I tried to get out a door leading to the rear of the embassy," he said, "but before I could cover much ground, they grabbed me and pretty soon blindfolded me."

On the top floor, the weapons-laden Marines reached the secure east wing. They were admitted, and Iranian employees were let out through the big steel doors. The Iranian employees were apparently not harmed and were allowed to go. The Americans, however, were trapped. There were closed-circuit television cameras inside, enabling the Americans to see what was happening outside the secure doors. But what they saw did not help.

At least one bound, blindfolded hostage, possibly Golacinski or perhaps Hohman, was being held in front of the television camera. Over a hand-held radio that had been taken from Golacinski, an Iranian told those inside that the hostage would be killed if they did not open up. It was sometime between noon and 1 P.M. The Americans had lost track of the time.

With the bulk of the group facing imminent surrender, 10 Americans, including Jones and Jerry Miele, a communications officer, and others who agreed to discuss what happened only with a promise of anonymity, locked themselves in the top-secret vault room at the far end of the wing and continued shredding material.

Frederick L. Kupke, a 34-year-old communications officer and electronics specialist who is one-quarter Kiowa Indian, had been in the vault shredding documents, but at the last minute, when the vault was locked, he decided to stay out. He grabbed an armful of shotguns and climbed an interior ladder to the roof, intending to hide the weapons from the militants.

The decision to surrender "just happened," according to Kennedy. "No one was really in charge," he said. "And anyway, to hold out longer wouldn't have changed things."

The outer doors swung open but the Iranians, eyes watering from the tear gas, did not rush in. Instead, they hesitated outside as one of their leaders decided what to do next.

"They had a guy at the door who seemed like he was pretty organized," said Sgt. Rodney V. Sickmann, a 22-year-old guard who had been in Teheran only a month. "He told everybody to stay back, and he told one person to come out at a time. So he grabbed us as we came through, put our hands behind our back and tied us with a plastic rope and blindfolded us."

The militants then began searching the eight-room, high-security area. They spent some time at the task before realizing that the vault room in the back was locked and that Americans were apparently inside destroying documents. Efforts to burn through the big doors with a blow torch failed.

Then, an Iranian leader grabbed a hostage, held a knife to his throat and threatened to kill him unless those in the vault surrendered. "It was now about 3 or 3:30 P.M.," Jones said — others agreed on the time — "and most of the classified documents had been destroyed." Before coming out, the last holdouts put all their weapons and the few remaining classified documents into several safes in the vault and locked them up.

The militants, finding all the available documents shredded and the safes locked, were enraged. They attacked some of the holdouts.

"They kicked me in the ribs, stepped on my hands and held a gun to my head," Jones said. "They wanted to know why I was helping Americans. They thought that as a black man I should be on their side. They said the papers belonged to the people of Iran, not to us."

Mixing polemics with blows, the Iranians "kept telling me that they were not angry with the American people, only the American Government," said Jones. "I tried to tell them that the government was elected by the people. They said 'No, it was elected by the Rockefellers and the Kissingers.'"

Others in the vault also were beaten, and some were threatened with guns and knives.

Kupke, who was still on the roof, waited a while until the violence subsided somewhat. Then he jumped down the ladder and surrendered. His hands were black from tar on the roof and grease from the shotguns he had carried up there, and the militants noticed it and demanded to know why. To steer them away from finding the weapons, he said the smudges were soot from having burned documents. That got him into worse trouble and a terrifying episode ensued. Kupke was beaten and threatened with a gun and a knife.

"They wanted the combinations to some of the safes," Kupke recalled. "I was kicked and knocked down on the floor. There were two or three guys on each leg and a couple of guys on each arm. One of them pulled out a knife, a pretty good-sized pocket knife. The guy in charge said, 'Open up the safes.' I said I couldn't. He said, 'If you don't we'll cut your eyes out,' and I said, 'I can't.'"

"The other guy," he said, "then put the knife blade against my eye — the bottom of my eye, and I proceeded to squirm and tried to convince them that that wasn't the thing to do. I was really scared."

Kennedy, a mild-mannered scholarly man, was horrified. "They got Kupke and started really beating and kicking him," he said. "They were trying to get the safe combination from him. They played Russian roulette with a pistol against his head. But poor Kupke couldn't give them the combination. It had been shredded."

There was more to it than that. There were several safes, and Kupke knew the combinations, or thought he did, but he wasn't sure he could remember them all with his life on the line. "If I did open one and couldn't open the others, it would have been worse then," he said. Apparently, however, they believed him: he was badly beaten but not mutilated.

Another of the holdouts in the vault, who asked to remain anonymous, said he had one safe's combination coded on a piece of paper in his wallet. A militant searching him found the scrap, but did not realize what it was. "Then he took a bill of lading, which was absolutely meaningless, out of the wallet and kept that," the holdout related. When he was alone later, the hostage said, he ate the paper bearing the combination.

Much later, the hostages would learn that their heroic efforts to protect the safes had been futile. The Iranians eventually just drilled out the locks.

Sgt. John McKeel also was beaten, apparently because he had sprayed Mace in the face of one of the invaders downstairs.

After these assaults, Jones said, "We were blindfolded and hoods were placed over our heads. We were then led out into the hallway and forced to face the wall or kneel or sit."

As militants began scouring the embassy premises, the new captives were pulled into the hallway, searched, bound with plastic tape and blindfolded. Then they were taken outside, where large crowds were screaming and chanting: "God Is Great!" "Long Live Khomeini!" and an array of anti-American vituperations.

Donald Hohman vividly recalled the moment:

"They took me to the outside of the embassy, removed the blindfold and made me face what looked to me like at least two million screaming Iranians. They were yelling, 'Death to the Americans!' over and over and over and over until it was like an earthquake, there was so much vibration from the noise.

"It sounded like the walls were going to come down on top of me. The whole building was shaking. I have never been so terrified of anything in my whole life. I must have turned white all over with fear. I muttered to one of the guards, 'Please, please take me back inside.' And pretty soon they did. But even so, I could still hear that screaming and feel the embassy vibrating."

Finally, the blindfolded hostages were marched across the embassy compound to the ambassador's residence. As they stumbled along, Kennedy said, some of the captors whispered in their ears: "Vietnam. Vietnam." Kennedy said he began to whistle "Rally Round the Flag," a catchy patriotic tune with overtones of the cavalry coming to the rescue. Other hostages picked it up as they moved across the grounds to the mansion. There, they were distributed to various rooms, tied to chairs and told to keep silent.

For the Americans, it was a complete rout, but Sergeant Sickmann said he felt the surrender had been handled as well as possible. "If somebody had fired a shot," he said, "we probably would all have been shot."

2

On the Edges

As mobs assaulted the chancery, several Americans caught outside hid behind the warehouse. A few others were off the compound on nearby errands. One of the latter, a Marine, said he had gotten word over his radio that there was a sit-in demonstration under way, and he was not overly concerned. Then he heard that the protesters had cut the chain bolt on the main gate and had rushed onto the embassy grounds.

He returned through the compound's north gate, which was open and unguarded, and was walking south toward the crowds around the chancery when he suddenly heard his name being called. A Marine and a civilian hiding near the warehouse just south of the apartment building had spotted him and were hailing him to come and take cover. He scurried over.

From their distant position, some 400 feet from the chancery, it was hard to tell what was going on. Much of the action was inside the chancery anyway. After listening a while to voices speaking Persian over the Marine's radio — the militants had by then seized several radios — the trio decided to send out a scout to see what was going on. One of the Marines crept out.

But as he approached the chancery, the scout was spotted by the militants and he ran back to his companions, inadvertently giving away their hiding place. Soon, all three were surrounded by a band of Iranians, some armed with wooden clubs and lead pipes. But the Americans did not give up without a fight. Fists began flying, and all three landed punches. Two Iranians tumbled to the ground and a third, as a Marine put it, was "plastered" to a wall.

But it was over quickly as other Iranians armed with guns rushed up. "I got a sawed-off shotgun in my face," said one of the Americans. A .38-caliber revolver was stuck in the chest of another. They were ordered to lie on the ground and remain silent.

The Iranians then searched the inside of the warehouse, where Steven Lauterbach, a 29-year-old general services officer, and two other Americans were hiding in the windowless basement known as the "Mushroom Inn." It was locked at both ends with vaultlike doors, but the Iranians had no trouble getting in.

They brought one of the other hostages to the door "with a gun to his head," Lauterbach said, and "forced us to open up."

Later, they and the men seized outside the warehouse were led off to the ambassador's residence, where, in a room with 35 other hostages, they were blindfolded and trussed to chairs.

Duane Gillette, one of the new captives, said: "Right after the takeover, I was waiting for someone to come in and get us out because it was such a barbarian act that I didn't figure the world would allow such a thing to happen. I was very optimistic. I was waiting for someone to come and say, 'There's been a big mistake. It's all over now. You can go home.' However, it did not happen for 444 days."

In the two-story consulate building, the place where American travelers went for aid and Iranian immigrants obtained visas for travel to the United States, 60 or 70 people were seeking help. On hand also were at least 14 Americans, including several Foreign Service officers.

Usually, two Marines were on duty at the consulate. But Richard H. Morefield, the consul general, had cut back visa services the day before because of the demonstrations, and as a result only one Marine, Sgt. James Lopez, was there.

With the exception of some military service, Morefield and Sergeant Lopez had almost nothing in common. Indeed, they represented opposite ends of the diplomatic community in Teheran, the civilian administrator and the military functionary. But both were to perform coolly, some said even valiantly, in the day's crisis.

At 50 years of age, Morefield was one of the most scholarly and experienced hands at the embassy. He holds a bachelor's degree from the University of San Francisco and a master's from the University of California. During his captivity, he would learn Spanish and study algebra. He had also spent two years in the Army in the early 1950's. A 23-year Foreign Service veteran, he had served consular tours in Colombia, Norway and Uruguay, and had arrived in Teheran in July 1979. Amid the uncertain prospects of postrevolutionary Iran, Morefield's wife, Dorothea, and five children had remained at home in San Diego.

Sergeant Lopez, at 21, had arrived in Teheran only a month before the takeover, an unmarried ambitious Marine out to see the world. A 1976 graduate of Globe (Ariz.) High School, where he played football and the trumpet in the school band, he attended Mesa Community College briefly and then dropped out to enlist in the Marines in 1977. He was the top Marine in his recruit class, and he had an undiscovered talent — it would be unveiled in captivity — for drawing cartoons. He couldn't have cared less about politics.

"When I got to that country, I didn't care one way or the other about the government," he said. "They wanted an Islamic Republic, that's their business, not mine. It's their country. Let me do my job and I'll let them get on with their lives. I had no feeling one way or the other about them."

Richard Queen, the consular official who was to be released after 250 days as a hostage because he was suffering from multiple sclerosis, also was on duty in the consulate. He said the first word that militants had broken into the compound was heard on Sergeant Lopez's radio. "The news we received was very sketchy," Queen said. "But shortly afterward, we started noticing that some of the militants were gathered around the consulate."

Gary Lee, a 38-year-old general services officer, was in his office. An Iranian consular employee came in and said: "Lee, you'd better leave. They're coming over the wall."

Kim King, a 27-year-old American tourist who was at the consulate because he had lost his passport, recalled: "We looked out and we could

19

see them coming across the motor pool area. I couldn't see any guns. They were carrying pictures of Khomeini on poles."

Shortly afterward, the window of a second floor washroom was shattered and a demonstrator on the roof tried climbing through. King said Sergeant Lopez went in, shoved the intruder back out the window and fired a couple of rounds of tear gas into the yard to temporarily scatter the crowds below. He then wired the washroom door shut with coat hangers and herded those inside to more secure areas in the back of the building.

In the gathering confusion, King said, "Someone asked the Marine if weapons were going to be issued, and he patted the pistol on his hip and said, 'This is all we've got and we can't use it.' " He had received word by radio that Laingen had ordered no shooting.

For a time, Morefield, who was in command at the consulate, resolved to barricade the doors and try to hold out until the police or Iranian Army troops arrived to repel the invaders. Later, the militants seized the embassy power station and cut off electricity to the consulate. Finally, Morefield concluded that no help was on the way, and when it became apparent that the demonstrators would soon break through, he "gave the word that we were to leave the consulate," Queen said.

Through a large sliding door on the north side of the building, away from the side where the demonstrators were gathered inside the compound, the consulate had direct access to Bist Metri Street. To their surprise, the consular officials found no protesters there and those trapped inside began moving out in small groups to attract less attention.

Iranian employees and Iranians seeking visas were the first to go. The Americans followed, a few at a time. Morefield and Sergeant Lopez would be the last men out. For the Americans, the plan was to slip away to another embassy. The Swedish and Austrian legations — both situated in a 15-story office building nearby that had previously housed the Canadian Embassy — were closest to the American compound. The most direct route from the consulate would have been two blocks south on America Street and one block west on Takht-E-Jamshid (Taleghani Avenue). But getting there would not be that easy. Iranian protesters still occupied the corner of America and Takht-E-Jamshid at the compound's southwest corner, so it would be necessary to take a series of back streets. It might even be necessary to turn elsewhere for refuge, some thought. Those who got away did just that.

As the Iranians and Americans left, Lopez continued to destroy equipment, such as the visa stamps, and to drive back the invaders with tear gas grenades. It was a madhouse scene.

"We were trying to get people off the compound, we were trying to keep people from getting hurt," Lopez said. "There were a lot of problems. The radios were captured by the Iranians, so that our [radio] net was full of garbage. We had trouble communicating through the landlines after they took the basement [of the chancery] because the phone exchange was down there. After a while, it was impossible to get a landline."

Most of the Americans, including Queen, were captured nearby. "The group I was in was about six people," Queen said. "We started walking and we got about two blocks when we noticed that a group of militants were following us, running after us. We were walking slowly." Any inclination to run was forgotten, he said, when a police officer appeared and "fired a shot over our heads." They were then led back by militants who shouted "C.I.A.!" and anti-American slogans.

But a few escaped. King followed five American consular officials on a circuitous route through the streets, then made his own way to Mehrabad Airport and left Iran without incident. The five consular officials were to have a more noteworthy adventure.

They were, in fact, beginning an odyssey that was to become one of the most celebrated episodes of the hostage crisis, one known as "the Canadian caper." The five — Robert G. Anders, Kathleen and Joseph Stafford, and Cora and Mark Lijek, spotted the demonstrators, turned the other way and began a long walk to Anders's apartment in north Teheran. There they were safe, at least for the time being. After days of wandering from one hiding place to another, they would be taken in by Canadian Embassy officials and eventually spirited out of the country.

Morefield, who had formed the departing groups and sent them out at intervals, was not so fortunate. With Lopez still battling invaders, Morefield, Gary Lee and the small last group stepped out. "We turned to the left and walked quickly, not running," said Morefield.

Several blocks away, Lee recalled: "Some kid saw us and yelled, 'C.I.A., C.I.A.' Somebody fired a shot in front of Dick Morefield."

"They surrounded us," said Morefield, "and said, 'Come with us.'

"I said, 'You've got the building — it's yours,' and they told me: 'You're a hostage.' "

"They marched us off at gunpoint," said Lee.

For those who got away, it was Sergeant Lopez's rear-guard actions that were remembered. "By keeping the consulate secure, he made it possible for us to go," said Lijek. "He was the one all of us looked to to tell us what to do. He may have been the most junior guy there, but he was certainly up to the occasion. He didn't get excited. He didn't lose his composure."

"He was standing there and overseeing the entire effort and putting his own safety last," said Joseph Stafford. "I'm grateful and I'm sure everyone in the consulate that day is grateful. He performed superbly."

Sergeant Lopez, a spit-and-polish but unduly modest Marine, said he regarded his actions in the consulate retreat as standard "emergency procedure," just part of "my job."

For all his heroics, it was finally time for Lopez to run.

"I had evacuated everyone and had torn the red stripes off my blue trousers and thrown an old windbreaker over myself and tried to look as scuzzy as possible to pass for an Iranian," he recalled.

The sergeant was somehow under the impression — a peculiar one, since no one else had it — that the Canadians had a car waiting outside to take the Americans away to their embassy on the edge of town. "If I had been two seconds quicker, I would have been in the Canadian Embassy," Lopez told CBS News.

"I was locking all the doors," he said, "barricading as much as possible to give them a hard time to get into the building. And the last door I locked I came out, and I found out later that as I was walking out the door, the car from the Canadian Embassy was driving off.

"So," he concluded, "it was the luck of the draw with me."

Four unarmed Marines, including 23-year-old Sgt. William E. Quarles and Sgt. Ladell Maples, 23, were in the apartment building at the north end of the compound when the takeover began. They overheard Cpl. Westley Williams's radioed warnings. But when they looked out they saw it was already too late to reach and defend the embassy gate at the south wall. The Iranians were pouring in.

ON THE EDGES

Following set procedures for an emergency, they donned fatigues and flak jackets, then they barricaded themselves in a room at the top of the 10-story building. The wife of an Iranian employee of the embassy joined them.

From a window overlooking the grounds, they watched in amazement as the Iranians moved over the compound. "It must be a joke," Sergeant Quarles told his companions. "They look like a bunch of school kids."

Sometime afterward, a band of Iranians entered and began searching the apartment building, which was almost vacant at the time. Led by a man with a pistol, they soon burst into the room where the Marines were gathered.

"Hands up," the gunman shouted. Their hands went up, slowly.

The woman was released, but the Marines were all searched, then led downstairs, where they encountered a contingent of Iranian national police officers. They apparently had come to turn the captors out and the prisoners loose.

As the Marines stood with hands over their heads, a heated argument developed between the policemen and the gunman. A police officer pulled Sergeant Quarles's hands down and the gunman shoved them back up again, and that is where they stayed. It was a symbolic victory for the militants, who were now clearly in command.

Sergeant Quarles was blindfolded, taken to the barracks and bound so tightly to a chair that rope burns were cut into his wrists and arms. He said he was not worried at first. He expected that more Iranian authorities would arrive quickly to evict the intruders. But as the hours passed, he realized that his hope was forlorn.

At 10:30 A.M., as the Iranian mobs were breaching the walls of the compound, the embassy's top officials, Bruce Laingen and Victor Tomseth, were just leaving the Foreign Ministry in downtown Teheran. They had gone there to discuss the future diplomatic status of the embassy's military personnel, a sensitive issue since it harped back to the historic and hated American military presence in Iran. As expected, the diplomats had made little progress on the question. They had left the Foreign Ministry and were heading back to their car when the first word of the intrusion at the embassy reached them.

NO HIDING PLACE

Michael Howland, their security guard, and two Iranian drivers were waiting at the car. As the two diplomats strode up, Howland told them he had just monitored a message over his radio. There was trouble at the embassy, he said.

Tomseth recalled: "We got in and started out, but we had not gone more than a few hundred yards when a second message came to the effect that there were hundreds of people pouring into the embassy compound and that it was advisable that we not return just yet."

Turning back to the Foreign Ministry, not so much to take refuge as to seek the help of the Iranian Government in ousting the intruders, Laingen and Tomseth found no one willing to take charge. They saw the chief of protocol, the senior undersecretary, the deputy to the senior undersecretary; all seemed unable to do anything.

By afternoon, Foreign Minister Ibrahim Yazdi appeared, but he had troubles of his own. Within 48 hours, he would lose his job to Abolhassan Bani-Sadr, and already his authority in revolutionary Iran was so vitiated that, as Tomseth put it, "Had he gone over to the embassy, he not only would not have gotten those people out of there, he might well have been taken hostage himself."

Laingen, Tomseth and Howland camped all day in Yazdi's office. "I staged a kind of sit-in at the foreign minister's desk, refusing to go and pressing throughout for assistance," Laingen said. By evening, Yazdi, apparently willing to promise them anything to get rid of them, told Laingen that the militants would be removed the next day.

"We didn't believe it," Tomseth said. "It was clear he wanted us to leave. He wanted us to go, anywhere; he didn't care. But we insisted on staying."

The irony of men about to become hostages insisting on staying in the very place where they would be held for 14 months was, of course, unappreciated by everyone at the time. "We weren't thinking about our safety at all, naturally," said Tomseth.

The exasperated Yazdi grew more blunt. "He suggested that I leave the ministry," Laingen said. "I reminded him that it was his obligation to provide me and my colleagues protection and that I could not be assured of that protection if I left the ministry." In another twist of irony, this same argument would be used two days later by the Iranians to justify holding the three men.

24

ON THE EDGES

The Americans, along with their two Iranian drivers, spent the night on couches in diplomatic reception rooms on the third floor. The next day, further efforts to gain government help to oust the embassy invaders proved futile, and another night was spent on the couches.

Then, 48 hours after the takeover, Iran's clergy-dominated Revolutionary Council ruled that the three Americans should be given "protection" at the Foreign Ministry. They were told they could leave, but that safe conduct anywhere could not be guaranteed.

The diplomats did not want to leave anyway. They believed that they could best work for their colleagues' freedom by staying in the Foreign Ministry and pressing government officials on the matter. In addition, they did not want an attempted "escape" of their own to jeopardize any avenues toward resolution of the crisis. So, they sent their Iranian drivers home and decided to stay put.

Soon, guards appeared, ostensibly for the diplomats' "protection," but in fact for their incarceration. It was unclear at what point their captivity began. Their status changed from guests to hostages subtly, almost imperceptibly, Tomseth said.

But Tomseth noted that there was one "critical watershed" in this transition. Three days after the embassy takeover, President Carter sent former Attorney General Ramsey Clark and William G. Miller, staff director of the Senate Select Committee on Intelligence, to Iran to seek a negotiated settlement. While the two were airborne, the Ayatollah Khomeini announced that he would not see them and made it clear that he expected no one else in authority to see them either.

"At that point," said Tomseth, "it became fairly clear to the three of us in the Foreign Ministry that it was going to be a sticky matter indeed."

Theirs was by far the most civil treatment accorded any of the hostages. For all but the last few weeks of the crisis, when they were sent to a prison, the three were housed in a well-furnished 60-foot former diplomatic dining room, with Persian carpets, gaudy French-period furniture and crystal chandeliers. They were given blankets, sheets, mattresses, bedrolls, cots, card tables, chairs, a couch, writing materials, a television set and a table for table tennis.

At first, they were also given a couple of 24-hour-a-day telephone lines, as well as access to the Foreign Ministry's Telex facilities. One of the lines was used to keep in touch with the six Americans hiding in the city and to make local calls to government officials. The other line was kept open to Washington around the clock at first. With no way to prevent eavesdropping, Tomseth, who had previously worked in Thailand, and a language expert at the State Department, communicated "secret" matters in Thai. Tomseth also used the language to communicate through a Thai cook with the Americans who had escaped from the consulate and were hiding in the city.

Laingen said he never thought the militants at the embassy would kill their American hostages. He said he was thus more concerned with the climate of public opinion in the United States. So his early messages to Washington urged restraint in dealing with Iran. That was, in fact, the public policy adopted by the Carter Administration, though secret plans for a rescue raid were begun almost immediately.

For the diplomats stuck at the Foreign Ministry, there was soon little left to say and almost no one to say it to. After the first hectic radio messages on the day of the takeover, they were unable to contact the rest of the hostages. Calls to the embassy went unanswered or were answered by militants who would hang up when they found out who was on the line. Eventually, even the six Americans hiding in the city managed to get settled and they, too, stopped calling. The telephones available to the diplomats at the Foreign Ministry became almost vestigial. "We found we didn't have that much to say most of the time," said Tomseth.

They focused instead on futile efforts to talk to Iranian officials about doing something for the embassy hostages. Their main contact was the chief of protocol; four men held that title during their stay in the Foreign Ministry, but none was helpful beyond answering their own custodial needs.

Life at the Foreign Ministry was soon humdrum, if not oppressive. There were newspapers and books to read, letters and memorandums to write and some amenities. Their furniture, Laingen said, was "elegant and French-style, heavy chandeliers, much of it rather dusty and dirty and rundown-looking because of the wear and tear of the revolution and because protocol had gone out the window."

The Iranian diplomatic staff — the career professionals, as opposed to the political appointees — looked in on them occasionally and "were absolutely appalled at what had happened and totally sympathetic to us," Tomseth said. But they could offer little but sympathy.

In contrast to the turmoil at the embassy compound a mile to the south, the office of the Iran-America Society on Park Avenue in north Teheran was almost somnolent. Kathryn L. Koob, the director, was holding a staff conference, talking of ways to put the educational and cultural exchange program back on its feet. It had been virtually shut down by the Iranian revolution.

Suddenly, the phone rang. It was an Iranian director of the society, whom Miss Koob declined to identify, with word of trouble at the embassy. Under instructions to wait for a call from the embassy in such an event, Miss Koob waited until she could stand it no longer.

"I called the embassy and I heard this strange voice at the switchboard say, 'Embassy occupied.' " She then called Laingen's secretary, Elizabeth Montagne, on a private line.

"I understand you've got company."

"You'd be surprised what's going on around here," Miss Montagne replied.

"Kate!" — it was Elizabeth Ann Swift, a political officer, on an extension — "we're under attack. Bruce is at the Foreign Office ——"

Suddenly, the line went dead. The compound had fallen.

Throughout the day and into the next, Miss Koob, her bilingual Iranian secretaries and William B. Royer Jr., a 48-year-old teacher who had formerly been director of the society, kept tuned to Iranian radio and television stations for news and, with an open telephone line to the State Department, sent summaries and recapitulations to Washington.

Late the first night, they had some unexpected visitors — Kathleen and Joseph Stafford and Cora and Mark Lijek, who had escaped from the consulate with Robert Anders. They stayed until nearly dawn, swapping tales of what had happened and helping with the summaries to Washington. The Staffords and the Lijeks then left to hide out at their respective apartments, while Miss Koob and Royer continued feeding information to the State Department.

The next afternoon, November 5, six Iranians arrived at the society office, but Miss Koob and Royer slipped out the back door with the secretaries and fled to the German Institute, just around the corner. Later, after the Iranians had gone, they returned to the office and resumed the calls to Washington.

Later that afternoon, however, a much larger group of Iranians appeared and surrounded the office. There was no escape this time. The Iranian secretaries were released, but Miss Koob and Royer were taken to the embassy compound. There, like the other hostages, they were bound, blindfolded and forbidden to talk.

Hurrying away from the din of angry crowds at the besieged American consulate, Anders, Joseph and Kathleen Stafford and Mark and Cora Lijek picked their way through narrow back streets north and west of the compound and headed for Anders's apartment in north Teheran.

It was a long walk, but they encountered no problems and arrived at midafternoon. There, safe for the moment, they began making telephone calls, trying to find out what had happened back at the embassy. They also called friends, whom they refused later to identify, to discuss possible hiding places. The calls were cut short when the phone went dead. Anders said the telephones in Teheran were always going dead, and they ascribed no special significance to the incident.

Over a radio such as all members of the embassy staff had in their homes, they tried again to contact the embassy. But the militants had seized the broadcasting apparatus and were using the frequency themselves. It was by now clear, if there had been any doubts, that the compound had been taken.

After dinner at Anders's apartment, they split up. Anders stayed home and the Staffords and the Lijeks went to the Iran-America Society on Park Avenue, which would not be seized by the militants until late the next day. The society director, Kathryn Koob, and her top aide, William Royer, were monitoring news broadcasts and sending summaries to the State Department over an open telephone line. The bill for this extended call would later come back to haunt Miss Koob.

The Staffords and the Lijeks stayed until 4 or 5 A.M. Then, in the predawn darkness of November 5, they slipped out and went to their respective apartments. They slept late.

The telephone at Anders's apartment was still dead in the afternoon, so the five used their apartment radios to communicate with each other, as well as with Bruce Laingen at the Foreign Ministry. They had

28

to share their radio frequency with the militants back at the embassy, but it was not a problem, Anders said.

"We used first names," he said. "The conversation was something like: 'Bob?' 'Yeah?' 'We're coming to pick you up.' 'Okay.' "

Friends — they refused to name them but said they were not Americans — supplied two cars and a temporary hideout, and the two couples, with packed bags, picked up Anders, who brought along an attaché case with some personal effects.

Over the next few days, the five Americans hid in several homes and apartments, including those of two of their colleagues being held hostage, gaining access through house servants. They moved frequently because they were afraid the militants might find lists of employee home addresses and raid the places where they were hiding.

Finally, they turned to the British for help. For a few days, they were put up in residences owned by the British Embassy, but that became, in Laingen's words "a bit of a burden rather quickly to the British." A new arrangement had to be made.

So Tomseth and the Thai cook who had worked for one of the diplomats worked one out. The Americans moved into an apartment in an isolated part of north Teheran that had been rented by an employee of the United States International Communications Agency. Even there, eventually, they began to feel they were being watched and grew restless to move on.

Laingen, in an effort to get them out of the country, nearly blew their cover. He simply told the Iranian chief of protocol and his colleagues one day that the five were free in the city. "We were in effect asking the government of Iran's cooperation in insuring their security and facilitating their departure," Laingen recalled.

The tip-off could have had disastrous results. But the Iranians were too busy to care. Laingen said: "They in effect threw up their hands, saying 'Oh, my God, we've got enough to worry about with all that compound situation. Let's not worry about this now.' We never raised it with them again."

It quickly became apparent that they should not have said anything because the government officials they were dealing with were obviously encouraging, if not cooperating with, the militants. But the Iranian diplomats apparently forgot the matter, and for good measure Laingen said over an open and presumably tapped line to Washington a few days later that the Americans outside the compound had left the country.

In fact, the five were still hiding in north Teheran, but were growing increasingly uneasy. Searching for a more secure hideout, Anders finally called a friend in the Canadian Embassy and said: "I just want to let you know I'm out. I'm not a hostage."

The Canadian was elated. "Why did you wait so long to call me?" he said. "Come on over."

It was a big breakthrough. Going to the Canadian Embassy on the edge of Teheran seemed risky, however, and the five never did so. Instead, on November 10, they were hidden in the unlikeliest of hideouts: the homes of Kenneth D. Taylor, Canada's ambassador to Iran, and his first secretary, John Sheardown.

Over the next 11 weeks, Joseph Stafford, 29, and his wife, Kathleen, 28, were harbored by Ambassador Taylor and his wife, Patricia, in their spacious, two-story north Teheran residence, which was ringed by a wall on a quiet street.

Not far away, Robert Anders, 54, and Mark Lijek, 29, and his wife, Cora, 25, were put up in the 18-room hillside home of John and Zena Sheardown. There, they were joined a week later by Lee Schatz, 31, an American agricultural attaché who had been away from the compound at the time of the takeover and had since been hiding in the Swedish Embassy.

All were given casual clothes and passed the ensuing November, December and January living in relative peace. They kept track of news, read, played games and occasionally visited one another. At the Sheardown home, Anders, Schatz and the Lijeks had to hide indoors two or three times a week when an Iranian gardener appeared for work.

There were a number of similar problems at the Taylors' residence. Seven Iranian servants worked there and were curious about the strange houseguests: They had come for an extended stay with no baggage. They never left the house. They seemed to vanish whenever Iranian visitors appeared. And they never attended the ambassador's dinner parties or at-home receptions.

"I said they were traveling lightly," Mrs. Taylor explained. "I told them they were tired. We still had to carry on an ambassador's functions normally. As time went on, the servants accepted the fact that there was something not quite normal going on, but they didn't pursue it."

There was one close call. Mrs. Taylor, a petite, Australian-born, 51-year-old research scientist with a doctorate in bacteriology from the University of California at Berkeley, was lecturing at the Teheran School of Medicine at the time, and had invited an Iranian friend from the university to dinner one evening at 6. She had arranged for the Staffords to leave for the Sheardowns' home at 5:45, but the Iranian friend arrived early.

"He walked in the front door as the Staffords were making their way toward it," Mrs. Taylor said. "I couldn't send them scurrying up the stairs, so I just said, 'Oh, these are friends of ours, Joe and Kathy.' He said he was glad to meet them and they went out the front door. I said to them, 'See you again soon.' "

The Taylors and the Sheardowns felt no compunctions about what they were doing. "We were not doing anything wrong," Mrs. Taylor said, "and they needed help."

All six Americans were deeply grateful to the Canadians. "They were sticking their necks out more than we were," said Anders. "They would be in more trouble for harboring us."

While the hideaways in the Canadian homes seemed secure, the Staffords late in January received an anonymous phone call warning that their position was growing precarious. It unnerved everyone. Soon afterward, on the basis of weeks of secret preparations, the six were spirited out of Iran with the help of the Canadians.

3

The First Weeks, the Worst Weeks

The first days and weeks in captivity were the worst for many of the hostages. Most were housed in the ambassador's residence, and were bound to chairs or handcuffed and blindfolded 24 hours a day. They were forbidden to speak and denied showers, exercise and activity of any sort, except for meager meals and trips to the bathroom.

In those first days, there were interrogations, death threats, humiliations before screaming crowds and television cameras, at least one mock execution, daily propaganda harangues and cruelties that ranged from incidents of Russian roulette to incarceration in a closet.

The women were separated from the men after a few days and the hostages were distributed in smaller groups to various buildings in the compound, but the rigors were unchanged.

A whispered word by Charles Jones, the communications specialist, to a fellow hostage drew swift retribution from a guard behind him who "grabbed my head, pulled it back, slammed it into a wall and told me to shut up."

"I shut up," he said.

There were random blows, too. "The first day I was tied up, I got a fist in the forehead," said Sgt. James Lopez. "Other times, during moves once or twice, I got a kidney punch."

Being blindfolded around the clock was a torment in itself to some. "When you can't see," said Moorhead Kennedy, "it comes as a terrible shock. I became disoriented, almost claustrophobic."

In the climate of fear and uncertainty that prevailed at the time, every move held terrors. "On the second day," Duane Gillette, the Navy petty officer, said, "they moved me from one room to another. They blindfolded me for it. One of the others was moved before me. When he went, I heard a shotgun blast. Then they came for me."

The blast was apparently an accident, and no one was hurt. What had seemed like a pending execution was simply a move to the next room, Gillette said.

Two days later, Jerry J. Miele, a 41-year-old communications officer, and several other hostages were paraded blindfolded before roaring crowds in scenes that were televised to a shocked world. "They took me outside to the crowd," he recalled. "I thought I was going to get it there."

Elizabeth Ann Swift, who was tied up and blindfolded for the first three weeks, said the guards knew she spoke and understood Persian and occasionally stood behind her and talked, in Persian, about executing the hostages.

The fear of death was present even in more relaxed moments. The captives were guarded around the clock by young Iranian gunmen, many of them students who were ill at ease with their weapons. "The first week, they had about five people in there with weapons — they were really paranoid," said Sergeant Sickmann, who feared that he would be shot accidentally.

The same fear gnawed at Sergeant Lopez. "No one was in charge," he said. The Iranians didn't know what they were doing. One guy would come in and tell us one thing, another guy would come in and tell us another thing. We were afraid they were going to come in and execute us and then find out later that they weren't supposed to do it."

In the middle of his second night in captivity, Morefield, the consul general, was awakened by gunmen.

"Are you Richard Morefield?" one asked.

"Yes."

"Come with us."

Morefield said he thought he was going to be executed. He and some other hostages were herded into a van and driven somewhere — he believes it was a student dormitory in northwest Teheran — and there he was subjected to the first of three mock executions that he would experience.

He and five other hostages were dragged into what appeared to be a shower room and seated on a plain wooden bench. There was a drain in the floor, and visions of their own blood flowing down the drain overwhelmed some. But Morefield, in what he believed to be his last moments, had another thought.

The oldest of his six children, 19-year-old Rick Morefield, had been executed by a gunman in 1976 during a robbery at a Washington area fast-food outlet where he had been employed. "I thought, 'How ironic that instead of the son's following in the father's footsteps, the father. . .'" and his voice trailed off as he recalled the horror.

"So I just started praying" — mostly Hail Marys, Morefield said, and listening in an agony of suspense as the captors behind him cocked the hammers and clicked the triggers of their weapons.

"It was absolute terror," he said.

On the same night, Moorhead Kennedy was also awakened about 2 A.M. and taken to a car. A blanket was thrown over his head, and he could hear weapons being loaded into the trunk. "Some other hostage in the car — I think it was a Marine — whispered when he heard the guns rattle that two people already had been shot," Kennedy said.

He was terrified. A scholar of Islamic law, an economics specialist fluent in Arabic and French, and the embassy's third-ranking diplomat, Kennedy was a native New Yorker with a prominent family background and patrician tastes that ran to sailing and mountain climbing. He had gone to the best schools — Groton, Princeton, Harvard Law — and had spent two years in the Army in the early 1950's. He and his wife, Louisa, had raised four sons. His 20-year career with the State Department had taken him to posts in Yemen, Greece, Lebanon and Chile, in addition to the War College and various desks in the State Department. He was an up-and-coming foreign service officer and one of the most able diplomats in the embassy — and he thought he was about to get his brains blown out.

But after a ride he regarded as his last, he and a few others were dropped off at "a very fancy home," where their lives as hostages improved. Though still under orders not to talk to one another, he and his fellow captives were able to whisper, pass notes in bathrooms and pass the time with chess, card games, books from the embassy library and an occasional censored news magazine.

There were, in the first few days, rare moments of levity. Frederick Kupke, a communications officer, and Donald Cooke, a vice consul, were in a group of about 15 hostages tied up in the consulate.

"You could hear a pin drop in there," said Kupke. "There was a guy with a machine gun at one end of the room guarding us. There was a guy with a G-3 machine gun guarding us. Very strict. We even had to look in a certain direction. The security rules were completely ridiculous."

At one point, Kupke said, their bonds were loosened briefly to get the blood circulating, and a militant clad in a new set of apparently pilfered U.S. Marine Corps camouflage fatigues "came strutting in and said, 'Okay, you may smoke if you have them,' and Donald Cooke jumped up and pointed to the 'No Smoking' sign on the wall and said, 'That's not allowed here.'

"Nobody said anything for a while, and then everybody broke up laughing."

Malcolm Kalp, whose duties in the embassy were never made public — the Iranians regarded him as a C.I.A. agent — was one of those held in the consulate. The captors there put an American flag on the bathroom floor, so the hostages would have to walk on it to get to the toilet. Kalp picked it up twice, but the Iranians put it back. A wiry man, 5 feet 9 inches tall who speaks with a thick Boston accent, Kalp adopted a belligerent attitude toward the Iranians right from the start. He tried to escape three times during the captivity, and was frequently left bound hand and foot and was kept in solitary confinement for more than a year. Each time captors entered his cell during that year, he routinely greeted them with: "Hello, assholes." Some of the Marines used even harsher language.

Visitors to the compound were rare, but on the third night, Robert O. Blucker, an economics officer, recalled that Ayatollah Khomeini's son, Sayed Ahmed Khomeini, came "to see the Persians and greet them and encourage them in what they were doing."

"He was fingering his 'worry beads' and smiling and talking to them," Blucker said. "He didn't want to look at any of us. We were allowed to stand around in this crowd of Persians and watch the proceedings, but he never acknowledged our presence in any way. I figured at this point that the whole affair had government backing." Other hostages would see the Ayatollah's son a few days later, and again in the summer.

For the first week, Sgt. Rodney V. Sickmann was bound so tightly that his wrists and arms hurt. He could see nothing, say nothing and, after a while, feel very little. As wearying hours passed into days, the dark-haired, mustachioed sergeant, who would later awe his captors with feats of arm-wrestling and calisthenics, grew stiff with inactivity.

Sickmann, known as "Rocky" to his friends, had been a high school football star in Washington, Mo., a small town 50 miles west of St. Louis, where his father drove a concrete-mix truck and his mother worked in a carpet store. He joined the Marines in 1976 and served in Okinawa and on aircraft carriers in the Mediterranean before volunteering for embassy guard duty. He had arrived in Teheran only a month before the takeover and could hardly believe what was happening.

"There was about 15 of us," he said, "and we were sitting at this long table, and I was tied to the back of the chair. You could never get out of this chair, except to go to the toilet. If you wanted to lay your head down, they'd put a pillow on the table. Otherwise, we just sat there until nighttime, when they'd put us on the floor. They'd tie our hands and feet and cover us."

For the first three weeks, Sickmann said, all the hostages in his group had their feet tied and their wrists handcuffed. After that, only the hands were bound with rags and these were loosely knotted. "They'd tie it just far enough to where you could hold a book," he said.

Similarly after the first few weeks, the treatment of most of the hostages improved. Blindfolds came off. Bonds were kept on some, but were loosened. Talking was still prohibited, but enforcement was relaxed. Meals were more regular. Exercise was permitted. Terrors were ebbing and life began falling into rigorous routines.

It was still a struggle. Kennedy said that when the captors finally began allowing him to read, he found a book containing Admiral Byrd's account of his survival at the Pole. It told how Byrd, facing howling winds and deep cold, was forced to decide whether to risk asphyxiation by leaving his leaky stove burning or death by freezing should he turn it off. "We talked a lot about how he managed to cope," Kennedy said.

For others, there was no relief in talking. "I remained blindfolded and bound and prohibited from talking from November 4, 1979, to March 17, 1980," said Charles Jones. "I remember that day because it was my wife's birthday and St. Patrick's Day."

Kathryn Koob also was kept alone for four months before being put into a room with Elizabeth Ann Swift, whom she had seen only at Christmas when they were brought together for a broadcast. Miss Koob had been raised by a devout Lutheran family on a farm in Jesup, Iowa, and had obtained her teaching degree from Wartburg College, a Lutheran school. She taught high school a few years in Iowa, then joined the United States Information Agency and served in the Ivory Coast, Upper Volta, Rumania, Nigeria and Zambia before being posted to Teheran in July 1979. Her religious faith had been a source of strength all her life, and in her months alone in captivity, she said her mind turned increasingly toward religion.

"I suddenly realized something that had always interested me," she said. "Something I'd always had questions about was the life of contemplatives. In the Lutheran Church, we don't have contemplative orders, but they've always fascinated me. I always wondered how people would live a life of silence, and I felt, well, 'Here's your chance to try it.' So I set up for myself a schedule of devotion."

Her schedule included the singing of hymns to herself, memory work on scriptural passages and large amounts of time engaged in prayer and meditation. "I tried also to remember there were a lot of people in the world a lot worse off than I was. I was warm and dry and had plenty to eat."

Col. Charles W. Scott, a 47-year-old Army attaché, armed himself with anger rather than faith to meet the rigors of captivity. He often erupted at his captors. His life as a hostage was just the reverse of that of most hostages: he was treated reasonably well for a few days, then subjected to solitary confinement, mock executions and other cruelties. The change apparently came as a result of interrogations when the militants "accused me of being a spy."

John E. Graves, the embassy's public affairs officer, said the Ayatollah's son paid a visit to the compound, apparently his second, about a week after the takeover. In an article written for *Stern*, a West German magazine, Graves said:

"The visitor spoke slowly and softly in Farsi and smiled often at the hostages. After he left, one of the student captors explained that he was Ahmed Khomeini, son of the Imam, and that he had come to see that the hostages were well, and to reassure them that they need not fear for their safety. In addition, said the student, the Imam hoped that understanding would develop between the hostages and their captors."

Graves said this signaled the beginning of a series of dialogues between himself and some of the students, including a tall young medical student named Ali, who spoke excellent English and was friendlier than the others. Like many of the captors, Graves said, Ali had studied in the United States.

Ali, according to Graves, said the students had never been serious in their demand for the return of the Shah. "We aren't interested in the Shah," Ali was quoted as having said. "That was just a curtain. The Shah is finished. We just needed him as a banner, a slogan to get the crowds going."

Graves said Ali claimed the students had four goals — furthering the Iranian revolution, making it a model for all Islamic lands, winning the poor people of Europe and the United States to the revolutionary cause and demonstrating to the world American perfidy in Iran and the Third World.

"We are not against the American people," Ali was said to have told Graves. "They are good. I know them. But they have no idea what their government does. They always hear lies. The press is controlled by the C.I.A. and the Zionists."

Then, Graves said, a dialogue unfolded:

"Did the Imam Khomeini know of your plans to attack the embassy?"

"No, we didn't tell anyone," Ali replied.

"What would have happened if we had resisted?"

"We expected that. We were surprised how simple it was. We were prepared for violence. We weren't afraid to die."

"What would you have done if the Bazargan regime had gone against you?"

"No problem. Bazargan couldn't do anything. He had no power or authority. He tried to get us out of here, but we just ignored him. We knew that the local committees and the militia were with us."

Then Graves asked: "What would you have done if the masses had stayed home, if Khomeini hadn't blessed your actions?"

"We only planned to stay three days," Ali replied. "If the Imam had not publicly supported us by then we would have gone home."

Some time after this conversation, Graves said he saw Ali again, and they had a brief talk.

"Shah, Shah, Shah — that's all they talk about now," exclaimed Ali, apparently tired and exasperated at his fellow students. "It's crazy. They really think it's important to get him back. They don't understand it has nothing to do with our revolution — that we just talked about him in the beginning to get the mobs moving. But now we have these engineers. . ." and his voice trailed off.

Graves never saw Ali again.

"From then on," he said, "we were in the hands of uneducated, erratic fanatics."

The interrogations, which began soon after the embassy takeover and continued for weeks, were harsh for some and easy for others. Some hostages were openly defiant; others were cooperative, a few to the deep resentment of those who were not. Most hostages fell somewhere between the extremes.

The treatment they were accorded in their captivity sometimes, but not always, appeared to be related to their performances in the interrogations and, of course, to whether they were perceived to be spies. There were other factors, too, including their positions on the embassy staff and the degree to which they complied with their captors' wishes.

The Iranians found two sources of information suggesting that some of the hostages were spies. One was a State Department document that the militants brandished on December 1 and said they had found in the embassy files. It was a cable written by Bruce Laingen that said Malcolm Kalp and William Daugherty would need "the best cover we can come up with." Kalp's duties were never disclosed, and Daugherty was listed as a political officer.

The militants also found a false Belgian passport in the possession of Thomas L. Ahern Jr., the embassy's narcotics liaison officer. The passport appeared to suggest that Ahern had a double identity and possibly a dual role in Iran. Later in captivity, the Iranians would produce alleged "confessions" from some hostages that appeared to support these documentary claims of espionage, but State Department officials called them sheer propaganda and "hardly credible."

Kalp, who spent 374 days in solitary confinement — more than any other hostage — denied under extensive questioning that he was a Central Intelligence Agency operative, but the militants never believed him. Later, it would be his contention that the harsh treatment accorded him in captivity had stemmed from his attempted escape and his belligerent attitude toward his captors.

Soon after the embassy fell, Elizabeth Montagne, Laingen's 41-year-old secretary, was taken roughly to a gunman who demanded the combinations of locked embassy safes, combinations that she did not know. In one of the most chilling accounts of the captivity, she told NBC News how he had put a gun loaded with one bullet to her heart.

"He went click, and the bullet went up one chamber — I could feel it go up," she said.

"And then he said, 'I'm a very good judge of character, and I know you're lying to me.' And I said, 'If you think I'm lying you're a lousy judge of character, because I'm telling you the truth: I cannot open those safes.'

"Then he went click and the bullet went up another notch." There was further dispute over what she knew and then "click — the bullet up another notch."

"Is this worth dying for?" the gunman asked.

"I said, 'No, it's not,' and he went click, and the bullet went up another notch.

"And I — this little game must have taken about four, five, minutes, it seemed an eternity — and I can remember my mind being very, very clear, and very, very sharp. I remember my heart trying to jump out of my chest. He kept pointing the gun at me, and the last — there was one click to go.

"And he said, 'Do you think I'll pull the trigger?'

"And the only thing I could think of was 'I wonder what it would feel like to have a bullet go through my chest.' Then, I thought, 'Well, it can't hurt for long.'

"We stared at each other, and then he — he put the gun down. He said, 'O.K., so you don't know the combinations.'

"I just kind of collapsed."

Elizabeth Ann Swift, a 39-year-old political officer, was accused by her captors of taking part in intelligence work. She also was subjected to the torments of a gunman seeking the combination of a safe.

A studious-looking woman with horn-rimmed spectacles and a serious mien, she was born and raised in Washington, D.C. After graduation from Radcliffe in 1962, she joined the State Department and served in the Philippines, Washington and Indonesia before going to Iran. It was her relatively high position on the embassy staff that apparently led the captors to believe she knew the combination of a safe in the chancery vault.

Her confrontation with a gunman was different from Elizabeth Montagne's, however. Miss Swift in fact knew the safe's combination.

"You've got five minutes to open the safe or I'll kill you," the gunman told her.

"I didn't think he would," she said. "I lied and said I couldn't." She waited five minutes and nothing happened.

It was a daring bluff, but it worked.

"I am very familiar with the kind of courage it takes to fight in combat," said Colonel Scott, who served in Vietnam and won the Silver Star and the Bronze Star. "But I say there is a different kind of courage to face interrogators when you are completely alone and don't know when you are ever going to see another American or whether you are going to get out of the situation alive and in one piece."

The colonel, under questioning by the Iranians, said his mission had been to help the Iranian Army obtain spare parts for nonlethal military equipment, but his captors did not believe him. As a result, he said, he was kept in prison throughout his captivity, including eight weeks in solitary confinement.

"I was never permitted to leave my cell except blindfolded, even to go to the toilet," Colonel Scott said. "In the entire 14½ months, other than the last 25 days, I had spent only 11 days in a cell where it was possible to see daylight. The rest of the time, I was in a cell that amounted to a closet — no windows, no circulation of air."

Michael J. Metrinko, an embassy political officer, was also accused of being a spy. He said his captors had seized many of his papers — files, classified reports and address books that listed many Iranian friends he had made in his service there — and regarded these as proof of nefariousness.

For Metrinko, who had been in Iran for the State Department since 1977, this was the second incidence of captivity. As the consul in Tabriz, he had been held hostage by anti-Shah demonstrators for five days the previous February. When he was freed, the consulate was closed and he moved to Teheran.

He had joined the Peace Corps in 1968 and spent time in Turkey and Iran. His State Department service had taken him to Syria and Greece and he was fluent in Arabic, Turkish and Persian.

He was amused rather than broken by his captors' interrogation technique. They had evidently been told that they could successfully break down a suspect by long periods of intensive questioning. Metrinko was, in fact, grilled for six hours at a time. But the captors then made the mistake of letting him sleep for long intervals between sessions.

Charles Jones was hauled before interrogators five times, but they wound up spending much of the time in naive-sounding polemics, trying to persuade him that America was evil. "They kept telling me I was black and should help the oppressed people of the world," he said. "I kept telling them that Iran was their country," he said, "and that I had nothing to do with their revolution — that I was an American first."

The duration of the questioning varied widely. Kennedy's interrogation lasted only a few minutes; after his captors found that he was an economics specialist, they seemed to lose interest in him.

Col. Thomas E. Schaefer, the defense and Air Force attaché, was questioned four to eight hours a day for two weeks and was kept throughout that time in what he called "cold storage" — an unheated room in a house in north Teheran where he could "see my breath." The room, which had fans that brought cold air from the outside, was 12 feet wide, 20 feet long and furnished with a single folding chair. He slept on the bare floor without a blanket, and he was fed only cold rice.

Schaefer, a 30-year Air Force veteran who had been a bomber pilot in Vietnam and had served with the Strategic Air Command, had been through "terrorist and survival school," which helped him cope, at least mentally. He said he was subjected to the lengthy interrogations and harsh treatment because the captors believed he had been sent to Iran to overthrow the revolutionary government. He said the interrogators were "the most paranoid people" he ever met.

They were naive, to boot, he figured. Once, they brought out a common radio that they had found in the embassy and contended that it had somehow been used to communicate with the former Shah's supporters in Kurdistan. The Iranian inquisitors, Schaefer said, "did not know how to interrogate." They poked and pushed him around, he said, but never struck him in the face or body.

Robert Blucker, a tough-talking, 52-year-old economics officer whose specialty was oil, was taken to the same house in north Teheran and kept in handcuffs on a cold floor for weeks. He repeatedly refused to tell his captors where his apartment was, certain that they wanted only to loot it. He was beaten by a group that included a "monstrous little dwarf" with a pistol stuck in his belt and "two or three terrorist thugs."

Capt. Paul Needham, an Air Force logistics officer, also was kept in the north Teheran house, bound in a bedroom for most of the time and forbidden to talk.

On Thanksgiving, Colonel Schaefer began a hunger strike to protest his harsh treatment and the lack of mail. "They were upset that I wasn't eating," the Colonel said. On the fifth day of his fast, the captors marched him into the kitchen, placed a plate of spaghetti in front of him and lowered an automatic rifle at him.

"You will now eat," the rifleman said menacingly.

It was a showdown. Schaefer looked down the barrel of the weapon. The rich aroma of the spaghetti sauce wafted up to his nostrils.

He ate.

"I was so hungry I was going to eat anyway," he said.

Interrogations grew less frequent after about two weeks, and the first major development of the hostage crisis occurred: On November 19 and 20, a total of 13 of the hostages — five women secretaries and eight black men — were released and sent home in what the militants evidently regarded as a propaganda coup. Unknown to almost everyone at the time, Yasir Arafat, the leader of the Palestinian Liberation Organization, had acted as a go-between and was believed to have been instrumental in negotiating the release of the 13 women and blacks.

The militants showed off the first three — Kathy Jean Gross, a secretary, and Marine Sgts. Ladell Maples and William Quarles — to hundreds of reporters at a two-hour news conference in an embassy courtyard. The three sat on plastic chairs on a platform, shivering in the evening chill. "They believe in what they are fighting for," Maples said guardedly as the militants watched and reporters scribbled notes. "We've been fed more than adequately," said Kathy Gross. "We've slept nights."

Some hours after those three were put on an airplane, it was the turn of the other 10 to be put in front of the television cameras for press questioning. A banner hung behind them. "Oppressed blacks, the U.S. government is our common enemy," it declared.

This group, too, was wary. Air Force Capt. Neal Robinson, a budget officer, said of the captors, "Based on their beliefs, their feelings with regard to the actions of the Shah, they feel totally justified." Terry Tedford, a secretary, said, "We heard the chanting all night. It had a very definite effect on me. I don't think I could have put up with it another week."

All 13, after being debriefed at Weisbaden, where the other 52 would follow them more than a year later, were meticulously watchful of their words. State Department officials spoke with them about the continuing peril of the Americans still being held.

Back in Iran, Ayatollah Khomeini said he had ordered the release of the 13 because Islam has a high regard for women and because blacks in the United States are "oppressed."

Charles Jones was the only black kept in custody; he never learned why he was not released, or why he was treated so harshly. Miss Koob and Miss Swift assumed that they were the only women not released because of their relatively high positions on the staff.

The release raised many false hopes among other hostages. For example, Metrinko, who had been kept with one of the blacks allowed to leave, said: "I could hear the guards discussing the release of the hostages. They kept discussing taking them out to the airport and having reporters talk to them about their treatment. I was naturally overjoyed."

Then, the crushing truth emerged. "I realized when the guards

talked the next day about the reception at the airport that they had left."
For Metrinko and the rest of the hostages, there would now be no easy
way out. The long, harsh ordeal of captivity stretched away into infini-
ty.

4

The Mushroom Inn

At 6 o'clock one morning in November, probably toward the end of the month, some of the captors went into the room where Richard Queen was being kept, his hands still bound, and took him and some of the others to a warehouse basement on the embassy grounds. It was the hostages' introduction to the Mushroom Inn.

"There were no windows," said Queen, a 28-year-old vice consul on his first assignment abroad. "It was like living in a tomb. You didn't hear the outside world. You didn't see the outside world. You didn't know what was going on at all. You were completely cut off, as though you were living in a tomb."

There were several rooms in the Mushroom, and Queen shared one until mid-March with Joseph Hall, a 30-year-old Army warrant officer in the defense attaché's office who had previously served diplomatic tours in Indonesia and Greece.

The hostages in the Mushroom were ordered not to speak to one another. And according to Duane Gillette, a Navy intelligence clerk from Columbia, Pa., in the rolling farmland of Lancaster County, "It was frowned upon if you looked at the other hostages."

Sometimes Queen and Hall and some of the others managed to whisper to a fellow hostage, especially on the infrequent occasions on which they were allowed to go to the toilet unaccompanied by a captor.

Gillette, a short, slender young man with rimless glasses, and 16 other hostages were put into an 8-foot by 12-foot room in the Mushroom. He was restricted to one corner.

"I was in a location where I had three of the militants in front of my bed with Uzi submachine guns and G-3's," he said. "I could not get involved with the clandestine communications that were going on — notes being thrown back and forth. That was the worst of it, to not talk to any of the other hostages."

"During the worst time in that room," he said, "the thought ran through my mind: If I die, would I be dying *for* America or *because* of America?"

Queen, who had grown up in the Village of Scarborough in New York's suburban Westchester County, said he was able to take a shower "every second or third day" in the Mushroom and that once a week he was taken to a "very small courtyard" near the ambassador's residence, where "we were allowed to exercise and see the sun and hear the traffic, hear the birds, for about 20 minutes."

While the hostages lived amid fear and confusion, diplomatic efforts to set them free persisted. On December 4, the United Nations Security Council, in a unanimous vote, called for their release.

About December 17, Richard Morefield, the consul general, was brought to the Mushroom with about 20 other hostages. Compared with the student dormitory where he had previously been held, Morefield said, at the Mushroom the food was better and the hostages had more contact with their captors. He and eight or nine others shared a big room that had been divided into small cubicles with temporary partitions. In his space, he was able to walk two steps in one direction, three in another. He, too, was prohibited from speaking with the others. But, through eye contact and gestures, he said, he was able to get some messages back and forth.

One of those apparently moved to the Mushroom at the same time as Morefield was John Limbert, the political officer, who had served in the Peace Corps in Iran, been an instructor at Pahlavi University, married an Iranian woman and was one of the most proficient speakers of Persian among the hostages. Limbert, 36 years old, recalled being kept in a room subdivided with bookcases.

THE MUSHROOM INN

"The program stayed very much the same," Limbert said of the experience in his new quarters. "Read, sleep, exercise. I asked some of the students to bring me books in Persian and they brought me some books by Dr. Ali Shariati, a kind of patron saint of the revolution. You kind of made your own routine. I dreamed about the future, past and future. I fantasized about what I would do when I got free. I kept track of time with pistachio shells. My hands were tied together but pretty loosely and I was getting 13 to 14 hours of sleep."

Queen busied himself in the Mushroom by organizing a lending library with embassy books. Others were able to volunteer to work with him and sometimes they would talk.

"We'd say we were talking about books," he said, "but a good number of them didn't speak English, so they didn't know better."

Morefield was one of those who helped out with the library and it was with Queen, he said, that he was able to have his only "extensive conversations" in the Mushroom.

Morefield said some of the hostages seemed to want to establish a dialogue with the captors, but that, initially, he "felt that I couldn't and didn't want to." And he limited his exchanges with them to requests for permission to go to the bathroom or to ask for more food.

Later, however, when he was being held in a small apartment building in a village about two hours north-northwest of Teheran, Morefield said he got into a running political discussion with some of his captors that sometimes became quite intense. One day there, returning from the toilet, he recalled, one of them started a conversation with him and "I just blew up."

Morefield said he told the Iranian his people might have the right to have the Shah returned to their country, but they were going about it the wrong way. "I told him there were obvious ways to get him through our American legal system," he said, adding that the person they should approach might not necessarily be the President, but perhaps "some judge some place."

Morefield said the young Iranian captors often talked about what they perceived to be the defects in the American political system. One of their themes was that the hostages were the tools of the economic and Jewish elite in the United States. Morefield had no patience with them. "You got rocks in your head," he would reply.

49

"I wasn't very good at one-on-one relationships with them," he said. He felt they could sense the anger in his voice and that he "turned them off," by being "too authoritarian."

"That was one of my weaknesses," he said. "If I had been good at that I would maybe have learned things that could have been helpful to me or others."

John Limbert, who had earned an undergraduate degree and a master's degree in Middle East history at Harvard, was exasperated with his captors' limited grasp of international politics, too. And he was as blunt with them as Morefield.

"One of them said to me," Limbert recalled, " 'Why is America the world's greatest enemy of humanity?' That's where the conversation would start. Then I'd say, 'No wonder you don't go to school. You know everything. You know that the U.S. causes droughts in India and floods in Bangladesh. I envy you. You have such simple solutions. My 8-year-old son thinks better than you do."

Early on in the Mushroom, Morefield said, he and one of the young military men took it upon themselves to clean the bathroom. He said he thought his captors saw this as a humiliating task, but, he added, "it didn't bother me."

At some point during his stay in the Mushroom, Morefield said the possibility that the United States Government might consider the hostages expendable began to haunt him. Once, he said, he and another hostage who apparently had been laboring under the same train of thought, looked at each other glumly and, without a word, made the executioner's sign with a finger across the throat.

In the first week in December, Moorhead Kennedy, the economics specialist, and his roommates were moved to the basement of the embassy from a luxurious suburban house where they had spent nearly a month. As they were being ordered out of the house, their captors told them not to bring any personal belongings and, for the first time, they were handcuffed instead of being bound with cloth and rope.

"We still thought we faced death at that point," Kennedy said. "We figured we were going to die the way they went about the move. I went peacefully. I guess that's the way you go. I mean, what else do you do?"

In the first months, Kennedy said, there were a number of "terrible scares" and he brooded a great deal about being shot.

"After that," he continued, "we began to feel they had too much invested in us to kill us unless something was done to really endanger us."

One of the scares, Kennedy said, occurred one day in December as he and others were being moved from one room to another.

"You could smell fear in the second room," he said, "You have to smell it to know what it's like. We thought it was the anteroom to death. Then, suddenly we were taken back to our original room."

"We got there," he added, "just as they were putting away the vacuum cleaner."

Kennedy was also unnerved by an anonymous message he spotted scrawled on a wall. It was in Arabic. But he reads some Arabic and it translated as "The Ayatollah Khomeini has agreed to the execution of the hostages."

And, on still another occasion, Kennedy misinterpreted a gesture by the students, who one day gave him and other hostages some writing paper. "We thought it was maybe for a last letter home, a last will and testament," he said. "But, instead, it was one of those infrequent moments when the students were in a mood to move mail."

Messages from outside were welcome, often eagerly awaited, but arrived quite erratically. "Letters I wrote were thrown away and letters they received for me were thrown away," said Duane Gillette. But there was often mail from strangers, Americans who simply wanted to let the hostages know their country was thinking of them, and Gillette remembered with affection a letter he had gotten from a child in New York. "There was Tom Daley," he said. "He is in fourth grade. But he came out and said I think we ought to bomb these bastards. 'Bomb' was misspelled. 'Bastards' was misspelled. It brought tears to my eyes it was so good."

Sometimes, though, letters from well-meaning Americans — the ones that began "Dear Hostage" or "Dear Friend" — became an annoyance. "They were the letters you hated to get," said Moorhead Kennedy. "You were thankful that people cared. But you figured they were using up your quota of letters. And, thus, you would get less from home."

"One time," he continued, "I threw all that kind of mail back in the mailman's face and said not to bring me any more of that kind, only letters from my family."

NO HIDING PLACE

Letters from home were desperately needed by some hostages, and their denial was an acute punishment. A few hostages said they had occasionally felt forgotten.

Having lived in cloisterlike conditions without close companionship, they were later often unable or unwilling to discuss their feelings of deprivation. There were no reports of homosexual encounters among the 50 male hostages held throughout the captivity. The two women, who were always separated from the men, reported no instances of sexual harassment.

When the released hostages held a news conference at West Point, Sgt. John McKeel joked: "As soon as they let us get home — so, especially the Marines, we can get back to chasing women — it's going to be perfect." He added: "We were all right, physically and mentally."

It was clear to some, however, that all the hostages were not all right.

There were at least two apparent suicide attempts, according to three of the hostages. One of these sources was a Foreign Service officer who asked that his name not be used. The others were Thomas Schaefer and Frederick Kupke. All three refused to disclose the identities of those who, they said, had tried to kill themselves. A fourth hostage, Steven W. Kirtley, a Marine corporal, said he had witnessed one of the attempts by a roommate. He declined to identify the roommate or to say what had happened other than that guards had called an ambulance.

"I know it for a fact," said the Foreign Service officer, "but I won't go into details of how I know it." He said one case involved a wrist slashing in February 1980. "I'm not sure just what he was trying to do at that point," he said. "In the other case, the man fully intended to kill himself," the officer added. He declined to say how.

There was some speculation that one reason for the guards' occasional middle-of-the-night raids on the hostages was a fear of suicide attempts. Malcolm Kalp challenged that idea. The Iranians left potentially dangerous instruments lying around, he said. Nine-inch scissors, used for cutting hair, were kept in the bathrooms, for instance.

But, after the suicide attempts, the captors took away all of the hostages' shoes, belts and razors, and replaced drinking glasses and plates with plastic.

52

THE MUSHROOM INN

Both the suicide attempts and escape attempts presented delicate problems for the Iranian captors.

"One of the leaders, Hussein, told us point-blank what their problem was," the Foreign Service officer said. "They couldn't shoot us. We were their stock in trade. And they couldn't do us much harm. We were gradually learning that. Of course, at that point, we didn't know."

"The Imam's instructions," he went on, "were specific — that our health had to be protected. They worked very hard at that. They were inept, but they certainly worked at it. So they had quite a problem in keeping us under control. And, according to Hussein, they thought they had to intimidate us, had to show us who was boss."

5

First Christmas

Christmas 1979 underscored the hostages' predicament and intensified their loneliness. They had been in captivity nearly two months. The initial terror had ebbed, but many were beginning to feel that they were in for a long ordeal.

Richard Morefield had been cheered to learn that the students were planning to permit American clergymen to conduct Christmas services. But his spirits plummeted, he said, "when I walked in and saw the obvious propaganda use that had been made of it."

The four visiting clergymen spent two hours negotiating with the captors before they saw the hostages. The Rev. Dr. William Sloane Coffin Jr. of the United Church of Christ, who is the senior minister of the Riverside Church in Manhattan; the Rev. M. William Howard Jr., a Baptist from Princeton, N.J., who is president of the National Council of the Churches of Christ in the U.S.A.; Msgr. Thomas J. Gumbleton, an Auxiliary Bishop of the Roman Catholic Archdiocese of Detroit, and Léon-Etienne Cardinal Duval, the Archbishop of Algiers, were brought to the heavily guarded embassy at 11:30 on Christmas Eve in a police-escorted caravan of Mercedes-Benzes.

The clergymen said later that they had told the militants they wanted to conduct an ecumenical service for the entire group of hostages, and they said they had almost walked out before yielding to a demand that they meet the captives in small groups.

Reverend Howard, the Baptist minister, presided over the session that Morefield attended. A table laden with food and microphones attached to Coca-Cola bottles dominated the room. On the walls, along with traditional Christmas decorations, were revolutionary and anti-American posters. As the hostages prayed with Reverend Howard and sang hymns, Iranian television cameras focused on them. Beyond the view of the cameras, Morefield said, were "about 40 of our captors who obviously were there, I think, to intimidate us."

His emotion, that Christmas morning, was "absolute rage." He was so angry, he said, that he worried later that he might have been rude to the minister.

For Richard Queen, who had spent hours working with Morefield in the little lending library in the Mushroom Inn and sneaking conversations, the clergymen's visit was pure joy. He, too, had seen Reverend Howard.

"I can't really adequately describe how moving it was and how important it was," he said. "One, for the spiritual strength it provided me, and also because, just because, well, Reverend Howard was from the United States, and that was evidence the world still exists."

As time passed, Morefield cooled off. Whatever else he felt, Morefield said when he got home, he believed Reverend Howard had gone to Iran because he felt it was his Christian duty. Others among the hostages were not so sure.

"Some priests upset us greatly," said Duane Gillette, the petty officer. "They were more worried about, I think, creating turmoil in the United States, rather than the condition of the hostages."

James Lopez, the Marine guard, described the Christmas services as "a dog and pony show," and he expressed bitterness about the visit by clergymen the following Easter, too. He was shocked, he said, to learn that the clerics were "saying conditions were nice and everything was copacetic and we were having such a good time in Camp Teheran. We couldn't believe they were actually buying that garbage the Iranians were putting out."

For Sgt. Rodney Sickmann, the political ramifications of the Christmas ceremonies had been telegraphed. Early in December, he said, "they started buttering us up, trying to get us to make statements and signing different documents.

"Stuff like this," he said. "We knew what they were trying to do, and every time they asked us to make a tape, we'd just say things for America, which really upset them."

William F. Keough Jr., the educator who had been in charge of the American School in Teheran before it was closed after the fall of the Shah, said he recognized that the Iranians had been trying to exploit the clergymen's visits for propaganda. But he added:

"Many of us thought we should go along with this because every opportunity we had to get our faces on camera was assurance for people back home. My feeling was your family needs to see you. You never say what the Iranian students want you to say. There are ways of not answering questions, frustrating questions, switching to the Red Sox. You get off the topic. The clergymen were obviously being exposed to artificial conditions."

Before going overseas, Keough had been superintendent of schools in Bedford, Mass., Burlington, Vt., and Huntington, L.I. He had graduated from Boston College. His second wife, Katherine, had been active in the group that lobbied on behalf of the hostages, shared information and generally tried to buck up spirits. They had made their home in Waltham, Mass.

By Christmas, Robert Blucker, a crusty 22-year veteran of the Foreign Service, had been moved back to the ambassador's residence in the embassy compound and had shared two separate rooms there with various colleagues. Blucker, a stern, studious man who read voraciously, refused to attend the religious services at Christmas, but he took part in the holiday dinner that the captors prepared.

"It was quite good, compared to what we had been having," Blucker recalled. "I think there was turkey and stuffing, two or three kinds of cake and pie."

"It was a bang-up meal," said Moorhead Kennedy. "Our morale was very high for the first time."

The hostages were given permission to talk to one another for the day and, at one point, Kennedy recalled, "Barry Rosen said to me, 'We're going home.' "

Like some of the other Foreign Service officers among the hostages, the 35-year-old Rosen, bearded and balding, had first seen Iran as a Peace Corpsman. He had returned in 1978 to serve as the embassy press attaché.

Kennedy beamed with admiration for Reverend Coffin. He thought the New Yorker had done "a marvelous job" and that he was "absolutely aware of what we were going through."

"It looked very black for us," he continued. "He hit just the right note as far as I was concerned. And I will always be in his debt."

On the other hand, Kennedy said, "The group that came out at Easter were a disaster. The priest said to one of our number, 'I sure would like to spend, say, 20 days with you fellows. It would give me a chance to meditate.'"

"Well, not long before then," Kennedy added, "we had been stood up against that wall, and we all said to ourselves, you know, we'd very much like to have had him with us."

Another visitor who came in for criticism in the early months was George Hansen, a Republican Congressman from Idaho who made two trips to Iran, one in November, one in December, on what he depicted as a personal mission to end the hostages' captivity. Many politicians dismissed Hansen's venture as self-serving. He was "out of bounds," said Representative Thomas P. O'Neill, the Speaker of the House. Except for some attention in the news media, nothing much came of Hansen's trips.

On Christmas Day, Kathryn Koob sat alone in the library on the second floor of the chancery overlooking the main entrance to the embassy and Takht-E-Jamshid Avenue. Outside, hundreds of Iranians were sounding their rhythmic death chants for President Carter and the Shah. Hour after hour, the crowd chorused.

Like the other hostages, Koob was thousands of miles from home, without family or friends. "But the message of Christmas," she said later, "was the same."

A deeply religious person, she had always believed that "Christmas is Christ. It's not tinsel, it's not the tree." That afternoon, her beliefs were being tested, and she remembers saying to herself: "If you really mean what you say, here's your chance, kid."

At 11 P.M. Miss Koob heard what she took to be a church bell ringing, probably, she thought, in a church across the street. It was the catalyst she had needed. "I had a worship service," she said, "and it was Christmas."

At the Foreign Ministry, Michael Howland, the security man from Alexandria, Va., had shaped a Christmas tree out of paper and trimmed it with ribbon. On Christmas Eve, Secretary of State Cyrus R. Vance telephoned from Washington. Then Laingen, Tomseth and Howland put in a call to the State Department and sang Christmas carols to their colleagues in the Iran Working Group.

Friends at the Nepalese Embassy had sent the three Americans a turkey. But they had no way of preparing it and they gave the bird away. Over their usual evening meal of commissary provisions, they raised a toast with glasses of water, and turned in early.

"We certainly had no expectation that first Christmas that we would spend another one there," Laingen said. "If we had known that, it would have been rather hard to take."

New Year's Day was the nadir of Miss Koob's experience. "Nothing particular happened," she said. "I had no different treatment that day, no different food. I suspect perhaps it was because two months had gone by and at that point I felt it was going to go on for several more months. It seemed to me that everything had hardened."

As Miss Koob's sense of despair deepened, United Nations Secretary General Kurt Waldheim began a four-day visit to Iran that would yield little. Waldheim would later deny allegations that he had bungled a proposal to establish a United Nations Commission to investigate past United States activities in Iran in exchange for the hostages. In any case, though, he achieved no substantive movement toward a resolution of the crisis.

A few days earlier, Moorhead Kennedy had been shifted to yet another room, this one in the basement of another embassy building. He was told there was a shortage of showers and that he would only be able to take one every 10 days.

His mood could not have been more different from Miss Koob's. At about that time, he recalled, "I began to think pretty much we would make it. I wasn't quite sure the guards could keep the mob out. But I still thought we'd probably make it."

In the ambassador's residence, Blucker had found that if he climbed up on the radiator in the bathroom he could catch a glimpse of the sky and the trees and could even watch the dozens of green parrots and the gray and black ravens waging their daily battles for sovereignty on the embassy grounds.

"Nice to watch," he said. "It was nice to see the outside."

But on December 30 he was moved to a room in the basement of the chancery that he was to share with three others: Barry Rosen, the press attaché; Robert C. Ode, at 64 the oldest of the hostages and a retired Foreign Service officer who been recalled to temporary duty in Iran, and Bruce W. German, the embassy's budget officer.

There had been an attempted escape at the embassy a few days earlier. "Whether that persuaded them that the ambassador's residence was not a good place to keep a bunch of people, I don't know," Blucker said. "I had heard one night an unusual amount of gunfire and wondered what in the world was going on. I found out later that was the night of the escape attempt, when they fired on Bill Belk."

There were a few attempted escapes, but none succeeded. The hostages never set up an escape committee as American pilots captured in North Vietnam had done, said Moorhead Kennedy, and he explained that there was good reason why. There was no command structure among the hostages. Most of them were civilians. And their leader, Bruce Laingen, was being held elsewhere.

Besides, Kennedy said, messages were difficult to pass and the hostages were kept so thoroughly apart that they rarely saw more than a few of their fellow captives.

"We were in watertight compartments," he said. "We were a platoon divided up. We were cut off from the world. Nobody got out. Nobody infiltrated in to help."

As early as December 23, 1979, William E. Belk made the first attempt to escape. Malcolm Kalp tried only a couple of hours after Belk failed.

It was nearly midnight when Belk wriggled free from sheets that bound his hands, cut through a window screen and slipped out onto the embassy roof.

Belk was tough. Forty-three years old, he had spent most of his adult life as a military man, serving two years in the Air Force and 20 in the Marines, schooled in their uncompromising "name, rank and serial number" code of conduct for prisoners. Five years after joining the State Department, he arrived in Iran to serve as a communications and records officer. That was just five weeks before the embassy takeover.

When Belk began his escape try, he had expected to emerge on the embassy roof in darkness. But, he said, "much to my chagrin, I found that the lights to the compound — lights that embassy workers had not been able to get working in recent days — were on. It was lit up like a stadium and here I was sitting on top of a building."

He climbed down to a courtyard where young Iranians were walking around in small groups.

"The only thing I could think of was to act like a student," he said. "I had a sweater so I pulled it over my head and pretended to be putting it on and started mumbling away. I walked right out behind five other students."

But as he ducked around a building, Belk was confronted by a female guard with an automatic weapon.

"Stop," she cried in Persian.

He lunged at the guard and tried to wrestle her gun away. She screamed and got off two wild shots, but he jerked the magazine out of her gun and broke away. He had made it to the top of the compound wall before patrolling guards spotted him and started shooting.

Startled, and winded from his sprint, the adrenaline pumping through his body, Belk toppled from the wall, injuring his leg.

"I couldn't run any further and I couldn't get back on top of the 12-foot wall," he said. "I tried to hide as best I could."

But the attempt was fruitless. In moments he was surrounded. The guards slapped him around, took him back to his room and blindfolded him.

Later, three Iranians returned to the room and accused Belk of having connections with the Central Intelligence Agency. One of them kicked his injured leg. Another jammed the barrel of a .45-caliber pistol behind his ear and told Belk, "People who try to escape get shot." Then he pulled the trigger. The hammer clicked on an empty chamber.

Belk spent the next 10 days in isolation.

The next morning, Elizabeth Swift asked a guard what the noise had been about.

"We shot a hostage," the guard told her. It was not until more than a

61

year later, on the airplane ride home, that she found out what had really happened.

The commotion stirred by the capture of Belk apparently alerted guards to Kalp's attempted escape two hours later. It was the first of three by Kalp, who tried again in May and June.

Kalp recalled the first night: "When Christmas came along and there was no Christmas relief, I decided that they would never release us as long as Carter was in." So when the guard fell asleep at about 1:30, Kalp walked out the door. But before he had gone more than a few steps, he was nabbed by hallway guards who apparently were extra alert because of the fuss over the capture of Belk.

"They tied me up for three days and nights and handcuffed my feet," Kalp said. "That's when I began my solitary confinement."

His second attempt came when he was being held in solitary in a private dwelling in Isfahan. In the back of a desk in the chancery in Teheran, he had found a 12-inch hacksaw. He carried it with him, hidden on his back between his shirt and trousers. The Isfahan room had sliding glass doors with bars on the outside and a blanket hung over the frame so that he could not see out. He began to saw the bottom of the bars. But his captors heard the rasp of the blade and took it away.

In his third attempt, a month later, he fed some tranquilizers, which he had been given to help him sleep, to a fierce watchdog that was chained below his second-floor window. At 3:15 A.M., believing that the dog was asleep, he picked the lock and jumped out. But the dog woke up and, straining against its chain, began barking loudly. Carrying a little sack of food and water that he had saved to sustain him on what he had hoped would be his flight, Kalp ran around a corner of the building. Turning, he saw a guard on his knees aiming a Q-3 rifle at his stomach. Kalp surrendered.

When guards put handcuffs on him, Kalp said, their hands were so shaky that it took five minutes. The guards, he thought, had orders to protect their prisoners and were nervous over what might have happened to him. But their possible nervousness was not reflected in kind treatment. His hands cuffed behind his back, he was blindfolded and taken into a bathroom, where his captors kicked and punched him. Then, for a day and a half, he was kept bound and cuffed and under constant surveillance.

FIRST CHRISTMAS

"He was a tough nut," Kennedy said of Kalp. After his last escape attempt, "they welded his windows shut."

Toward the end of captivity, some of the Marines agreed that if they were not freed by February 12, 1981 — time enough, they thought, to let President Reagan secure their freedom — they would try to escape, even though they realized it probably would not work.

"I don't want to sound John Wayne-ish," said James Lopez, "but it wasn't going to be a breakout. It was going to be a kamikaze mission."

Sgt. John McKeel, a square-faced, slow-spoken, 26-year-old Texan who had arrived in Iran a week before the embassy takeover, said the attempt would have involved about half a dozen hostages. He told of making homemade fire bombs and other improvised weapons. "We'd mixed detergent and kerosene, razor blades and pins and things of that sort," he said.

Did he think it would have worked?

"No," Sergeant McKeel muttered.

"I doubt that I could have gotten out of the country alive," said Warrant Officer Joseph Hall, "but it had gotten to the point where I was seriously thinking about it."

Moorhead Kennedy got the impression that the Marines planned a "suicide breakout" every week or so. "It never took place," he said.

In the opinion of the Foreign Service officer who asked not to be named, the attempted escapes were not serious efforts, but rather appeared to be part of the psychological need of some hostages to offer resistance.

"There were many such attempts — most of them phony," he said. "People knew damn well they weren't going anyplace. It was a gesture. It had to do with the military notion that somehow they had an obligation to give their name, rank and serial number and escape if they possibly can, and harass the enemy. And with that kind of mentality, they did all kinds of what I would call idle gestures."

After the first attempted escapes, Belk and Kalp were thrown into solitary confinement and Blucker and some of the others were put into the basement of the chancery. Life in the basement was rougher. There were no windows and the guards seemed more hostile. After a while, one of Blucker's roommates was moved out.

"We were known as the bad people in that room," he said. "Next door to us were the good people. They had no guard sitting in their room. They had cards, tennis balls to bounce, picture puzzles to play with, access to a tape recorder with some tapes. At a certain point they decided one of ours was a good man, a good boy. So they moved him into the room with the good boys."

"I can't prove anything about the good boys," Blucker continued. "I am satisfied I know who they are, but I can't prove it so I'd better not say. They were young people, unideological, with no high position in the embassy. I suspect that what they did was that they just didn't resist. That they were politically inert."

On the other hand, Blucker said, "A bad guy was somebody who followed my kind of conduct. They passed a petition around calling on the U.S. Government to return the Shah. I refused to sign that. It wasn't appropriate. I refused to write any letters to senators or newspapers demanding that actions be taken to get us out. I was generally hostile. I made no remarks against the Shah or against David Rockefeller or Henry Kissinger. In fact, I didn't try to be anything but the bourgeoisie, the reactionary. And I fussed at them, I snarled at them."

Blucker referred to those who had "collaborated" with the Iranian captors. Then he corrected himself and said "cooperated." In their initial days home, neither Blucker nor any of the other hostages reported any instances in which they felt their colleagues had behaved disloyally to the United States.

Pressed to distinguish between cooperation and collaboration, Blucker replied, "I don't know. I don't know. The words are hard to define. Where does one stop and the other start? Cooperation includes collaboration and other things. It's just too complicated to go into."

One of the former hostages, who asked that he not be identified, said: "I know that a lot of people did things that I wouldn't do and I didn't approve of and I wish they hadn't done. But I don't want to label them. There were several people, perhaps. I shouldn't say a lot."

Colonel Scott, one of the decorated Vietnam veterans, called it an "all or nothing situation."

"You are either totally loyal, you do not cooperate or aid and abet your enemies, or you do." he said. "The Code of Conduct says it all."

6

Television Shows

In television footage arranged by the captors, some of the hostages were shown making statements that were critical, in varying degrees, of the Shah and United States policy, and to some extent portraying better conditions than actually existed for the captives. The Iranians also made public some tape recordings containing critical remarks by hostages. After their release, some of those who appeared in the television films said they had done so under duress and that they had tried to give clues that they were not being sincere.

Sgt. William Gallegos, a quiet 22-year-old Marine guard from the industrial city of Pueblo, Colo., 100 miles south of Denver, was the first hostage to be interviewed on television. And his appearance on NBC on December 10 brought a crescendo of controversy.

All the networks had been negotiating with the captors for three days for the opportunity to conduct the interview. Eventually, NBC struck an agreement in which the captors would pick the hostage to be interviewed and have the filming done by an Iranian crew. Two NBC correspondents, George Lewis and Fred Francis, would be admitted onto the embassy grounds to question the hostage and an NBC producer, Walter Millis, would edit the film in Teheran. In addition, the captors stipulated that the film include an unedited, five-minute propaganda speech by an Iranian woman whom some of the hostages later referred to as "Mary the Terrorist," and that the film be broadcast during prime time. ABC and CBS would not accept those terms.

As the camera began rolling, Sergeant Gallegos, who had played football and run track in high school but dropped out to join the Marines, was seated in a straight-back chair between a large picture of Ayatollah Ruhollah Khomeini and an anti-Shah propaganda poster. He was wearing a sturdy windbreaker with a fur collar over a striped sweater and a white shirt, open at the collar. He looked healthy, but, perhaps understandably, somewhat ill at ease. Early on, he said that "most of the students" had been "really good to us."

"It's hard to believe, I know," he went on. But "we haven't been asked any questions as, you know, what we were doing here, what really our job was. There was just: What do you do here? You know, What's your name, What do you do here, How long have you been here, and that's it.

"And," he continued, "nobody's been mistreated. All of us can see each other. We're — everybody's getting enough food to eat, we're — the cleanliness is really great. You know, it's — they come and clean up. And clean clothes. Everything we need. Everything — toothbrushes, combs. I know everyone here wants to go home. I don't know what negotiations are toward this — what's happening between the Iranian students and the American Government. I know that they keep telling us that they want the Shah to return to Iran and we'll be released. Other stipulations were that if the Shah wasn't released that all the hostages would be put on trial. I don't know what would happen after that. But I hope, I'm leaving it up to my country, and my people. I have faith in them."

As the interview continued, Sergeant Gallegos was asked how he personally felt about the issue of returning the Shah.

"Myself," he said, "as a Marine guard, you all know I'd give my life for any American, any American, any President of the United States — present and past — for any of my friends. And I just — I can't see it now. I just think of all the people that have given their lives before — Americans given their lives for a good cause. In some way I don't see this as a good cause."

The following dialogue ensued:

TELEVISION SHOWS

Q. Do you know there's a well-known psychological observation that a hostage very often assumes the political feelings of and is very often sympathetic toward his captors?

A. Yes, sir, I feel that way as a Marine. You know how I feel. I hope you know how I feel. I know my superiors know how I feel.

Q. Why are you here? I think that's a question a lot of . . .

A. Why am I here, sir?

Q. Why were you the one singled out to do this interview?

A. I don't know. There are many of us. I was called upon. I didn't know what was going on. I was reading a book. Next thing I know, they say, come with me. They told me to stand up. And I went into the hallway and they said, all right, you're coming with us. So the next thing I know, they bring me over to a little room over here and then they said you're going to be interviewed by one of the TV stations. And then they brought me here.

Q. What if you said no?

A. I thought about saying no; but I felt that many of the people don't know what's going on, I think. I want them to know that we're O.K. I want them to at least fight, you know, do something. I want President Carter to know we're all right, you know. I want him to know that nothing's happening to us. Not as of yet. I want him to know that we're relying on his decision to let us go home.

Q. All right. You've told us about your conditions and the people across from you. What about the psychological strain of being in that room? How do you see your fellow hostages? Are they holding up? Are any of them having problems?

A. The strain is tremendous on all of us. We're holding up, though. It's really, the Marines themselves are holding up great. The hostages looked at each other. They looked at the Marines and the Marines give 'em a smile of confidence. And they looked at us and they just, they wonder what's going to happen. You know, the strain is showing; not physically, but it's there. In the eyes. You can tell. As far as, it's not really taking any effect yet. I mean, they haven't gone to drastic measures, no. A lot of the hostages have been ill, but have been taken care of by doctors. Doctors come down at least twice a week to see us and give medication if it's needed.

A. Did they accuse you of being a spy?

A. Yes, sir. I was accused of being a C.I.A. agent. I was accused of working in a spy den. I was accused of many types of spy activities.

Q. Are you a spy?

A. No, sir, I'm not. I'm a United States Marine security guard.

Q. What would you like to see the American people do? Can you tell them that you're ready to hold out here forever, I mean what would you like to see them do?

A. We're not ready to hold out here forever. I don't know how much longer we can take this. And especially if the Shah's not returned. I would imagine that it would get a little worse. I don't know. As far as the people, I would imagine I want the people to know, to find out the truth. You know, I want them to find out what's going on here.

Photographs of Sergeant Gallegos and excerpts from the interview appeared on front pages of newspapers across the United States the next day.

That morning, President Carter said over breakfast with the Democratic leaders of Congress that he had been personally upset by the broadcast. Later, Thomas P. O'Neill Jr., the Speaker of the House, said he was "bitterly disappointed that an American network would take a poor young boy who probably means well and allow him to be trotted out before American television and the American people."

Executives of the two networks that had turned down the interview joined in the criticism.

Roone Arledge, the president of ABC News, said he was "surprised and disappointed that NBC did it."

"It was not television's proudest moment," he continued. "I don't know how much harm it did to television journalism to have one of the networks knowingly participate in the students' quest for a forum. It's a setback for those of us trying to operate responsibly in a sensitive terrain."

Bill Leonard, the president of CBS News, said he had easily rejected the interview offer. "As long as they were dictating the spokesman, the cameras, the hostage and when we could televise it, they were asking us to be a conduit rather than a journalistic organization," he said. "I didn't spend three seconds with that decision."

TELEVISION SHOWS

William J. Small, the president of NBC News, said he felt confident his network had done the right thing.

"We did it," he said, "because it was a very important interview, because no one has talked to any of these hostages for 35 days. The American public has the right to know what's going on there. Obviously, we knew we'd have to do it in the presence of the students. They're not going to let you take a hostage home for Christmas.

"I don't know what better proof there is of its importance," he continued, "than the page one play it got in newspapers across the country. For all the criticism, I'd do it again — tonight, no question about it."

The morning after NBC broadcast the interview in an excerpt on the Nightly News and for its full 18 minutes later in the evening, CBS and ABC presented another, shorter interview with Sergeant Gallegos that had been conducted by one of the captors and been given to the networks by a so-called "student committee."

"This is different from what NBC did," said Richard C. Wald, the executive vice president of ABC News. "As long as we identified it as handout film, explaining where it came from, and as long as we were free to use it or not use it, as we saw fit, we were eligible to put it on the air. It does not breach editorial integrity. We didn't have to pay for it with a five-minute vehicle for propaganda."

Small, the NBC news chief, smiled at what he called the "righteousness" of the rival networks. As he saw it, it was no easier to justify taking a handout prepared by the Iranians than to make concessions to them for an interview by a network reporter.

"We all did what we did for the same reasons," he said, "to serve the immense interest in what's going on in Teheran.

"If you look at the history of kidnap victims and hostages generally, one of the things you realize is that if there were a total news blackout, the people holding these hostages would do something more dramatic. Coverage is the escape valve for the steam. I'm not saying that we're trying to be an escape valve — that's not our mission, even if it serves that purpose."

In Teheran, correspondents for ABC and CBS confided to colleagues in the press corps that they had spent a jittery night waiting for executives in their New York offices to decide whether they had been courageous or stupid when they rejected the interview. They knew the line had been very thin.

Back home after his release, Sergeant Gallegos said he had been "forced in various ways" to go before the camera. "I was not beaten," he said, adding, "I did it for my military superiors. I'm sorry the public didn't understand."

"I was saying that the treatment was good for my fellow colleagues so that they would not be mistreated," he continued. "But also I was trying to say that we were not being treated well."

Jerry Plotkin, who had been visiting the embassy when it was seized and who identified himself as a 45-year-old California businessman on his first trip outside the United States, shied away from reporters after regaining his freedom. In late November, during the fourth week of captivity, the Iranians gave a Los Angeles radio reporter a seven-minute tape recording of a message made by Plotkin.

"In the name of God," Plotkin was heard saying, "return the Shah and free the hostages. Let the world know no tyrant or dictator can ever find safe harbor in the U.S."

"We have been treated humanely," he continued, "The students treat us kindly and with respect."

On February 3, the Iranians released another tape which they said had been made as Elizabeth Ann Swift, one of the political officers, was speaking to her family on the telephone. It was not clear whether she was aware that the tape was being made.

At one point on the tape, she said, "You know, I don't know what the C.I.A. was doing here, but it was doing things that it shouldn't have been doing, and I just wish the United States would realize that too."

Referring to her captors, she said, "The guys had a certain point when they came here. But, anyway, don't worry about that. I just wanted to make sure you understood how I felt, because I will not defend this sort of nonsense."

On the first New Year's Eve of the captivity, all three networks broadcast segments of a film made by the Iranians showing four hostages seated at a long table and reading from handwritten notes statements that criticized alleged American "spying in Iran" and depicted the Shah as "a puppet of the United States" and "an accused criminal" who had taken "billions of dollars of the peoples' money" when he fled Iran.

One of the four was Jerry Plotkin. The three others were Marine Sgt. Kevin J. Hermening, at 20 the youngest of the hostages; Steven M. Lauterbach, a 28-year-old embassy administrative officer with a master's degree from the University of Michigan; and Staff Sgt. Joseph Subic Jr., a 22-year-old military policeman in the Army. At various times during the captivity, the two sergeants and Lauterbach, all single, had been roommates.

The film showed Sergeant Subic saying that he had arrived in Iran as a defender of the Shah, but that after seeing "more and more poor people — people without homes, food, education — my thinking started to turn around."

The State Department characterized the film as "a cynical propaganda ploy," but it did not criticize the networks for presenting it.

At first, the Iranians insisted that the film, which ran for an hour and had been made during the Christmas visit by the clergymen, be shown in its entirety without preview. The television organizations said no, but they changed their minds later, after the Iranians agreed to let the networks slice the film into chunks they considered appropriate. On the air, the networks explained how the film had been produced. They noted that only excerpts were being shown, that the captors were anxious to have the film shown and that the hostages might have been forced to make the statements. All of them, it seemed, had learned from the Gallegos interview.

Lauterbach and Sergeants Hermening and Subic also wrote letters to newspapers saying they had seen photographs and documents that had convinced them that their captors' demands for the return of the Shah were justified.

"Basically, the reason for doing that," Lauterbach said after his release, "is that we were trying to — we had been told at that time that they were seriously considering letting some of the hostages go and that if we cooperated in this respect it might expedite their release. And so, we did send some of those letters. I now wish that I hadn't done that. I feel kind of bad about that. But at the time I felt it was the right thing to do because it might bring about the release. I also thought that these might be recognized for what they were in the States. That is, orches-

71

trated propaganda that wasn't to be taken seriously. That's the reason I did it."

As a counterweight to the Iranian propaganda efforts, the United States mounted a diplomatic offensive early in 1980 to build world reaction against Iran.

The United Nations had acted earlier, but to no avail. Less than a week after the hostages were seized, the Security Council issued a call for their release. Three days later, President Carter ordered a halt to oil imports from Iran and froze Iranian assets in the United States, a step that, it turned out, set the stage for the eventual arrangement that led to their release more than a year later.

On January 13, as a result of the American diplomatic campaign, the United Nations Security Council voted to impose economic sanctions on Iran because of the continued captivity of the Americans. But the resolution was vetoed by the Soviet Union.

There would be another Iranian propaganda push on April 10, when the captors offered to sell the American television networks a 34-minute videotape featuring Sergeant Subic, the son of a retired master sergeant. The Iranians insisted, as a condition for turning over the tape, that it be presented in full, without editing. If the networks agreed, the Iranians promised to provide 11 more hostage "confessions." The networks refused to buy it, and it ran only on the Iranian state television on April 9. Americans learned the contents from reports by foreign newspaper correspondents who saw it.

On the tape Subic was shown criticizing the American Government and confessing that he had spied for the Central Intelligence Agency. He also purportedly told of United States surveillance flights over Iran and pointed out computer equipment concealed in the floor and ceiling of the embassy warehouse. At one point, the sergeant named several hostages who he said had carried out espionage work. Among them were Colonel Schaefer, the 49-year-old defense and Air Force attaché for whom he had worked; Thomas Ahern, 47, who was listed as the narcotics control coordinator on the embassy staff, and two men, William J. Daugherty, 32, and Malcolm Kalp, 41, whose job descriptions were not made clear by the State Department and who, early on, along with Ahern, had been accused by the Iranians of being C.I.A. agents.

Initially after his return home, Sergeant Subic was not willing to discuss this tape. But in an interview several months later with *The Red-ford Observer*, a weekly newspaper in the Detroit suburb of Redford Township, where he was staying at his parents' home, Subic said the Iranian film had been "faked."

"The militants spliced used film footage of me taken on various oc-casions during my captivity, and one of them faked my voice in the film where I supposedly admitted to the militants as being a C.I.A. agent," he said. "Everything we did on film was either manufactured or staged by militants for propaganda purposes."

Subic said that he and other hostages had been badly beaten by in-terrogators in Iran and that he suffered recurrent stomach pains caused in part by a bleeding ulcer. "The interrogators were very professional," he said. "They punched me under my ribs, but their beatings left no marks on my body. I still experience stomach pains."

The sergeant made no effort to conceal his bitterness over news coverage of the film on which he allegedly confessed. He said he planned to leave active military service shortly, but he insisted that the Army believed his version of what had happened in Iran. "If the mili-tary really suspected that I had admitted to being a C.I.A. agent, I would have been arrested for a military court-martial," he said. "But there has been, and there will be, no military investigation to my actions in Iran."

If there was no military investigation, there were at least serious of-ficial reservations about Subic's actions in Iran. Among the 21 military hostages held through the entire 14 months of captivity, Subic alone was not awarded a Defense Department Meritorious Service Medal for his conduct. The Defense Department did not say why he had been denied an award. It said only that Subic's actions while in captivity did not measure up to the standard required for a decoration. The Meritorious Service Medal is usually given to service personnel who distinguish themselves in joint activities in noncombat situations.

On January 18, John Limbert, the political officer most capable in the Persian language, was moved from the Mushroom to solitary con-finement in the basement of the embassy. His windowless 10-by-12-foot room was illuminated with fluorescent lights and furnished with a bare mattress, a small typewriter table and two chairs.

"They said they were doing this because they thought I was important," Limbert said. "I don't think this was a sort of thought-through thing though. It was like they had read that this is the way hostages are treated in Solzhenitsyn, treat them in random ways. It was like they had taken a course, Hostages 101, and they were doing it badly. I'd have given them a C-minus."

Limbert discovered that his room was next to one occupied by William Belk, the communications and records officer, and Specialist Hohman, the Army medic. The rooms were separated by a thin partition that came about an inch short of meeting the permanent wall, leaving a gap like a mail slot.

"We could slide notes through there," Limbert said. "We'd trade news, sort of, 'What did you see? What did you hear?' It could be anything, whatever the students might have let slip, anything. One of my neighbors was able to smuggle a radio to me. He left it in the bathroom. It was about the size of a cigarette pack. We had news for about a month then, broadcast in Farsi. They were never able to discover the radio, but, of course, I couldn't take it with me when I moved."

7

Escape

On January 28, the six embassy employees who had been hiding with the Canadians — five members of the consular staff and an agricultural attaché — flew out of Iran bound for Zurich. The Canadian Government had issued them diplomatic passports and, according to a diplomat in Washington, the Central Intelligence Agency helped forge Iranian visas for them.

Kenneth D. Taylor, the 45-year-old career diplomat who was Canada's ambassador in Teheran then, had struggled for six weeks to find a way to get the Americans safely out of the country, consulting frequently with superiors at the Ministry of External Affairs in Ottawa in coded Telex messages. In turn, Ottawa was conducting a running dialogue with Washington.

At first, Taylor had considered driving the four men and two women to the city of Tabriz, in the northwest, then across the border to Turkey. Later, he thought they might be able to make a dash for a port on the Persian Gulf and slip aboard a friendly tanker.

But both solutions would have meant more than 400 miles of overland travel in regions where disorder and lawlessness were as unpredictable as the desert winds. Furthermore, Tabriz and the Province of Khuzistan, which lay between Teheran and the Persian Gulf, were in even greater turmoil than the rest of the country. It was Khuzistan, with its independent-minded Arab majority, that eight months later would become the main battlefield in the Iraq-Iran war.

"So, we decided to confront the Iranians head-on," Taylor said later, and to send the Americans out of the country directly through the Teheran airport.

By early January, Taylor said, he and officials in Ottawa and Washington had agreed that the Americans should be spirited out of Iran by the end of the month. The Cabinet, in a secret session, agreed to the highly unusual procedure of issuing Canadian passports to the Americans.

Taylor and the other officials had been spurred on by several factors. For one thing, "at least three or four" journalists as well as the diplomats in Ottawa and Washington were already aware that the Canadians were sheltering the Americans. And, while the journalists had agreed to keep the secret, Taylor and some of the others worried that word might inadvertently get out. Taylor also wanted to move while the Americans were still in a "confident, resilient mood" and were prepared to take the risks in getting out.

Furthermore, Taylor said, he worried: "What would happen if the situation was suddenly resolved, and the Iranians took everybody to the airport and we rushed out and said, 'What about our six?' "

Perhaps, he said, "They'd say, since the six were harbored surreptitiously, they are obviously C.I.A. agents, so the rest of them can go but you six and the Canadians have to stay."

In mid-January, as the documents were being prepared with "technical assistance," from Washington, the group had a fright.

A man, speaking in unaccented English, telephoned the Taylor residence, where Joseph and Kathleen Stafford were staying, and asked to speak to them. Mrs. Taylor, who answered the phone, said she didn't know what he was talking about. He persisted and she held her ground. The man finally hung up, but they were all shaken.

When the passports arrived in the diplomatic pouch, one of Taylor's Persian-speaking aides, Roger Lucey, discovered that the visa-makers had erroneously followed the calendar used under the Shah and not the traditional Islamic calendar reintroduced by Ayatollah Khomeini. According to the false documents, the Americans would have been leaving the country before they had arrived.

"We might have argued it out with immigration, and told them, 'Don't blame us for your administrative foul-up.' " Taylor said months later after he had taken up his next post as consul general in New York.

Instead, he said cryptically, "We fixed it up."

All preparations for the getaway were complete by the weekend of the Iranian national elections, in which Abolhassan Bani-Sadr won the presidency. Taylor thought the election would add to the confusion in already chaotic Iran and would help cloak the departure.

The Iranians went to the polls on Friday, January 25. The vote-counting went on through the weekend. And on Monday morning the Americans were driven to Mehrabad Airport in two Canadian Embassy cars, a gray Chevrolet Caprice Classic and a red Peugeot 404.

Taylor worried as the Americans left the Canadian residences. "After three months with us," he said, "the six were healthy. But their degree of resiliency, their ability to respond to the unexpected, was limited."

In revolutionary Teheran, getting through roadblocks on the airport approaches and check-points in the terminal had become a three-hour ordeal. The Americans passed through five of the check-points smoothly. At still another inside the terminal, an immigration official took their passports and disappeared into a private office. It was a critical moment.

Finally, the bureaucrat returned, handed the Americans their papers and waved them toward the plane.

Suddenly, another hitch developed, barring their way. The jet aircraft, they were told, had developed "mechanical difficulties."

Twenty tense minutes ensued.

Taylor had anticipated trouble like this. Each of the Americans had tickets on other flights, and even if the airport had been shut down, they could have returned to Teheran. A rented four-bedroom house was awaiting them.

The contingency plans were not needed, however. The "mechanical difficulties" were cleared up. And finally, after nearly 12 weeks of hiding and gnawing uncertainty, the Americans boarded the plane and soared away.

Taylor had also anticipated the possibility of retribution from Iran and had in recent weeks pared down the staff of his embassy to eight: himself, his secretary, one political officer, a woman communications specialist, a military police sergeant and three corporals.

On the day of departure, Taylor took one other precaution. At his behest, the sergeant, a short, husky, ox-boned M.P., took a sledge hammer and pulverized the Canadian Embassy's cryptographic machinery. "He nearly drove it through the floor," another Canadian diplomat said.

Shortly before the Americans left, Taylor's secretary, Laverna Dollimore, and the three corporals departed on a British Airways flight to London. A few hours later, the M.P. sergeant, Taylor and the two other Canadians took off on a Scandinavian Air Service jet bound for Copenhagen. In Ottawa, Prime Minister Joe Clark announced that the Canadian Embassy in Teheran had temporarily been closed. More than a year later, Canada still would have no diplomats in Iran.

Back in the United States, the six Americans tumbled into the arms of their families at Dover Air Force Base in Delaware, then quietly faded into the fabric of the land. The State Department had told them, they said, "they'd rather we didn't talk too much," and they embraced the guidance.

For days afterward, though, the rest of the country toasted Canada. Flowers, candy, cakes and thousands of "thank you" messages, poured into Canadian diplomatic offices. Maple leaves — the symbol of Canada — sprouted in lapels and everywhere Canadians were treated to free meals and drinks. In New York, Mayor Edward I. Koch said the Canadian assistance "rivals the heroic action taken by the Dutch and the Danish in World War II, when they saved Jews from the barbarism of the Nazis." And he invited Taylor to City Hall to receive the key to the city.

The Iranians did not take the getaway lightly.

"Sooner or later, somewhere in the world, Canada will pay," the Foreign Minister at the time, Sadegh Ghotbzadeh, raged at a press conference. "Any hardness, harshness or changes which may be imposed on the hostages," he added menacingly, "it's only the Canadian Government which will be responsible for it."

Indeed, less than a week after the six Americans had fled, the hostages were subjected to a new episode of terror. The captives, who did not learn of the good fortune of their six colleagues until months later, said they never found out what brought on the renewed harshness. Moorhead Kennedy said he thought it might have been in retaliation for an attempted suicide. Richard Morefield said he thought it might have been related to another escape attempt.

Steven Lauterbach, the administrative officer, Sergeant Subic and Sergeant Hermening had tried to make a break on Wednesday, January 30. The three, who were being held in the chancery, had been taken about 100 yards across the embassy compound to the ambassador's residence for a hot shower, an event that had become a part of their routine every three or four days. Once inside, they tried to climb out a window but were caught.

"They apparently were very angry with the attempted escape," Lauterbach said. "I was roughed up and I was beaten. It was not a severe beating. I was roughed up. After that I was in solitary for about six weeks."

The Iranians may have been more angry than Lauterbach knew. They never explained. In any case, at 1 A.M. on February 5, a group of the hostages was abruptly confronted with the first of a series of incidents that left them shaken and terrified.

Seven Iranians wielding automatic rifles and wearing white masks, green fatigue uniforms and combat boots burst in on 21 hostages sleeping in the Mushroom and herded them together against a wall, spread-eagled.

"They told us not to talk, not to move," said Paul Needham, the 30-year-old Air Force captain who had gone to Teheran on a temporary assignment as an adviser to the Iranian Air Force.

"One of the guards barked out an order," Needham said. "A round was chambered in each weapon. He barked out another order. I could hear the safety catch go off. He barked another order about 15 seconds later and a round hit the floor. It was ejected and fell to the floor. I thought I was dead as the last order was barked out. I thought it was to fire. I do not speak Farsi and I thought he had said to fire."

Gary E. Lee, the administrative officer, later recalled thinking as he waited for the bullets to tear into him, "Boy, I sure hope they hit me in the head and not the back, so I go quickly."

NO HIDING PLACE

Colonel Scott, the military liaison chief, was certain he heard someone cry out in Persian, "Get ready."

"My knees were knocking," said the colonel, a veteran of two combat tours in Vietnam. "I thought things had deteriorated so badly that they were just going to get rid of us."

The men in white masks had put the hostages against the wall in two groups, Queen said.

"When they moved the first group in, they had everybody lie down," he said, "but, one, Commander Sharer, said, 'You're going to shoot me standing up, not lying down.' He refused to lie down. And they were all standing up when I came in."

"When we were all in the room against the wall," Queen continued, "there was dead silence. Then I heard the metallic clicking of the weapons, locking the bolts, removing the safety. I don't know which. It was just this harsh metallic click. And I really thought that was it. I just stood there. I knew it was my last moment. I said the Lord's Prayer and tried to give myself the last rites, because I was sure that we had just breathed our last."

How long he stood there, Queen does not know. What inscribed itself on his mind, however, was the "deadly silence."

"No one said anything," he added, "No one sobbed. Just pure silence."

Eventually, Queen began having trouble holding one of his arms high in the air as he and the others had been instructed.

"The multiple sclerosis had started to hit me by then and I couldn't keep my arm up, and so it started to fall," he said, "At this time they relaxed the weapons a little bit. One of the militants realized I had a problem. So the guy came up and slapped my arm down.

"Then," he continued, "we were taken individually into a small room and stripped to our underpants, searched. While this was going on, another group went into our little rooms and tore them apart. Then we were taken back individually to our rooms."

In the next few days, more of the hostages were terrorized by the men in white masks.

Moorhead Kennedy and some of the others sharing his basement room at the embassy were preparing for bed late one night, he said, when two of the masked men charged in yelling, "Savak! Savak!" Savak

was the Shah's brutal secret police organization, triumphantly disman-
tled by the revolutionaries.

The hostages were hauled out of their rooms and forced to strip to
their undershorts in the cold night air. Inside, other Iranians were ran-
sacking their clothing and personal belongings.

The sharp clack of rifle bolts resounded in the night.

"The masked men chambered rounds into their weapons," Kennedy
said. "They tweaked our elastic bands on our shorts as they walked
back and forth behind us. They poked their cold guns into our backs."

Death seemed imminent. Kennedy said he had trembled, but had
otherwise managed to control himself. When he and his roommate,
Frederick Kupke, realized there would be no shooting, Kennedy said,
they "jumped for joy."

Before the men were returned to their rooms, their belts were taken
away, Kennedy said, and they found that their razors had been seized.
Later, the hostages would refer to that night of terror as "the panty raid."

Another night, Sergeant Sickmann and some of the others were
blindfolded by men in white masks and marched down a hallway. One
at a time, Sergeant Sickmann said, the hostages were taken into a room
by the masked men and told to strip down to their underwear. Then
their blindfolds were removed.

"We just had our face against the wall," the sergeant said. "He told
us not to look. So here we are, we've got our eyes closed, myself and the
other hostages, sitting there, shaking like a leaf against the wall. You
hear these rifles cocking. We thought we were goners then."

In December, Sergeant Sickmann and some of the others had been
shown films, he said, of people "who were killed lying on the ground
with their heads blown off."

"All these images started showing, you know? They kept coming
into my head," he continued, "and the rifles being cocked and stuff like
that. It was sick. I thought I was going to be the same way."

One of the masked men "started searching private parts of your
body," Sergeant Sickmann said, and, finally, he and the others were told
to get dressed. A week later, he said, there was a similar search.

The seeming futility of the hostages' situation was reflected in the
departure on March 11 of a United Nations Commission that had gone to
Teheran to seek the release of the hostages. The commission left with-

out even seeing them and without any apparent impact on the conditions of their captivity.

On March 13, Captain Needham recalled, he and some others again stood before a firing squad that did not fire. This time, however, the gunmen did not crank ammunition into their weapons.

Robert Blucker was one of the few hostages put up against the wall who did not believe that an execution was under way. "I didn't think they'd shoot us in that fashion," he said later. In the search, Blucker said, the Iranians found $1,020 in cash on him. They had known about the money, he said, and had told him previously they did not want it. They were not thieves, they said. That night, however, they pocketed the money.

Colonel Scott said that after he experienced one of the mock executions his fear of being killed disappeared.

"You can just get so scared," he said, "You get angry and once you get angry it sustains you through many sorts of stress. I refused to think about death after that."

The midnight raids and the firing squads constituted probably the most concentrated punishment the hostages endured after the first days of their captivity. Many of them apparently shared that fright.

But generally the treatment varied greatly. Hostages suspected of being intelligence operatives and those few who tried to escape had a hard time. At least to some extent, the behavior of the hostages, their personalities and the personalities of the captors who confronted them figured in their treatment. But not always.

Two of the hostages, William Keough, who at 6 feet 9 inches was much taller than the Iranians, and Robert Blucker, were determinedly aggressive. And the Iranians stayed at a respectful distance.

"We complained about the hotel service," Keough said, "that the bathroom was dirty and said, 'When the Ayatollah comes around I'll tell him how dirty this place is,' or 'Send in your sister to clean up.' "

Keough said he had never been physically threatened "because I made it obvious early on that this was not the thing to do."

"When a man would open a door of the cell and hand in food," Keough continued, "I would demand more bread or oranges. They would back away immediately and say, 'Bread is finished,' or 'Oranges is finished,' and my large foot would be in the door and the door some-how wouldn't close until such time as we got bread and oranges. There was a lot of testing going on."

Donald Hohman, the Army medic, was thrown into solitary con-finement many times. "Why?" he asked rhetorically. "Because I dis-agreed with anything the terrorists told me to do. I refused to let them use me. I would not be an animal. I refused to be an animal. They didn't like it."

John Limbert said he was once told he had "broken the rules" by writing notes, and was punished with solitary. "The whole thing was absurd," he said, "You'd say to them 'There are no rules. What rules?' and they'd just say, 'You've broken the rules again.' It was absurd."

"If you sort of held your dignity," he continued, "it infuriated them. They'd say to me, 'We think you've forgotten you're a hostage. You're talking and acting as if you were a diplomat.' It wasn't just me they said this to. They said it to the military and to the other people involved."

Perhaps as draining over the long run as the cold rifle barrel in the back was the daily worry of being accidentally shot. Many of the young guards, the former hostages said, were as awkward with their automatic rifles and submachine guns as a ballerina on a tractor.

"When we were taken outside," said Michael Metrinko, the political officer, "there were 20 or 30 guards who kept their G-3's and their Uzis pointing at me." The guards usually formed a ring around them, and Me-trinko mused on what might happen if there were any gunplay. "I al-ways thought it would be funny," he said, "if one of them were to go off. They would have a massive blood bath, killing each other because they were also pointing at each other. They were very incompetent."

"Those guys were nervous," said Keough, "They'd keep cocking those rifles. I was afraid they'd make a mistake."

Sergeant Lopez found it "slightly nerve-racking because we had all these little kids running around with shotguns. They were 17, 18. They had no weapons training and they're walking around playing John Wayne and Audie Murphy and what-have-you."

In mid-February, Kennedy's group was moved out of the embassy basement to an upstairs room that "had a few windows" and was given a stove on which to heat the food that sometimes had been arriving cold from a command kitchen somewhere else.

"Once," Kennedy said, "we ate by candlelight. We were living the good life."

Toward the end of the month, conditions improved, too, for some of the others. Blucker and his roommate at the time, Robert Ode, were moved to an upstairs room with a window, a desk, two leather chairs and a pair of mattresses. They "also had the privilege," Blucker said, "of asking for tea and dates. You might not get them, but you could ask for them."

In March, two of the hostages were visited by a man who implied that he represented the government. Blucker said he later discovered the man was associated with the Red Crescent Society, the Islamic equivalent of the Red Cross. The purpose of his visit, Blucker said, was to "assure us that things were going to be better."

"I thought at least that perhaps the government was taking control of the situation," Blucker said. "There were no serious confrontations at that point. They were doing their best to be kind. People who were usually very solemn put on sort of frozen smiles."

At about the same time, Richard Morefield was shifted from the Mushroom, where he'd been confined for nearly two months, to the main embassy building and given a room with Sergeant Lopez. Many of the hostages were told they could openly talk to one another. "Now that," said Kennedy, "took some getting used to."

Morefield said he had seen Sergeant Lopez once before in the Mushroom, but when they met in the new room he did not recognize the Marine.

"He'd lost a lot of weight as a result of, I think he said, chicken pox," Morefield said.

As February blended into March, the hostages with Kennedy were allowed to make telephone calls home, but not before one of the Iranians had nettled them a bit by asking, "Who will be the first to give up his turn to call to his friend?"

They all deferred to one another. Kupke was finally chosen by the guards to go first. Kennedy saw this as another "ethnic act" on the part of the guards, in this case because of Kupke's partial Indian ancestry.

Kennedy said his call went through on March 22 at 4 A.M. Eastern Standard Time. He talked about eight minutes to his wife, Louisa, who had taken a leading role among the hostages' families. He placed the call "at that hour because I figured that would guarantee that my one chance to phone the States would result in talking to Louisa."

"We had a very nice talk," he said.

In mid-March Blucker said he asked "the chief terrorist in charge" for a nearby private room with a sunny exposure. He said he was told that a C.I.A. agent was being housed there, but that a change could be arranged.

"I assumed that having been unable to get anything out of me, he was trying to bribe me with kindness," Blucker said. "So I went into that nice little room by myself, sunbathed every day for a few hours. I was able to throw down the window from the top and finally have perfect fresh air. That brought on a million mosquitoes, of course, and, for a while, my face looked like a battlefield. But I left it open anyway. And I never paid off. I never did a thing for them. I never wrote a letter for them."

8

Aftermath of the Raid

 T he arrival of April brought spring and mounting hope to the imprisoned Americans. "Spring was in the air," recalled Moorhead Kennedy. "They [the students] began taking pictures of us, as though gathering souvenirs before it was all over. The Red Cross came and checked on us. Everything seemed to be coming up roses."

A Swiss government airplane was on a Zurich runway on April 1, ready to fly doctors to Teheran to prepare for the imminent release of the hostages. Cots had been brought to the Iranian Foreign Ministry for the hostages to rest on before they left for the airport.

The reason for all this activity was cryptic. Unknown to nearly everyone at the time, secret negotiations for the release of the hostages had been under way since January in London, Bern and Paris. The key participants were President Carter's chief of staff, Hamilton Jordan, and the Iranian Foreign Minister, Sadagh Ghotbzadeh, though Ghotbzadeh's position was so shaky that he at first asked Jordan not to disclose their meeting because he literally feared he might be killed by resentful zealots of Ayatollah Khomeini.

Nonetheless, a way out of the deadlock began to emerge. A United Nations Commission would be set up as a forum for Iran's grievances against the Shah and as a vehicle for releasing the hostages. The Carter

Administration agreed to it, and Ghotbzadeh finally got the endorsement of the Ayatollah and his Revolutionary Council, made up mostly of Islamic clerics who, together with Khomeini, held the real power in Iran.

A five-member United Nations Commission was formed and went to Teheran in late February, but the scenario fell apart. Khomeini, with no explanation, announced that the fate of the hostages would have to be decided by the Iranian Parliament, which had not even been elected. And at the Ayatollah's request, the captors refused to let commission members even see the hostages. Later, the Iranian Government appeared to be inching toward another settlement, but backed out in early April. That was too much for Carter, who severed diplomatic relations and secretly gave the go-ahead for a military rescue raid.

April also brought one of the more unusual events of the captivity, the visit by Barbara Timm to her son, Kevin Hermening, at 20 the youngest of the hostages.

Mrs. Timm and Hermening's stepfather, Kenneth Timm, flew to Teheran on April 18 in defiance of a ban on travel to Iran by President Carter. Some of the militants took the couple to a cemetery where they said victims of the revolution were buried. The Timms took pictures. On the way back they stopped for lunch at a Kentucky Fried Chicken stand.

Then, all of a sudden, with only 20 minutes' notice to Hermening, mother and son were brought together. While silent guards watched and Iranian television cameras rolled, Hermening and his mother sat together on a couch for 45 minutes, holding hands and talking about basketball and their family.

For most of the hostages, spring brought an abrupt change. It happened on April 25.

"All of a sudden there's running up and down the hallways," said Sergeant Lopez. "There's vans being backed in, the door kicks open, and they tell us, 'Pack, you will be leaving soon.' They were very frazzled, they were very nervous, which made us nervous because these clowns were running around with automatic weapons, fingers on the triggers, locked and loaded.

"Something had gone down. We didn't know what."

It wasn't until much later that Sergeant Lopez and his fellow hostages learned that the upheaval on April 25 had been caused by the abortive American rescue mission that ended in a conflagration on the deserted salt flats of the Iranian desert.

Planning for the mission had begun almost immediately after seizure of the embassy in Teheran the previous November. Within days President Carter had ordered the Pentagon to begin contingency planning for a rescue effort. Volunteers were enlisted from the four services. Helicopters and planes were commandeered for test runs in the desert regions of the United States and aerial reconnaissance pictures were taken of possible landing sites in Iran.

By the end of January, Secretary of Defense Harold Brown informed the President that the Pentagon believed it had a feasible plan. In early April, while Moorhead Kennedy was noting the improved conditions in the embassy, President Carter received word that mission commanders were ready to move.

On April 7, the United States Government broke diplomatic relations with Iran and four days later, President Carter convened a meeting of the National Security Council and after an hour of discussion ordered the rescue plan into motion.

The plan called for a surprise commando assault on the embassy after dark on Friday, April 25. The key to success was getting American troops into a position outside Teheran, from which they could slip into the city unnoticed. To do that mission planners designed a two-stage approach. The first stage called for a rendevous of helicopters and C-130 transport planes, carrying the commandos and fuel, at a remote airstrip in the Great Salt Desert, 200 miles southeast of Teheran.

From there, the refueled helicopters were to ferry the troops to a landing zone in the mountains north of Teheran. After a day of rest in hiding, the troops were to drive into Teheran in unmarked cars and trucks prepositioned for them by American intelligence agents, who had entered Iran under false passports in the preceding weeks.

The commando unit, according to the plan, would assault the embassy under air cover provided by several of the C-130's which were equipped with high-powered cannon. Once the embassy was secure, the helicopters would fly in, pick up the freed hostages and the troops, and speed to another desert rendezvous with the transport planes. From there, everyone would be flown to safety.

NO HIDING PLACE

Not everyone familiar with the plan thought it feasible or wise. Secretary of State Cyrus R. Vance feared the raid might escalate into a major military confrontation with Iran, possibly causing the Soviet Union to intervene. Even if it was successful, he warned the President, the Iranians might respond by rounding up other Americans in Teheran and holding them hostage. Vance told the President he would resign if the rescue plan was carried out.

The rescue, as a dejected President Carter told the nation shortly after midnight on April 25, ended almost before it started when four of the eight RH-53 Sea Stallion helicopters used in the mission broke down either en route to the first desert rendezvous or on the ground. Faced with a decision to abort or proceed without the number of helicopters considered necessary for a successful mission, President Carter ordered the Pentagon to abort the operation. As the troops prepared to board the airplanes in the desert, one of the helicopters collided with a C-130 transport. The resulting fire and explosions killed eight members of the rescue team. Their bodies had to be left in the desert with the wreckage.

Mrs. Timm was still in Teheran when the rescue mission took place, trying to arrange a meeting with Ayatollah Khomeini. "I am very angry," she said, "that the President of our country would do something so stupid."

All of this, of course, was unknown to the 53 hostages held in the embassy compound. Some of them had just finished eating a dinner of chili found in the commissary when their captors announced the Americans should pack up, according to Rodney Sickmann.

Sergeant Sickmann recalled that the captors told them to use the bathroom because it would be 10 hours before they had another chance. "They blindfolded us and took us down to a van they had waiting," he said. "We got in and they handcuffed us." With Sergeant Sickmann were Sergeant Gallegos and Jerry Plotkin. Through their blindfolds, they could see the bursts of camera flashbulbs. "They put us in there, handcuffed us, took pictures of us," Sickmann said. "It was really weird."

"I don't know how many cars were with us," he went on, "but we drove from about 11:30 that night 'til about 7 o'clock the next morning.

The roads we were on, they felt like they were cow pastures. We were bouncing up hitting the top of the van with our heads.

"You can't sleep. You could lean on somebody else's shoulder, but then he'd move, and everybody would have to move because you were handcuffed together. We finally got to Isfahan that morning. We didn't know this until about a month later, when they told us where we were."

Other hostages experienced similarly disorienting, uncomfortable journeys. Moorhead Kennedy remembered hearing a lot of noise outside on the night of April 25. "We were told to pack," he said. "We were blindfolded again and taken outside into the hall. From under the blindfold we could see that our gear was being piled up. We thought that maybe the Shah was dead, that maybe it was all over."

Kennedy's hopes expired when he heard the sound of handcuffs clicking. He was driven off into the night, certain only that the upward tilt of his darkened van meant that he was being taken to the hills outside Teheran.

Blucker, the economics officer, was put in a van with Colonel Scott, Donald Sharer and Duane Gillette, the Navy communications specialist. "We didn't know where we were going," he recalled. "We went through a series of maneuvers, stop, go back, stop, to shake anybody that might be following us. We were handcuffed to the vehicle and to each other. We went about ten hours without a rest stop.

"We were shouting at them to stop so we could relieve ourselves, but they wouldn't allow it, even when they stopped to rest." Blucker and his fellow hostages finally were dropped off in a city they later learned was Tabriz, in the northwest corner of Iran.

Colonel Schaefer remembered that post-raid move as "one of the more traumatic experiences" of his captivity.

At 11 P.M., he was taken from his room and thrown into a van, blindfolded, his hands cuffed by plastic strips. "I'd rather have had handcuffs," he said.

Driven for about four hours, he believed he was being taken south or southwest because the air grew warmer and the terrain did not seem to be mountainous.

"They were going so damn fast," he said, "we were banging around like piles of wood. And they wouldn't let us go to the bathroom."

NO HIDING PLACE

There were about eight people in the van with him, he said. Their destination seemed to be a military base, he thought, because there were a lot of revolutionary guards about. The rooms were small and dirty, he said, but the place was not a jail. It was a one-story, four- or five-room structure. The prisoners called it "the white hole" because the Americans were kept in a white tile room that might once have been a bathroom.

After about a week, Schaefer said, they were moved about a 10-minute drive to a place they called "the pink palace" because the room was pink. There was an attached bathroom, which meant they did not have to be blindfolded when they went there. The place appeared to be a private home. It was near a railroad yard. The hostages could hear the switching engines.

As far as Schaefer could tell, the house was in a small town near Qum. But, as was the case with most of the hostages who were shunted about Iran after the rescue mission, no one told him where he was or how long he might be kept there.

Treatment of the hostages after the raid was erratic. Some of the hostages who had been shifted to Tabriz were allowed several hours of fresh air a day. Some of them even were permitted to take short motorcycle rides.

For one period of nearly three months, in the spring and summer, Blucker and several others were held in the American consulate in Tabriz under the control of an especially pleasant and helpful guard. He replaced the Western-style toilets that had been ripped out and put in oriental ones that more resemble paved holes in the ground. He installed a shower, a washing machine and a dryer, and fenced in a big section of the garden to create a recreation area.

"He hung blankets on the barbed wire so that theoretically we couldn't see out," Blucker said. "But you could see in all directions. They took us out most days for an hour or two hours of sunshine. I don't think this happened to anybody else. We could jog, play badminton, sit under the trees and read, watch eagles soaring overhead. It astonished me that he did this. After two or three weeks he told us he had been fired. But within a week he seemed to be in charge again. A number of the boys gave us quite personal attention. We could demand this and demand that. I don't understand why it occurred."

As the Americans were being moved out of the consulate in early July, Blucker recalled, some of their captors had said to them, "Perhaps they release you."

"I think they were trying to be kind," he said, "but it turned out to be a cruel disappointment nevertheless because we landed the next morning in a prison, a terrible prison, somewhere on the outskirts of Teheran where the treatment again was bad, impersonal, like animals again. The noise was terrible, steel doors slamming and banging day and night. Lights were on practically all night. It was a little bit hot. Most of the prisoners there had perverted hours, sleeping all day and staying up at night.

"I had a bad time there," Blucker continued, "because I liked to sleep at night. I was with one other, I don't want to mention his name. I don't want to talk about him. We had nothing in common and didn't get along. We were stuck there for 77 days."

Months later, after he and several of the older hostages had been shifted to a "strange place with tiny little rooms" situated over a bakery that bustled day and night and near a garage where they could see young men changing tires and siphoning gas, Blucker met up again with the guard he had come to think of as "the good guy," and who, for the protection of the guard, he referred to as "Mr. X."

Mr. X seemed to be in charge of the new place, which Blucker thought might possibly have been the servants' quarters of some rich man. But the kind guard was seldom around. Once though, Blucker said, he asked for some magazines and "he brought me a whole stack of things going back over a year."

Kathryn Koob said the treatment of all the hostages ought to be seen in the context of the Iranian culture.

"They thought they were treating us very well by their standards," she said, "and, as one of them told us just before we left, 'We could have treated you a whole lot worse.' "

Elizabeth Ann Swift said she thought the interrogations in the middle of the night might have been as much "the Iranian way of doing things," as deliberate "psychological warfare."

"They run odd hours," she said, adding that one of her "keepers" often came to her room with "treats" — anything from lollypops to nuts stolen from the embassy commissary — at one or two in the morning.

For the two women, Elizabeth Ann Swift and Kathryn Koob, who were brought together in the embassy in March and kept together there for the rest of their captivity, the day of the raid brought certain signs that something unusual had happened.

"We could hear all the movement and shuffling up and down the hall," Miss Koob remembered. "We knew people were being moved from their current rooms. We didn't know why or where or what."

Nor did they learn anything immediately. Their treatment changed slightly. An embassy cook who had been preparing their main meals left and the student guards started doing the cooking.

But there was nothing to explain all the activity until, about six weeks after the raid, they got a letter from a schoolchild — one of the thousands of messages from Americans who wrote to the hostages. "We're sorry the rescue failed," it read. "We hope they try it again."

The Americans at the Iranian Foreign Ministry, Bruce Laingen, Victor Tomseth and Michael Howland, also lost some of their privileges after the raid. The Iranians took away their ping-pong table.

The senior diplomats among the hostages had a far more comfortable captivity than the others. Not only that, they got along well among themselves. "We were remarkably compatible," Laingen said. "We were a good combination in that we all had inner resources that carried us through. We knew each other well and we were friends."

The three of them would reach their decisions by informal consensus, but Laingen continued to perform as leader. "I thought it was important that I maintain it," he said, "for the benefit of the Iranians with whom we dealt, that they knew that the chief of mission was still there and that he was available as a mechanism to deal with the government of Iran."

It was important, he said, to maintain dignity, to show that "we were not cowed, we were not bowed."

And to insist, too, on continuing to act like diplomatic officials.

At first, Laingen insisted on wearing a necktie every day. One day the British Ambassador stopped by and, Laingen recalls, he asked, "Could you get me a tie or two? I'm tired of the one I'm wearing."

He gave up on the neckties within a month or so. But he and his roommates never settled into prisoner habits, growing beards and such.

"We were determined to look our best," Laingen said, "to maintain this facade, if you will, of dignity as American diplomats.

"I was the resident optimist," he went on, "Vic the resident pessimist, deliberately so, perhaps, because he appreciated more than anyone else how difficult it is to get a decision made in Iran under any circumstances, particularly revolutionary ones."

Tomseth noted that, within 48 hours of the initial takeover, the Revolutionary Council had decided that the senior officials were technically the government's "guests."

Their guards were older and more settled than the unpredictable student militants who watched over the other hostages. "I look back with affection on some of these men," Laingen said. "They did their best to make our lives comfortable." The guards even permitted Iranian friends to send in sweaters and watercolors, he said.

Like the hostages in more Spartan quarters, the trio in the Foreign Ministry had what Laingen called "structured" days.

They rose at 8, breakfasted at 8:30 or 9, read newspapers and listened to the Voice of America. Then they worked on their diaries, most of which, it turned out, were left behind in the commotion when the time came for their release, and on letters home, many of which their guards never sent, until lunch at 12:30.

For a time, they were allowed a couple of hours on a balcony to get some sun.

At 2 P.M., Tomseth would listen to news broadcasts in Persian, then tell the other two what had been said. Tomseth, 38 years old, the senior political officer, had been in the Foreign Service since 1967 and in Iran since 1975. He was the senior official of the embassy in point of time served in Iran. During a three-year posting in Thailand, he met his wife, Wallapa. He was fluent in Nepalese, having been in Nepal in the Peace Corps, and in Thai as well as Persian.

Laingen would nap each afternoon. Then they would exercise for an hour or two before dinner at 6:30 which was Western-style and served neatly and cleanly. They would read, play backgammon and work on jigsaw puzzles provided by the British. Laingen and Howland painted watercolors.

"We wound up spending the entire time we were in the Foreign Ministry in one or another of the reception rooms," he said. "It was a complex of rooms on the third floor. There was a restroom that had sinks and toilets but no bathing facilities. The first bath we got was after we had been there about 10 days and they brought us a tub into the kitchen area in the back and filled it up with hot water. We took turns bathing. They didn't change the water between baths so we rotated the schedule, who would go first, who would wind up in the dirty water."

The three eventually settled into what had been a formal dining room, he said, about 40 feet by 60, with cots and card tables, a couch and some chairs.

The Iranians moved them there, Laingen said, because they had become "an embarrassing fixture" during the Foreign Minister's occasional news conferences. There was Iran's chief diplomat, officially speaking for his country, and there, his listeners well aware of it, were three Americans who were being held in what most of the world agreed was an illegal captivity.

"We were a complication," Laingen said. The briefings were held in a room entered through the main salon. Whenever one was held, he said, "the guards made sure we were tucked behind the drapes, inside this dining room, and couldn't be seen by anybody." But everyone knew the captives were there.

Because of the newspapers they read and the Persian broadcasts that Tomseth monitored, the three were aware of efforts to transfer them to the custody of the student militants. But Iranian Government officials assured them that their status was different. "As they often said to us, 'You are a guest of the government'," Laingen said. "We took that with a grain of salt because the term guest usually implies a certain degree of freedom to move about, and we were not free to leave that room except to go to the bathroom."

Living, as they were, close to the people who were trying to conduct Iran's foreign affairs, the three — skilled observers of the diplomatic scene — had a different view than their lower-level fellows who were in the custody of student militants.

"Bear in mind," Tomseth said, "that there were essentially two groups in the Foreign Ministry, the professional people, the equivalent of our Foreign Service, and then I guess what we would call the political appointees."

To prevent their captors from knowing what he was talking about in conversations with Washington, Tomseth said he occasionally spoke in Thai.

Did the guards ever figure it out?

"I doubt it," Tomseth said. "I'm sure they were working on the basis that it was Chinese. It's a strange dialect."

The senior officials were allowed at first to keep telephone lines open to Washington, then to use the Foreign Ministry's Telex machines.

"We had the kind of information available to the public," Tomseth said, "because we had newspapers, radio and television."

But the three in the Foreign Ministry had no way of sharing their knowledge with their fellow hostages. "The first day after our people had surrendered in the embassy," Tomseth said, "I called the switchboard and one of the students answered. But he would not talk to me. I tried several times thereafter. But each time it was the same reaction. They would answer the phone and an initial question or two, but as soon as it was clear to them that I was trying to find out what the situation was, they just hung up."

"Eventually," he went on, "they just stopped answering the phone." And so, he said, three Americans in the Foreign Ministry had no contact with the other hostages until the January night when all were released.

Unlike Laingen, Tomseth and Howland, most of the hostages found life crude, confusing and almost totally bereft of information about the world, about events that might be affecting their lives and about their fellow captives.

Yet, incongruously, there were hints — a glimpse out a window, a snatch of sound wafting in — that normal lives were being lived just outside the walls of their impromptu prisons. Moorhead Kennedy concluded that the places where he was kept were part of a network of dwellings used by revolutionary students who had been involved in a kind of domestic peace corps, whose task was upgrading Iranian villages.

Thus, some sites were fancy and some were little more than hovels.

NO HIDING PLACE

At various places of captivity, hints of the unsuccessful April 25 rescue effort came to their attention.

Richard Morefield, who had been moved to a solitary confinement cell in what he believed to be a maximum security prison north of Teheran, was told without explanation: "You are here because of something your President did. And you'll learn about it later on."

Kathryn Koob and Elizabeth Swift, who had learned of the raid from an American schoolchild's letter, got more details from a censored copy of *Time* or *Newsweek*. The article about the raid had been torn out but was, inexplicably, stuffed inside the rear cover.

James Lopez recalled that "someone in Europe had written to Gary Lee, who was one of my cellmates, saying something to the effect that so far eight had died, but many more were willing to give our lives to save you.

"So," he went on, "we figured it was more or less a rescue attempt. We weren't quite sure. We didn't really find out all the details until we were released."

Jerry Miele was cleaning the embassy library, probably sometime in August, when he found what he called "an American socialist newspaper" that mentioned the failed rescue. Later, in a letter from a young American girl, he said, he learned that eight Americans had died in the attempt.

Rocky Sickmann's captors showed him news magazine photographs of the wreckage and the bodies that had been left behind in the desert. He knew that he was not going to stay long in his new quarters, he said. "They were buying us food, bringing us sandwiches, little hot dog sandwiches, and we knew this couldn't last forever, because they hated to spend money on us. Back at the embassy, they just took everything out of the commissary."

He was right. In a few days, he was moved to the old United States consulate in Shiraz. By the first week in June, Sickmann said, he had been taken back to Teheran, where he spent three days in the chancery, then to prison.

After they got home and had time to think about the attempted rescue, some hostages wondered about its risks and the threat it had posed to them.

AFTERMATH OF THE RAID

"Thank God for the sandstorm," said Kathryn Koob. "There was a certain risk and a certain number of the hostages might not have made it out. And I just felt from my location in the embassy at the time, I might not be one of those who made it out. I was on the second floor. There was no escape route."

Laingen said diplomatically: "Based on what I knew, based on the compound, the atmosphere in that city, the geography of the compound, people scattered all over it, the number of guns in the streets around the place, even at night, I find it very difficult to see how any such operation could have resulted in the safe evacuation of all my colleagues. If that couldn't have been done, I would have had strong reservations about it."

Tomseth agreed: "While not being opposed to the concept of rescue per se, I have great difficulty in understanding the desirability of that effort at that particular political moment. If for no other reason, the timing seemed particularly bad. The context in which it occurred, of course, was in the immediate aftermath of the break in diplomatic relations and a concerted effort on our part to line up support from Europeans and the Japanese for economic sanctions against Iran. And to make a rescue attempt under these conditions struck me as likely to have a serious deleterious effect. I think that some of the reservations that I later learned Secretary Vance had about the mission were the same kind of reservations that I had. There were all kinds of Americans running around Teheran at that time who could be taken hostage and simply take the place of us — even if the rescue mission had succeeded."

On the other hand, some hostages cheered the attempt.

"It did my morale a lot of good, knowing the raid was attempted," said Thomas Schaefer. "Dammit, they were doing something."

"The message came through," said John Limbert. "We were cared about and something was being done."

Charles Scott said that whenever he thought of the rescue attempt, "what burns in my mind are Theodore Roosevelt's words: 'Far better it is to dare mighty things, to win glorious triumphs, even though checkered by failure, than to take rank with those poor spirits who neither enjoy much nor suffer much, because they live in the gray twilight that knows not victory nor defeat.' "

"I was jubilated," said Robert Blucker. "It was good to know they were not prepared to leave us there forever, that they were prepared to try something even though it might mean some of us would be killed. I thought it should have been attempted even if a large percentage of us were killed."

Sickmann said that later, when he was shown *Time* magazine photos of the wreckage in the desert, "I was really sad." But, he went on, "It really made me feel good that the U.S. tried their best to get us out. Those guys risked their lives to come over."

Richard Morefield felt "sadness that somebody had died trying to save me."

William Keough said that his captors had been shaken by the rescue attempt. "They pretended to be a lot more confident," he said, "but, having worked with young people all my life, I knew they were even a lot more frightened than I was."

Some of the hostages believed that the moves after the raid were a tactic to upset them psychologically. Commander Sharer told *The Virginian-Pilot* of Norfolk, Va., how it was:

A guard would come into the room and say: "Pack your stuff."

"Why do we have to pack our stuff?"

"Just pack your stuff."

"Are we going home?"

"Just pack your stuff."

Sharer recalled, "Then all through your mind it would go: They're going to take us out and shoot us."

9

Coping: Killing Time

Sometime in early May, while he was being kept with two others in a bedroom-bathroom combination, an excruciatingly hot place with sealed windows, Michael Metrinko was visited by the Ayatollah Khomeini's son, Hojatolislam Ahmed Khomeini. He told the hostages not to worry and asked about the conditions they were living in.

Metrinko complained about the stuffiness and Ahmed Khomeini ordered the guards to take their captives outside and to let them exercise. The guards protested they were already doing that. "I told him he was being lied to," Metrinko said.

"In the next month and a half," Metrinko said, "I was outside three times for air and exercise." He said that each excursion lasted precisely 10 minutes.

Scattered about the country, teased by a scrap of information here, a scrap there, the hostages spent the middle months of 1980 trying to cope with the reality of a life without benchmarks, of a tedious imprisonment that showed no signs of ending, and of all too frequent reminders of their precarious and hazardous situation.

Kennedy told how, through an open window in his Teheran jail, he could hear the gasps and screams of prisoners being beaten and tortured. Metrinko said that from his quarters "I could hear people outside

101

being flogged. You'd hear proclamations being read about why they were being flogged, their misdeeds, you know. Twenty lashes. You could hear this going on."

In her quarters in the embassy compound, Elizabeth Ann Swift could hear the blare of at least three huge public address systems. They were always "ranting and raving," she said. At first, these noisy demonstrations lasted all night. After a while, they were cut off by 2 A.M.

"It was a barrage of hate," she said. "I never realized the depth of hatred against the United States in that country. In their eyes, the United States was tied completely to Savak."

The outside world knew of events that had enormous potential importance for the hostages — the release of Richard Queen on July 11, the death of the Shah in Cairo on July 27, the announcement by the Ayatollah Khomeini on September 12 of terms for the release of the hostages. But for them, after the disruption and dispersion following the failed rescue mission, one dreary day of captivity was much like another.

Occasionally, amid their constant fears, there would be a touch of the ludicrous.

There was, for instance, the matter of Kathryn Koob's telephone bill. On the day of the embassy takeover, she had kept a telephone line open for hours between her office in the Iran-America Society and the State Department in Washington. Sometime after mid-March when she and Miss Swift became roommates, there was a knock on the door and an Iranian guard entered and asked, "Did you make a phone call to the United States November 4 and 5?"

"Yes, I did," she replied.

"Fine," he said. "Then you will take your checkbook and you will write a check for 60,000 tomans [about $6,000]."

"Wait a minute," she replied. "There are two problems. I don't have a checkbook and I don't have an Iranian bank account and, number two, that wasn't my phone call."

They argued. Finally, the guard told her they would "find" her account and take the money from it. "I told him to please bring me what was left," she said, "but I never saw him or the money."

For the most part there was not much to laugh about. The hostages coped in various ways.

COPING: KILLING TIME

"I often considered writing a poem," said Duane Gillette. "Its title would be, 'Killing Time Is Killing Me.'"

"I determined to live as normally as possible," said Moorhead Kennedy. "I made up my mind I would keep myself and my things clean and tidy, that I'd keep myself as presentable as possible, sort of like the British dressing for dinner." And so, he said, he swept his room until not a grain of dirt remained. He scrubbed his toilet so clean that his guards started using it. Moved to a new place, he immediately posted family pictures and began scrubbing up.

The schoolmaster, William Keough, treated his captors like recalcitrant pupils. "Once we got over the initial pushing around, we established early on that this was not the thing to do," he said. He advised some of his fellow hostages how to behave. "I spent quite a bit of time instructing people on certain things they should know: How to push the limits, explaining to them that Iranian students understand confrontation, that we should be training the students, that we should be capturing the students rather than having them capture us."

As Keough's birthday approached, he teased the captors for six weeks, saying he was expecting a cake. When the day came on September 11, the guards delivered a cake. After Keough and the others had finished the cake, he said, he turned to the guards and asked, "Where's the ice cream?"

Toward the end of the captivity, Blucker said of his guards, "I had them so scared they were afraid to come into my room. I wouldn't let them in with their shoes on because they tracked in too much dirt. I yelled at them or I snarled at them. You could get to them by bitching at them. They told me, 'You're like an old woman. You say, "Do this, do that."' That didn't upset me. I told them they needed an old woman to tell them what to do."

For some, skill at games became a mainstay of life. Bert Moore, an administrative consul, said he had dominated the gamesmanship among his summer roommates, Sgt. Paul Lewis, Phillip R. Ward, a communications officer, and Sgt. John McKeel.

"We had cards and checkers," Moore recalled. "After the first couple of games, they refused to play checkers with me. When you win and still have eight men left, they didn't think that was a very good game. Finally, I got them all so they played gin rummy. I started out slow and went hard, and they decided they didn't like that game."

On the 4th of July, Colonel Schaefer cheered his roommates — Robert Engelmann, Steven Lauterbach and Barry Rosen — by using a red pencil and a blue pen to make an American flag on an 8- by 10½-inch sheet of paper. The four held an Independence Day celebration with the flag. "It was just a recognition," Schaefer said. But he kept the hand-drawn emblem wherever he was taken until, before he and his fellow hostages were finally released, his captors took it from him.

Malcolm Kalp said that the guards where he was held from July until the day he was freed fastened charts on the door of each cell, like those on the end of a bed that note a hospital patient's progress. In this case, they referred to behavior. The prisoner's treatment reflected the behavior report on the chart.

Kalp found the food often unpalatable. "How many legs does a raisin have?" the hostages asked each other, referring to the insects they would find in some of the stuff they were served — apples, grapes or dates with worms, fleas or flies, boxes of graham crackers or chocolate chip cookies full of ants.

He said that he got fresh fruit no more than once a month and, on Thanksgiving Day, his dinner consisted of two pieces of baloney and one piece of bread. Sometimes, he said, the guards spat in the food before they served it.

Or, he said, a guard would ask, "Do you like cashews?"

"Yes," he would reply.

Then they would dole out ten or twelve to Kalp while they wolfed down handfuls themselves.

"In September," Kalp said, "they gave me a Carnation instant breakfast, strawberry. I tried so hard to keep it until my birthday at the end of October, for something special. But they moved me October 24 and they stole it."

Every seven to ten days, the hostages were taken out for a shower. "They'd take us out to the residence," Kalp said. "The tub was black."

To pass the long weeks, he said, "books were my life. If I had a book for the next day, it was going to be a bright day. If I didn't have books, I'd get kind of depressed." There was a big library in the embassy and the guards would bring books from it to the hostages. But the selection was up to the guards and it was, at best, whimsical. A hostage was likely to be given a Nancy Drew mystery or a physics textbook.

Then there was the amusement of making elaborate plans, no matter how fantastic. Moorhead Kennedy got in trouble with his captors for passing a note to other hostages only once. His message dealt with the possibilities of a class action lawsuit "to get hostages some sort of compensation for the ordeal once we got home."

The Iranians, unaccustomed to such terminology, thought this referred to a mass breakout. "They berated us a lot about that," Kennedy said.

Laingen concocted a mental timetable, commencing on various dates when, he fantasized, the hostages would be freed. In the beginning, the date he fixed on was December 17. "I was going to be in Annapolis for a concert," he said. Then he wrote to his 14-year-old son, Jim, promising to be "home for Christmas."

James Lopez found that "day-to-day life was pretty much boredom."

But he enlivened it for his fellow captives by sketching cartoons that, according to Richard Morefield, became "a tremendous morale factor. Some of them were just devastating."

At first, the sketches were passed around surreptitiously. Then the captors — who presumably did not catch on to some of the fine points — permitted them to be posted on a wall.

Michael Metrinko remembered feeling "extremely good" when he saw one Lopez sketch depicting a mullah with a belfry in the background and bats flying around it. The artist signed it, "Political prisoner being illegally detained by the Iranian criminals."

Morefield laughed at one drawn for his 51st birthday on September 9. "It showed an old doddering captive flanked by two equally old doddering guards," he said.

Many of the hostages' recollections of this middle period of their captivity, though, were of the fussy domestic details with which they filled their days.

Kathryn Koob and Elizabeth Swift recalled a regular routine. They would get up anytime between 8 and 10 A.M. They would visit the bathroom, wash their faces, brush their teeth. Then their captors would bring breakfast, which was bread with cheese, jam or butter, tea, sometimes juice. Then they would study, pray or read Scripture. Between noon and 1 P.M., Miss Swift would exercise. They would lunch, wash the dishes and read some more. Miss Koob would do some needlework. At 5:30 they would exercise for 45 minutes, then eat supper. After evening devotions they would do what Miss Koob called "junk reading" — pulp novels, Gothics, mysteries, Regency romances. At 10:30 they would exercise for 45 minutes more, running figure-eights or circles around their room, then go to bed.

Colonel Schaefer set himself a daily schedule in which, he said, "I allowed myself very little free time."

Up at 8 A.M., he had a breakfast of tea with bread and either butter, jam or cheese. From about 9 to 11:30, he would study German from textbooks that he had been given. Then there was an hour or so of yoga and walking about his room.

Then came his main meal, lunch. When he was imprisoned in the embassy, lunch was American food, including roast beef, stew, hamburger, turkey, potatoes or rice, with a vegetable and sometimes fruit. After the rescue raid, when he was in "the white room" or "the pink palace," it was Iranian food, including rice with beans or lamb sauce or greens.

Afterward, he read a novel, a biography or whatever he had. "It always seemed they would have books," he said. He read a couple of hundred books. He could read a novel in a day, but he spent several days on *The History of the Peloponnesian Wars.* Then he would nap or play cards. He played solitaire and sometimes bridge, playing all four hands himself and found he was taking the schizophrenic competition seriously. "I found after a while I was leaning to north-south," he said. "It would upset me if east-west won a slam bid."

Then Schaefer would go back to reading and to another hour of exercise. "I can stand on my head for 30 minutes now," he said.

Supper, usually soup, was served at about 7 or 7:30 P.M. "When we asked for seconds, we normally got it," he said. "If they did not have seconds, they would give us bread and cheese. Something to fill us up."

Then he would read some more, usually until midnight or 1 A.M., until he was tired enough to go to sleep.

COPING: KILLING TIME

He would sleep for seven hours or so. And then he would start a new day that was almost identical to the previous day. And the next day. And the next.

Sgt. Gregory Persinger recalled: "I would wake up at 10 in the morning, walk an hour, exercise for close to 2½ hours, doing 1,000 situps to begin with, pushups and regular calisthenics. After that, I would sit up and read maybe, a couple of hours until the food came for lunch." Then more walking, more exercise, more reading and, finally, to bed.

Richard Morefield said that he had been overweight — 210 pounds when he was captured. He exercised, touching his toes and performing other simple routines when his captivity began, then gradually increasing the program until, by the end of his captivity, he was doing 50 off-the-wall pushups, numerous squat jumps and situps and an hour's jogging in his room. He weighed 178 pounds when he reached Wiesbaden, he said, "and if I'm smart, this might have added 10 years to my life."

Rodney Sickmann said he "walked about three miles a day, back and forth across the room, touch the wall, go back and touch the wall."

Most of the hostages said that they had come through the experience surprisingly well, but there were tensions.

Had there been conflict among the captives?

"Obviously," said Morefield, "there were quirks or characteristics that were very annoying."

Did anyone ever come to blows?

"Yes," he said.

Seriously?

"No."

10

Coping: Secret Messages

The cruelties inflicted on the hostages might have been part of a tactical effort at controlling them through intimidation. The captors apparently were under strict orders not to harm the captives.

There were at least two other reasons for the harsh treatment inflicted on some hostages, according to the Foreign Service officer who asked to remain anonymous. "There were a few that were treated much worse than the others because there was good reason for the students to think they were C.I.A. or spies or something else," he said. "But many had a psychological need to bring trouble on themselves."

Others challenged their captors for good reason.

Colonel Schaefer said that his experience in terrorist and survival school had made him less susceptible to pressure than some younger prisoners the Iranians regarded as "weak links." In his case, Colonel Schaefer said, the captors knew that pressure was not going to work.

"We took our antagonisms out on them," Bruce German said of the guards. "We were determined we would stand tall, proud to be Americans. We tried to destroy them with a sense of humor. We gave them names and they answered to them. We laughed at the most absurd things, the guards primarily."

Keough intimidated some of his captors. At 6 feet, 9 inches tall, he towered over all of them. In addition, he had a naturally belligerent personality, compounded by a schoolmaster's air of imperious authority over young people. His favorite tactic with the captors was passive resistance, but he described it as "totally relentless and unreasonable."

"I feel that I abused the fact that I was about a foot and a half taller than most of them," he said.

As the days dragged on, the hostages became more resourceful in frustrating their captors' efforts to prevent them from communicating with each other.

"We had the pony express going through the head," said James Lopez. "We would leave notes in the toilet paper rolls, under the toilet, in the sink, behind the mirror, under a loose tile. We snatched a thumbtack off a wall one time and we were sticking them underneath a little end table they had in the head. And we had a telegraph system, knocking through the walls. And we also had the system where when you knocked on the door and talked to one of the guards, you talked loud enough so that everyone in the hallway could hear you and you used little acronyms and jargon the Iranians would half understand but everyone else would catch it."

Two of the Marines, Rocky Sickmann, from the village of Krakow, Mo., and William Gallegos, from the south-central Colorado community of Pueblo, developed their own communications system, peculiarly American and particularly puzzling to their captors. It employed a kind of hog call. They started it when they were kept in the large partitioned room in the Mushroom Inn.

When one of them had something to say to the other, he would oink four times, Sickmann said. Then they would shift to a position where they could make eye contact. For the most part, they would lip read. But sometimes they would oink — twice for "yes" and once for "no."

Sometimes, to harass and confuse their captors, they would bark and woof like dogs.

Sickmann said that one of the books the hostages were allowed to read had instructions for a tapping code, in which letters were arranged in a grid so that 1-1 is the letter A, 1-2 the letter B. So they would use that to pass messages between rooms.

Steven Lauterbach could see prisoners in a nearby room and, when his guard got into the habit of nodding off to sleep, they would use a system similar to the tapping code, but silently. "We'd just flash it with our fingers," he said.

After the unsuccessful rescue raid in April, in what seemed to be a gloating gesture, several hostages were shown color photographs in *Time* and *Newsweek* of the wrecked helicopters and the charred bodies of members of the rescue team. Some hostages were allowed to read the stories, others were only permitted to look at the illustrations.

Generally, however, the Iranians tried to keep the hostages ignorant of world events, especially those relating to the hostage situation.

The barrage of news that inundates most Americans reached the hostages only in accidental and sporadic snatches. They did not know of the things that might interest them, much less the things that might affect them. They did not even know what impact their continued imprisonment was having on their fellow Americans — how, for instance, when he said good night each evening to the millions who watched his CBS television news show, Walter Cronkite would remind viewers how many days the Americans had been held in Iran, with the number flashing on the screen, creeping higher every day.

On rare occasions, the hostages were given copies of the news magazines, crudely censored with many pages torn out. But sometimes the censors would forget to cut out the table of contents in a magazine.

Some of the hostages learned in that way of the failed rescue mission, of the Shah's death, of Ronald Reagan's election as President.

But most knew nothing of what was going on.

Even before the hostages had been seized, the American Presidential campaign had commenced. While they were still blindfolded and being brutalized, just two days after the militants overran the embassy, Senator Edward M. Kennedy had challenged President Carter for the Democratic nomination. Two weeks later, several hundred members of an ultra-conservative Islamic group seized the Grand Mosque in Mecca.

A mob of Pakistanis stormed the United States Embassy in Islamabad, killing two American servicemen and two Pakistani clerks. But it was not to be a repetition of Iran. Pakistani helicopters rescued the other 90 members of the staff from the embassy roof.

Pope Paul visited Turkey and appealed to Christians to seek a better understanding of Islam, saying it shared many beliefs and moral values with Christianity.

In December, the Soviet Union invaded Afghanistan and soon got bogged down in warfare that would persist until long after the hostages had been freed.

And the American captives knew virtually none of it.

President Carter began his march to renomination by winning the Democratic caucuses in Iowa in January, but on the Republican side, George Bush, the former head of the C.I.A., upset Ronald Reagan.

Violence grew in El Salvador and the Roman Catholic Archbishop was assassinated in March. There were race riots in Miami in May. In London, a British commando team stormed the Iranian Embassy to free 19 hostages. The International Court of Justice ordered the immediate release of the hostages in Iran.

And the American captives knew hardly anything about it.

Shadowed by the frustration and national humiliation of the captivity of the hostages, Americans nonetheless continued a process of choosing their leaders that had not been interrupted, even by war, for two centuries. The Republicans nominated Ronald Reagan and George Bush. The Democrats renominated Jimmy Carter and Walter Mondale.

Strikes in Poland forced the Warsaw government in August to grant workers the right to organize unions, stirring fears (which persisted after the hostages returned to freedom) that the Soviet Union might invade Poland.

Egypt and Israel agreed in September to resume talks on Palestinian autonomy. China underwent the most sweeping peaceful change in its leadership since Mao tse-Tung's takeover 31 years earlier.

In November, Ronald Reagan was elected President. Many commentators believed that the Iranian crisis — and the splash of stories and pictures in newspapers and on television about the first anniversary of the hostages' captivity — turned what pollsters had thought would be a close election into a Republican runaway.

And still the American hostages knew almost nothing about it.

The hostages were offered a quick summary of the news they had missed after they landed in Wiesbaden, West Germany, their first stopping place on their journey home.

COPING: SECRET MESSAGES

But in captivity there were only odd glimpses, hints of what the rest of the world knew. Someone in the Boston area, who never identified himself, began sending Keough, who comes from Waltham, Mass., the sports page of a local newspaper.

"Every day the sports page went out and it would come in in clusters," Keough said. "Sometimes on the back of the sports pages would be news. Sometimes it would be the comics. The Doonesbury comic of December 28, 1979, let me know that this [the captivity of the hostages] had become a subject of widespread discussion in the U.S. Garry Trudeau is an astute political commentator and just reading that cartoon strip about Iranian students let me know the extent to which this was being handled in the U.S. On the back of the sports pages we would see an advertisement for one of the channels running a television show, tucked in there was a statement about the recent rescue attempt. We would pick up news that way. The August 14 issue of *Sports Illustrated* — tucked in that was the announcement that the game had been interrupted with the anouncement that the Shah had died in Egypt."

In December 1980, Keough said, Algerian diplomats brought him a Christmas package from his wife that contained underwear, socks and three books. The captors withheld a book on the Presidential election in the United States, but they let Keough have a book of crossword puzzles and a copy of a 1981 world almanac, which, to the delight of the hostages, contained a summary of the major news events of 1980.

"That sort of thing was taking place all the time," Keough said. "Information was coming through. You cannot suppress a group of strong Americans who are an intelligent group."

It was toward the end of her time in Iran that Kathryn Koob found out about the Canadian-assisted escape a year earlier. While she was sharing a maximum security cell with Elizabeth Ann Swift, a "compassionate" guard brought a magazine account of the incident to Miss Koob and told her that he hoped it would help keep her spirits up. It was "the most incredibly beautiful thing I've read in my whole life," she said.

Letters from relatives and even, in some cases, strangers also provided news on their situation. Usually, the information from relatives was guarded, as if they sensed that direct reports on the hostages would be blocked by the captors.

"Letters were getting through with one-liners stuck in the middle of this big, long thing about Aunt Thelma's apple pie recipe," said Sergeant Lopez.

Gary Lee, the 36-year-old administrative officer, said his wife, Patricia, let him know about the death of the Shah by reporting that a nonexistent "Uncle Shaw" had died.

Donald Cooke, a 24-year-old vice consul, said he understood the rescue effort had failed after he asked his family to send him a set of "Curtis LeMay stoneware," a reference to the American Air Force general who once advocated bombing North Vietnam back into the Stone Age. To this veiled appeal for an American raid on Iran, Cooke's family replied, "We sent the stoneware, but you didn't get it. It got all broken."

On July 11, Richard Queen was set free.

Early in his captivity, in December or January while he was being held in the Mushroom, Queen had his first attack of what, it turned out later, was multiple sclerosis. It is a degenerative disease of the central nervous system that can be aggravated by stress. "I didn't know what this disease was before," he said in a CBS interview later. "I'd never heard of it. And there was no medical treatment. There was a quack doctor who just gave pills and laughed."

The symptoms eased, he said, and he told his captors, "Fine, okay, I can live with a slightly paralyzed left arm."

Apparently worried, they moved him to more comfortable quarters in the chancery. There he could see the light in the morning and hear people outside. "I remember," he said, "there were a couple of schoolgirls, I guess, walking along and talking and singing." He said he was unable to describe what it was like "to feel life again, to be taken out of that tomb."

By early summer, his illness began to worsen. In late June, he began vomiting and stumbling about. "I was lying in bed all day and I would be vomiting," he said. "I couldn't eat." A conscientious, sympathetic Iranian medical student and Hohman, the Army medic, were caring for him. Queen thought he might have had a stroke, but Hohman said that his symptoms did not seem to suggest that. The militants feared he had a brain tumor. And, as had become clear to many of the hostages, no matter how bad their treatment, their captors were terrified that one of them might die.

So the medical student brought in a doctor and, according to Queen, "they said, 'Let's go.' "

He was taken to Martyrs Hospital in Teheran for about five days, then Ayatollah Khomeini made a decision to send him home.

"I woke up one morning and they said, 'You're going back.' And I thought, 'Well, I'm going back to the compound.' And I couldn't see going back with all these [intravenous] tubes.

"And they said, 'No, you're going back, back to the United States.' "

On the 250th day of his captivity, one year to the day after his arrival in Iran, Queen was freed.

The Ayatollah had sent President Bani-Sadr a message: "Considering the humane reasons that are seriously observed by Islam," he said, Queen "should be handed over to his parents so that they may provide treatment for him wherever they wish."

On a leaden morning in Zurich, an ambulance met Swissair Flight 363 at Kloten Airport. Two male nurses entered the airplane and emerged carrying Queen. He was wrapped in a plastic sheet. His face was pale, his hair and beard bushy and tousled. After tests at the United States Air Force hospital in Weisbaden, the diagnosis of his illness was announced.

On July 18, he was flown to Andrews Air Force Base and met by his brother, Alex, and Secretary of State Edmund S. Muskie.

"I really can't express with words what it's like to be back in America again," Queen said. "I really can't say much more. I just wish there were 52 more with me."

But the other 52 had months of additional captivity to endure. Most of them did not learn for some time that one of their fellows had been freed.

Some of the hostages discovered that Queen had been sent home when Richard Morefield's wife, Dorothea, wrote that Queen was suffering multiple sclerosis. How, they wondered, could she know that?

"We put two and two together," said Rodney Sickmann, "and figured that he had gotten out, and had an interview on television, and that's what Mrs. Morefield was trying to tell us.

"She didn't come right out and say it," he continued, "because they hated whenever someone wrote and gave us information like that."

Sergeant Sickmann said one of the guards told them that Queen was still among the captives. "Then a month later," the Marine said, "we found out from a letter that he really was released."

It was when the meals they had been preparing were cut back that Kathryn Koob and Elizabeth Ann Swift got hints of Queen's release. When their captors had difficulty cooking — burning food and such — the women took over the preparation of meals for six people. Then, all of a sudden, they found themselves cooking for just five. At first, they had no idea who they were cooking for; they eventually found out by reading notes hidden in a wastepaper basket. Or occasionally the guards would allow a note on the tray, signed by "the boys in the backroom" and asking for more salad or whatever.

Queen's own circumspection in his public comments drew the gratitude of Donald Hohman. "I know that Richard Queen wanted to talk after he got out of there," he said. "But, if he had, his words might have jeopardized the rest of us. So good for him for keeping his mouth shut."

Except for Queen, none of the hostages reported any critical medical problems. Some of them came down with food poisoning and Sgt. Gregory Persinger was so sick with stomach flu once that he was fed intravenously.

"They were good about getting doctors," said Duane Gillette.

But, according to Sergeant Persinger and some of the others, the Iranian doctors were sometimes wanting in medical skills. The one who saw him when he had the flu, for example, had trouble getting the intravenous needle into his arm.

"After three or four tries," Sergeant Persinger said, "I took the needle from him and started my own I.V."

One of the hostages, who would only discuss his captivity if guaranteed anonymity, said there was "a total lack of understanding of hygiene among the terrorists. No concept of dirt or filth."

He was in a group of 18 who drank from the same glass, he said, and all of them bathed in the same dirty tub. "I got strep throat twice in the first two months," he said.

Bert Moore, the 44-year-old administrative consul, apparently had

116

the worst case of food poisoning. He was stricken, he said, after eating "some local green-type soup" while being kept at a place that had initially taken them 18 hours to reach from Teheran by car. After four days of fever over 102 degrees, he was trundled into an ambulance and raced to a hospital in the capital. The ride proved almost worse than the poisoning.

"There were six of them and me in the ambulance and they were flooring it," Moore recalled. "We got to Teheran in 13 hours. I got scared everytime I went out with them in a vehicle. They don't drive very well."

When Gillette's two roommates in the American consulate in Tabriz got a case of food poisoning, he said, a doctor came and "gave the students hell because of the food they were giving us.

"Things got better for a while," he continued, "It was like a yo-yo. They weren't consistent with what they fed us or how they treated us."

When Gillette himself caught a cold, he was given Coricidin. Most of the time, Robert Blucker said, he was able to get aspirin to relieve the pain of "a little arthritis of the spine." And, after an initial delay, the Iranians kept Richard Morefield supplied with Maalox for his nervous stomach.

Charles Jones, the communications specialist, suffered from high blood pressure and hypertension and, every day, he said, a medical student would check his blood pressure.

"He was friendly," Jones said. "We would hear rumors about things happening and I would ask him if they were true."

Donald Hohman, the Army medic, tried to minister to his fellow hostages. But he was constantly battling with the captors.

"I got into an argument with a couple of the guards over something having to do with my treating Queen," he said, "and the guard put his hands on me, which I didn't like at all. So we scuffled a little bit.

"Another time, one of the hostages was slightly ill and I asked permission mission to get some medicine out of the dispensary. But the guards wouldn't let me. Finally, I just screamed at them to let me do my work and they sent one guard with me to get the medicine. They never liked me at all."

To Elizabeth Ann Swift, Donald Hohman was "a true hero. He should get medals for some of the things he did for people," she said.

11

The Captors

The Shah died July 27.

Quite a while later, Michael Metrinko read about it "from a line in *Sporting News* — something about a horse race." At first, he said, the realization "raised our hopes, 'til we found that he had died quite a while back. And if he's dead, what were we doing here?"

It was a good question. And puzzling. Somehow, as the months of their captivity dragged on, the Shah's whereabouts and his well-being had become irrelevent to the hostages' treatment.

On December 15, 1979, the Shah had left the United States for Panama. It made no difference to the hostages.

On March 23, he flew to Cairo. And it made no difference.

When he died, the United States Government issued a brief statement, offering sympathy to his family and expressing the hope that a period of peace and stability would settle over Iran. It did not.

In Teheran, there were public celebrations of the Shah's death. Teheran Radio called him "the bloodsucker of the century." But there was no apparent change in the treatment of the hostages.

The hostages were struck by the depth of the hatred their captors felt for the Shah and the United States. During the long middle months of their captivity, they had time to study the people who had seized them, to differentiate among the various levels of command, even to confer nicknames upon their guards.

William Keough, the schoolmaster, did not have much respect for his captors. "You have to remember," he said, "that we were dealing with radical boy students, who were perhaps the most spoiled babies of the Mideast. In the Iranian family setup, the boys are revered." So when captives insisted on special treatment, he said, their captors knew what they meant "because they had been getting it all their lives." He said that some of the guards "were old enough to be graduate students working on their fourth or fifth degrees."

But many of them seemed to be genuine students. "I don't think the terms 'student' and 'terrorist' are necessarily mutually exclusive," said Col. Charles Scott. "They were Islamic fundamentalists and very radical and very militant. Most of the philosophy they espoused to me in Persian was of people with a high degree of militancy."

A Foreign Service officer who asked not to be identified said the students had told him of being trained in the summer at Palestine Liberation Organization camps on how to handle hostages. He said they might even have had a manual on the subject.

"It was something we assumed," he said, "because they couldn't possibly have thought up all those things by themselves. They had some kind of instruction, some kind of guide, something more than their training, which they admitted to."

Many of the militants were incompetent gunslingers, he said. Guns often roared in the compound and, while many hostages feared being shot accidentally, they could not resist joking about it. "We'd laugh and say, 'There goes another toe'," the Foreign Service officer said. "They were playing around with the firearms and didn't have good training. They ended up by having accidents. I know for a fact that one student was shot in the foot or the leg in the Mushroom Inn."

Charles Jones also had a low opinion of the captors. "The majority of the so-called students were young unemployed kids," he said, noting that unemployment among the young in Iran was 70 percent. "Many of them called themselves students because they had no better names to call themselves," Jones said.

John Limbert said two interrogations he underwent persuaded him that his captors were incompetent. In the first, he was blindfolded; in the second, the interrogator had a bag over his own head. "I don't think they had any idea how an embassy actually works," he said. "It was so amateurish you couldn't believe it. It was silly, blind-alley stuff."

He recalled one captor's interrogation: "He asked me, 'Did you meet with Hassan so-and-so?' and I said, 'I don't know Hassan so-and-so,' and we argued for 15 minutes."

"He said, 'You're lying,' and I said, 'How do you know?'"

"It was this kind of searching questions that went on and on," Limbert said sarcastically.

He described his captors as "fascists."

"A lot of them reminded me of my students," he said. "Some of them were decent enough. Most of them were somewhere in the middle. And some of them were real cases. I'm not a psychiatrist or psychoanalyst but I think a lot of them were suffering from a cultural or historic sense of inferiority vis-à-vis America. It's a very simple thing. On a military level, the U.S. was selling military technology to them, and this rankled because they couldn't do it themselves. You know, you don't like the person who's always helping you. Ironically, many of them had had Peace Corps English teachers."

The women prisoners felt they fared better than most of the men and, said Kathryn Koob, the probable explanation was that their captors' Islamic beliefs demanded different treatment for women.

But treatment of the men varied, too. Laingen, Tomseth and Howland at the Foreign Ministry were in a separate category, of course. As for the variations in treatment among those held by the student militants, it depended, according to Thomas Schaefer, on the captors' impression of what the hostage's job had been.

Schaefer was interrogated — and not very skillfully, he said — because his captors believed that he "was part of the so-called coup d'état against the current Government of Iran."

"The treatment did seem to vary widely," said Michael Metrinko, speaking of his own experience in the hands of different captors. "We were divided into two groups — using their terms, the 'important' prisoners and the 'non-important' prisoners. The important prisoners were those who headed sections or had their names on documents."

As a political officer, Metrinko was treated differently from the Marine guards. "A Marine guard does not rate intelligence memos," he said. "Many had no interrogations. We were far more likely to be put in solitary confinement."

Elizabeth Swift said that, despite their captors' claims to the contrary, it was clear to her that the women were subordinate to the men. Whenever she asked a woman guard for something, the woman would ask a male guard for permission. One day, furious at this, Miss Swift told a woman guard to get a man so that she could ask him for something. When the man appeared, he gave her a severe lecture on how men and women students were completely equal.

Her first guards were medical students; her second — a more suspicious, hardline group — were students of various sorts. "I talked to them quite a bit about religion," she said. "That was a neutral subject." Occasionally, however, captives and captors also discussed the role of women in the modern world. Miss Swift said that the Iranian women did not seem to grasp the unmarried, professional status of her or Kathryn Koob.

Miss Koob divided her captors into three groups.

First, she said, were students — elite, very conservative students, 16 to 22 years of age, men and women, who had been picked from the various universities around town. They were the guards.

This group took the female captives to the bathroom and to the library, brought them books and took their clothes to be laundered. Most of them wore chadors, the traditional Islamic dress for women. "These girls took care of us," she said. "We couldn't get tea ourselves, and one time one of the men felt it important to tell us we shouldn't treat them like servants. We told him we'd be quite happy to get the tea ourselves if he could arrange it."

One young guard who had just gotten married kissed Miss Koob on both cheeks and proudly showed off her wedding ring. Many of the female guards were curious to see how the American women cooked. Miss Koob showed one of them how to make garlic bread sticks.

Sometimes, the guards would give speeches in what Kathryn Koob called "Third World rhetoric." They would criticize the American role in Vietnam. "They tried to convince us we weren't getting any mail because the American Government was stopping our mail to try and drive us crazy," she said. "Just before we got out, they told us we couldn't have our mail because the C.I.A. was poisoning it."

The second group of captors, in Miss Koob's classification, was all male and ranged in age from the mid-20s to the early 30s. They were administrators. "They all said, 'We're all equal, we have no bosses,' " Miss Koob said. "But they plainly did."

The third group, in her opinion, was the interrogators. They were highly trained and motivated, she said. "They were the people who did the interrogation, who were trying to analyze the things that they found out at the embassy, who were trying to make the decisions for the group about the direction the group was taking."

There was, for instance, Hamid, known as "Tooth" because of a gap in his front teeth; he said he had studied computer science at the University of California at Berkeley and he spoke fluent English.

The "chief terrorist," said Robert Blucker, was named Ahmed. Blucker called another "Pretty Boy." Rodney Sickmann remembered one guard called "Butler," another "the Taco Kid." Another was known as "Little Hitler."

One guard was called "Plowboy," another "Bozo the Clown," remembered Richard Morefield. "They were all, I think, committed revolutionaries," he said. Philip Ward, who had served in Vietnam, told how Green Berets there had trained a monkey and named it "Jocko." One of the Iranian guards had a slightly simian appearance so that nickname was given to him. "He'd come in and you'd say, 'Hello, Jocko,' and he'd sit there and smile at you," Sickmann said. "He didn't know what the heck was going on."

Moorhead Kennedy thought the nicknames were a bad idea. It got some of the guards angry, he said. "A polite approach is the way I was brought up in life," he said. "I didn't kowtow. I didn't grovel. I treated them like you treat a waiter."

Some guards were compassionate, said Duane Gillette, particularly those who had been in prison themselves. But even these were careful not to let others see them being friendly, he said. "To speak out against the treatment would have allowed the other militants to turn against that student and his life would have been in jeopardy."

Some guards achieved an off-and-on rapport with the hostages. Rocky Sickmann, a high school football star, had beaten one of them repeatedly in arm-wrestling, and one night in June the guard challenged the sergeant to a real wrestling match, with two hostages and four guards as spectators. Sergeant Sickmann threw the guard across the room. "They had to take him to the hospital and he came back with a sling on his arm," the sergeant said.

Other guards would argue with their captives. John Limbert regarded them as irrationally biased against the United States and hopelessly naive about its influence in the world.

Richard Morefield said that the students simply did not understand America and its pluralistic mix. They told him the hostages were tools of America's "economic and Jewish elite."

Morefield's mother is of Mexican descent and he said it bothered his captors when he told them, "You just do not understand minorities in the United States. You think I'm part of the elite. I'm not."

Other guards used their captives as tutors. "We helped them study for their exams," said Kathryn Koob. "We helped them with their English. One girl was learning English for medical purposes and was studying the names of bones."

Some guards tried to stir dissension among the hostages, Sergeant Sickmann said. First they would favor one of his roommates, Sergeant Gallegos, by delivering letters from home, then they would favor him in other ways. "But we'd sit down and talk it out," he said, "and say this is just what they're trying to do. Because we knew there were people writing to us." The attempt failed, he said, because the hostages agreed among themselves to share all the letters.

Elizabeth Swift remembered that "the students were quite willing to die for what they believed and during the first four or five days they repeatedly told me they were going to be martyrs because the United States was going to come in militarily and rescue us."

It was, of course, not until the spring that the rescue failed.

Unknown to the hostages, however, diplomatic efforts to free them continued. On May 24, a month after the raid, the International Court of Justice ordered Iran to free the hostages. Then, in September, the pace of the diplomacy increased at the same time that border skirmishing between Iran and Iraq built toward war.

On September 9, Washington received a secret message from the West German Government that a distant relative of Ayatollah Khomeini wanted to meet American officials in Bonn to discuss the release of the hostages. The next day, President Carter sent a team to talk. It was headed by Warren M. Christopher, the Deputy Secretary of State and the key American negotiator in the eventual release.

The Iranian, Sadegh Tabatabai, whose sister is married to a son of the Ayatollah, established his credentials by disclosing to the Americans the four conditions that the Ayatollah planned to announce for the release: the return of the Shah's wealth, the cancellation of American claims against Iran, the unfreezing of Iran's assets in American banks and a promise by the United States not to "interfere" in Iranian affairs.

On September 12, the Ayatollah listed those conditions publicly in a speech. But by then the Presidential campaign had begun to preoccupy America and the pace of the hostage negotiations stuttered.

For the hostages, there was one notable change. After months of settling into the tedium of a seemingly endless captivity, suddenly there came the sound of airplanes overhead and of gunfire outside.

"There was shelling and blackouts and stuff like that," Sergeant Sickmann recalled.

Kathryn Koob remembered wondering if there was a new power struggle in the country. "I knew something was afoot," she said.

The border skirmishing between Iran and Iraq had somehow blossomed into war and, as the hostages began to realize what was happening, they felt renewed hope — and fear — of its impact upon them.

12

Whispers of Hope

After 11 months of captivity in which vitriolic mob denunciations of the United States had become routine, some of the hostages suddenly heard a most outlandish sound waft into their cells one day: a stirring orchestral recording of the quintessentially American march "Stars and Stripes Forever."

"Three cheers for the red, white and blue" was being played through the streets, not for the benefit of the hostages, but to stir Iranians to patriotic heights in the new and sudden war that had erupted with Iraq's invasion in late September.

Immediately, Moorhead Kennedy deduced the meaning of the familiar martial music.

"We figured Iran must be involved in a local war of some sort, probably with Iraq," Kennedy recalled. "The guards didn't react to all the war sounds in a way that threatened us, so we knew we weren't involved."

Frederick Kupke listened in fascination to the Sousa music and then tried to decipher the chants of the new street demonstrations outside — rallying cries that reminded him of nothing so much as a familiar football cheer: "Get tough, Big Red! Get tough!"

Kennedy had no certain confirmation of the war until a letter arrived weeks later from his wife, Louisa. Meantime, other hostages closer to the war action heard the thump of shells and saw tracer bullets slashing through the night sky as they peered through the tiny windows of their cells.

"We could feel some of the concussions," Sergeant Sickmann remembered. "There was shelling and blackouts and stuff like that. They were telling us that this was just their practice, that they were practicing for war." Nobody believed them.

Captain Needham, the Air Force officer, leaped happily to the conclusion that a nighttime bombing was the work of the United States. "Not knowing the planes were Iraqi," he said, "that these were not American planes, we put our candles in our windows and said, 'Here we are. Come and get us. Help put a hole in the wall so we can escape.' "

As it became clear the trouble was with the Iraqis, hostages dared to hint at bias in discussing the new war with their captors, Sergeant Sickmann said. "We would sit there and have discussions about how they were getting beat, and they would say no, no, they were just preparing for an attack."

Michael Metrinko, the political officer, could not resist the didactics of a lesson for his captors; he told them that the Iranians' preoccupation with holding the hostages had left them vulnerable to outside attack.

"I took great joy in telling them all the people who had been killed had been killed because of their stupidity in taking the American Embassy," he related, "that if the American Government had relations with Iran, Iraq would never have attacked because they would have been afraid."

As it was, the Iranian Prime Minister, Mohammed Ali Rajai, visited New York on October 17 and, in a speech to the United Nations, accused the United States of helping Iraq in the war.

From the places where they were being held, the Americans could sense the sudden shift of Iranian attention. Richard Morefield, a former artillery officer, heard the Iraqi bombs land in Teheran and overheard guards discussing casualties. Even more, he saw increasing evidence of what Americans at home and a few of the hostages knew were trade sanctions against Iran. Food and kerosene became limited and long blackouts were ordered, as much to save energy, it seemed, as to wage war.

Kennedy's wife, in addition to confirming news of the war in a letter, told her husband in veiled language that the United States had imposed the trade sanctions against Iran.

"It was working," Morefield said of the American countermeasures. "I was sure of this."

Such stirrings of fresh anticipation fed into the final month of the Presidential elections back home, an event marked well by both hostages and captors.

The Iranians began predicting President Carter's defeat and saying it would mean freedom for the Americans.

"They would come in and say, yeah, Carter has to do something before the election to get us out that would make him look good in office," Sergeant Sickmann recounted, annoyed at the notion that domestic politics might intrude into a life-and-death issue. He said he was hoping instead that the President would send in bombers and "blow the country apart."

Each day of the far-off campaign was echoed in the jail cells of Iran by some of the same questions about President Carter's quandary that were fascinating political analysts back in the United States.

"We kept telling them that he [Carter] didn't have to do anything," Sergeant Sickmann said. "And they said, 'Oh no, no. It will be for sure, he will do something.'"

For the hostages, such talk meant primarily that they had better steel themselves for the likelihood of another siege of hope and disappointment coinciding with the first anniversary of their captivity.

On November 2, two days before the anniversary and the American election, Iran's Parliament voted to endorse the Ayatollah's four conditions for release of the hostages and asked Algeria to serve as an intermediary. Warren Christopher traveled to Algiers a week later with the United States response.

Soon after Ronald Reagan's election victory, guards in Iran gleefully appeared to announce the defeat of "the great Satan Carter." But the prospect of a Reagan Presidency apparently worried some of the captors, one of whom had told Charles Jones, "You want Ronald Reagan to win so it will be boom, boom, boom." Moorhead Kennedy recalled that his main reaction had been a new sort of worry, that the change in Administrations in Washington might require restarting the entire negotiating process with the Iranians.

By this time, at the beginning of their second year of imprisonment, the sporadic talk by some hostages of an attempt to escape began to interest such an earlier skeptic as Col. Charles Scott, the embassy's military attaché. He did not think an escape could work, but he indulged the talk nevertheless because he decided that he could not wait "forever." Accordingly, he and other hostages began to discuss a breakout deadline set sometime after the new Administration took over in Washington.

In retrospect, incidents of resistance to the captors would be recounted with pride by the repatriated Americans. "When they attempted to give me the story about how religious they were, I would tell them they were a bunch of criminals," Michael Metrinko said, recalling that some of his worst confinement was suffered in the final months because of his pugnacious attitude.

"I was being punished by the guards for my inability to establish a polite rapport," he said, telling of a final stretch of 17 consecutive days in a "special punishment cell" with no light, heat, bedding or books. For four days, he was kept on a diet of bread and water. The cell was "freezing cold." He had a sweater, but "no coat, no shoes."

"I was keeping warm by constantly jogging in the cell," he said. "There wasn't enough room to walk."

The wall in Metrinko's cell was "wet, always wet, and rotting," he said. "The plaster just came off in streaks."

When he demanded a heater, Metrinko said, he was "always being told, 'You don't need a heater. Families in Iran don't have heaters.'

"Of course," he continued, "that was a lot of bull because the guards had a heater outside. They came to the door in heavy parkas. Of course that made me feel colder than ever."

In that dank and miserable cell, Metrinko kept up the verbal counterattacks on his guards that had won their enmity so frequently during the long captivity. He yelled at them in Persian. He called them thieves. He hammered at their piety.

"If you let me stay here without heat," he told them, "may God curse you and your families who have heat."

"I commented frequently on the fact that their treatment to us was far worse than Savak would have treated them," he said. "It was true. Part of my job was to visit foreigners who had been jailed. I had a great many Iranian friends who were Savak prisoners and I talked to them about their experiences. I know what it was like. The followers of the Imam, so-called, were not treating us with the same standards that prisoners had been treated before.

"When I would complain," Metrinko continued, "they would say, 'You're not prisoners.' I would say, 'I'm not free so I must be a prisoner.'

" 'You have no rights,' they would reply, 'You're a criminal.' "

Sometimes, Metrinko said, the guards would tell him, "If I had been a foreigner or an Iranian who had killed someone I would have been allowed family visits. I would have been allowed to retain my money and would have been allowed to supplement my diet by shopping in prison shops. I would have been allowed freer access to doctors, hospitals, exercise and would have been allowed mail, radios and news."

Metrinko saw some of the guards wearing clothing from his apartment and playing a tape recorder he owned, and he objected.

"Of course we looted your house," one guard told him. "This is war."

As Christmas approached, the Iranians began collecting the hostages from their cells and bare rooms and bringing them together in comfortable surroundings they considered reminiscent of the Shah's era. Some were lodged in a palatial house with carpeting and chandeliers and red marble bathrooms with gilded fixtures. Others were taken to what they thought was a luxury hotel or motel that some surmised might have been the Foreign Ministry's guest house.

"We were quite comfortable," said Moorhead Kennedy, who had become a resident of the sumptuous house.

Shortly before Christmas, some of the hostages were visited by the Algerian ambassador and his aides. Kennedy and some of the other career diplomats were especially heartened. The neutral Algerians, they thought, could possibly provide a bridge between Teheran and Washington.

In rapid French that he hoped the guards would not be able to follow, Kennedy asked the ambassador if he had come in an official capacity. The United States Government "knew" of the visit, the diplomat replied. Kennedy was thrilled.

Richard Morefield spoke with the Algerians, too, and even his skepticism about the approach of freedom began to subside. "My impression was that they were true professionals and hard as nails," Morefield said. "I told them that I understood the difficulty of being a mediator. When I saw that they were professionals, that's when I had hope."

Morefield handed a letter addressed to his wife to one of the Algerians, and watched him put it in his diplomatic pouch. For the first time, he was certain that one of his letters home would be delivered.

The second Christmas in captivity was more subdued than the first. There were no American clergymen and some of the hostages were in a more belligerent mood.

On Christmas Eve, three Iranian Christian clerics and the Papal Nuncio in Iran, Msgr. Annibale Bugnini, who had been blindfolded for the trip, visited some of the hostages. Others were visited by a pair of Iranian ministers, the Algerian ambassador and his aides. And some were invited to participate in Iranian-led services on Christmas Day.

As at the first Christmas gathering, almost everything was filmed.

Kathryn Koob, meeting with one of the delegations in a room of the hotel or guest house, sang the third verse from "Away in a Manger," in a segment of film that was broadcast in the United States. She had chosen to do that, she said, because she wanted to share a prayer with the nation and with her nieces and nephews.

Moorhead Kennedy boycotted the services. He refused the gifts and candy the Iranians offered. Give it to the poor, he told them. "I refused at that point," he said, "to be used for propaganda purposes anymore."

Michael Metrinko scolded the clergymen.

"I told the ministers they were incredibly hypocritical for taking part," he said. And he taunted: "Where were you all year long when we were being treated so badly?"

At the Foreign Ministry, Bruce Laingen, the chargé d'affaires, Victor Tomseth, his deputy, and Michael Howland, their security man, celebrated their second Christmas together in relative splendor. As the holiday neared, friends in the diplomatic community brought them greeting cards and homemade cakes. They also smuggled in bottles labeled aftershave lotion but filled with whiskey. Howland again made a Christmas tree, this one of styrofoam, and decorated it with gold cutouts.

Two days before Christmas Laingen and his roommates were told to pack their belongings, that they were going to join the other hostages. At midnight, five to ten young militants, accompanied by a handful of Foreign Ministry officials, led the Americans downstairs and out through a courtyard to a waiting van.

As they were about to enter the van, Howland, apprehensive over what might lie ahead, suddenly resisted the move. He lunged at the leader of the group and kicked him in the groin. Laingen jumped between the two men, "mouthing diplomatic inanities," as he recalled it. But the damage had been done. The militant leader was humiliated. Abruptly, he ordered the Americans back to their old quarters. As they were reentering the Foreign Ministry, he put his pistol to Laingen's head.

"If your friend tries that again," he said, "he'll get this treatment." Alone again in the Foreign Ministry, Laingen and the others stayed up until 3 A.M., expecting more trouble. But no one was to come again for them for 10 days.

In December and January, as the negotiations for the hostages' freedom hurried toward a resolution, the talking point was money. Iran asked for $24 billion on December 19. On December 30, the United States pressed for a smaller amount. A week later, Algeria let the American team know that Iran would settle for $9.5 billion in frozen assets, provided they were turned over immediately.

On January 15, Iran cut this demand to $8.1 billion. The United States countered with an offer of $7.9 billion. Iran agreed.

But, as they endured the ordeal of a second holiday season in captivity, the hostages knew almost nothing of this.

Christmas came. New Year's came.

On January 3, the militants returned for Laingen and the others. They were frisked, marched out to the van, ordered to sit on the floor and sped to a prison somewhere in Teheran. They were led off to separate cells, each furnished only with a folding chair, a sleeping pad and some blankets. They were searched again. Their shoes were taken and they were left alone. There was no heat.

On the floor of Laingen's cell was a pile of toothpicks. Laingen said

133

his first thought was that they had been used for torture. "It was another of the dark moments," he said.

The next day, Laingen was moved to a larger cell. "If you behave," he was told, "you'll get privileges." Eventually, he was given books and the watercolors he had worked with in the Foreign Ministry. While in the Foreign Ministry he had executed a painting of three brown birds on a leafless bush — symbolizing himself and the two other Americans, he said — and sent it to his son, William, for his 21st birthday. Laingen's wife, Penelope, used the painting as the family's 1980 Christmas card.

Victor Tomseth said there was no effort to physically abuse the three men. There was not even an interrogation, which, he said, seemed to suggest that "we were in the last act of this drama."

Six other hostages had scrawled their names on the thick walls of Laingen's cell. And William Belk, the communications officer who had tried to escape a year earlier and had spent long months in solitary confinement, had etched on the dirty cement the cry of a desperately lonely man: "Angela, my love, my life, my wife."

On the 15th or 16th of January, Laingen and Tomseth were taken out to a car and driven to a large, well-appointed house. They were put in what they took to be the master bedroom. But the windows had been barred and painted over, and Laingen found the room more claustrophobic than the jail cell. At least in the cell, he said, "if you looked carefully you could see a patch of blue."

But there were amenities. Now they were getting food from the embassy commissary. For the first time in a year they had chili, and there was Land O' Lakes butter at breakfast. They were having their first long encounters with the young Iranian militants. There were a lot of them, Laingen said. They were not abusive, but he said he dramatized his attitude toward them by acting cold and angry.

In the last days of captivity, with the inauguration of Ronald Reagan drawing near, there were endless rumors about the prospects of freedom for the hostages, both in the United States and among the hostages in Iran.

The final pieces of the deal to set the hostages free were put together in the closing days of the Carter Administration. In Algiers, Warren Christopher, the Deputy Secretary of State, signed three documents on behalf of the United States. Iran balked at two technical additions. Eventually, these were dropped and, on January 20, as Ronald Reagan was about to take the oath of office, the frozen Iranian assets were deposited in an Algerian escrow account in the Bank of England, clearing the way for the release.

But as far as the hostages were concerned, nothing convincing happened until January 19, the day before they were set free.

Then, several things happened. First, a group of Algerian doctors appeared and gave all the hostages medical examinations. Next a familiar figure from the opening weeks of captivity, "Mary the Terrorist," reappeared. Some of the hostages then were asked to make propaganda statements for Iranian television cameras to the effect that their captors had treated them well. Some did and some did not.

It was the sight of the Algerian doctors that persuaded most of the hostages that the day of deliverance was at hand.

"We had been given exams before by Iranian doctors," Moorhead Kennedy said, "but this was a serious medical examination. We sensed that this was for real."

"They had taken blood tests," said Duane Gillette. "They took an EKG. They wouldn't do that just to play a head game. It was very encouraging."

Bruce Laingen, having spent most of his captivity in relative ease, was so incensed at his first experience in the hands of the militant students that his anger spilled over in the presence of the Algerian doctors. He refused to speak to the doctor who examined him.

The ever-belligerent Blucker wasn't cooperative, either. "They came around and said we were going to have a medical examination and blood and urine tests. I refused. By that time, I was almost totally rebellious. Then, that son-of-a-bitch Ahmed [the chief militant] — I was no longer speaking to him — he came in the room. I told him I didn't trust their needles, that I didn't need hepatitis."

Blucker had to be led out to the examination, which was conducted in another building. "Ahmed wanted me to wear his shoes," he said, "but I went barefoot across the ice."

At the examination building, Blucker was told he was going to have an electrocardiogram.

"I don't want any of that," he shot back.

135

"We're the Algerians," said one of the doctors.

Blucker was taken aback. He reconsidered and finally decided to cooperate.

Later, Ahmed and another captor Blucker had dubbed "Pretty Boy" asked Blucker to go on videotape. "He was almost pleading with me to go before the cameras," Blucker said.

He refused.

"Oh," said Pretty Boy, "you're so stubborn."

"Some of the hostages thought that if they didn't cooperate, they might not be released," Blucker said. "But I figured they would have to release all of us."

With Mary the Terrorist was a man who instructed some of the hostages that "candidates" for freedom were about to be interviewed for television. The implication was clear that benign comments from the Americans would hasten their release, or perhaps even determine whether they would be set free.

When Donald Sharer, the Navy commander, was told he was a "candidate" for freedom he replied: "I haven't believed you the last 10 months. Why should I start believing you now?"

"Well, you're going to be talking to 300 newsmen," the Iranian said, as if ever-conscious of the public relations aspects of the event.

Moorhead Kennedy, with the cameras rolling, said that some of his guards had been kind, and he even named a few of them. But when Mary the Terrorist asked whether he had learned anything from his captivity, it was just too much. His anger boiled out:

"I said that there was no excuse whatever for taking an embassy or for holding its staff as hostage, and that this was much larger than this one episode — that international relations, the peace of the world, depended upon the exchange of embassies and the security afforded to their personnel to do their jobs, and that Iran would suffer in the long run."

Kennedy feared his outburst had spoiled his chance for freedom. "I left the interview wondering whether I had blown my chances of getting home," he said. "But I knew darned well I wasn't about to play their propaganda game."

Sergeant Lopez didn't want to cooperate either, but he did. "Myself, I felt I'm not going to help this guy," he said. "I'm not going to say anything just to get out. So we went in the room with Mary the Terrorist. I told them, 'I don't want to do anything.' It was just talking to a brick wall. So they put me on camera.

"Honestly," Lopez said, "if you were given that choice and she said, 'How were you treated?' What are you going to say if you think you might get released if you say the right thing? Are you going to say 'I was beaten'? You're not going to say that. You're going to say, 'Some of the guards were mean, some of the guards were okay.' "

After the interview, Lopez was taken back to his room. He and his roommates began a game of bridge, refusing to believe that the promised release was imminent. "We figured it was just another dog-and-pony show to get the interview from us, to build up America's hopes and dash them again."

Sergeant Persinger decided freedom depended on the interview, and he said he had not been mistreated by the Iranians. "I was not forced," he said. "It was on the view you either do it or you're not going to be released. Let's say we were under pressure."

Immediately after his examination by the Algerian doctors, Master Sgt. Regis Ragan said, he was taken to a room and beaten severely. It happened, he said, because he had refused just before the medical exam to cooperate with the Iranians in making a propaganda tape.

In the room where videotaping equipment had been set up, the Iranians coaxed him to say "the treatment is good, the food is good."

Ragan kept silent.

There was more coaxing, then harsher demands: "We want you to speak," one said. But Ragan continued to sit on a chair and said nothing. They then showed him a newspaper that indicated that the United States and Iran were near an accord on releasing the hostages.

"What they were saying was if I did what they wanted me to do, I would be released, and if I didn't I would not."

After one of the militants outlined aspects of the proposed hostage agreement and again instructed him to answer questions for the cameras, Ragan told them: "I have nothing to say to you people."

At that point Mary the Terrorist, who had supervised several other videotaped interviews with hostages, attempted to question him without the cameras rolling.

"I told you people I have nothing to say to you," he responded.

Then, the klieg lights and cameras were turned on and Mary tried again. Again Ragan sat impassively — it was the pose in which he was seen when the film was finally shown.

"Then they took me downstairs to be examined by the Algerian doctors and after the examination they took me upstairs and took me into another room." There, he said, "they physically abused me. They hit me in the face and they told me I was going back into that room to make a statement. I told them I had nothing to say to them."

Ragan's voice cracked and his eyes filled with tears as he went on: "They called me a fucking pig. They called me a motherfucking pig and they threw me around." Then, he said, the blindfold was put back on and he was returned to his quarters.

No one slept that night. And the morning and afternoon of the next day dragged past with no word, and still no word.

"We were all kind of low that day," Commander Sharer said.

13

January 20, 1981

Finally, at 6 P.M. on January 20, after 14½ months of captivity, and at the height of the final day's confusion and doubt, the hostages were given a half-hour's notice of their departure.

"The guards just showed up," said Kennedy. "They said, 'You're going home. Pack up.'

"There wasn't any cheering," Kennedy said. "We just did it."

For Blucker it was just one more opportunity to offer resistance. "Ahmed came in," he recalled, "and told us we were leaving Iran and that we could pack one small bag. I told him I was going to take two bags. He didn't argue."

Blucker said that by this time, after months of forced moves all around Iran, the hostages had collected bags of string, drinking glasses and other odds and ends. "We were like the vagabonds who live on the sidewalks of New York," he said.

Despite the invitation to pack a bag, Blucker was still skeptical about getting anything out of the country. He was right. When he got his bags packed, they took them away and that was the last he ever saw of them. He left Iran with nothing but his clothes and a souvenir blindfold.

Colonel Schaefer put his letters, a flag and his Bible in a box. He had kept copious notes in the Bible in a kind of code, by making pin dots over words that conveyed his thoughts. The box was tied up and handed over to the captors, supposedly to be returned to him at the airport. He never saw it again.

At the captors' behest, Schaefer and the others then went downstairs to pick out a pair of shoes. Most of the hostages had had their shoes taken away early in captivity and had worn none since. The shoes that awaited them were their own. Five pairs of Schaefer's own shoes were there to choose from, and he picked out a pair of his black loafers with buckles.

He slipped them on — and quickly the blindfolds went right back on.

The blindfolded hostages were then put aboard buses and vans bound for Mehrabad Airport. "I had to sit on the floor, almost under a seat," said Sharer. "Everybody was kind of stacked like cord wood."

Schaefer was still skeptical about what was going on. He feared that Iranian extremists — of the right or left — might attack the Americans on the way to the airport. "I honestly felt there would be an attempt to shoot some of us and embarrass Khomeini and his Government," he said.

There were no attacks, but there was some trouble en route. A guard tried to take Laingen's bag, but he hung on and refused to give it up.

"Don't you trust us?" the guard asked him.

Laingen, flabbergasted, just stared at him.

Michael Metrinko, the embassy political officer who had been beaten, left shivering in cold cells, kept in isolation and denied virtually everything but food, had one last violent encounter with his captors on the way to the airport. Riding in a van, he exchanged curses with a guard. When the guard seized him, he shoved back and the guard went down. Metrinko was thereupon taken out and, as he put it, "roughed up a little."

When they got to the airport, an anti-American demonstration was waiting for them. So was an Algerian jetliner, a Boeing 727. Still, some hostages were not convinced they were getting out.

Sergeant Lopez said, "We were sitting in the bus wondering, 'When are they going to call this off and take us back?' 'What are they pulling?' 'Are they going to shoot us?' "

The hostages came out of the buses and vans one at a time. Looking dazed as the blindfolds were removed and put away, some were roughly shoved and hurried through what they took to be a token gantlet of final vituperation.

It would be the last opportunity on both sides to vent the rages, frustrations and pent-up hatreds of their long relationship as captors and captives, their last chance to lash out at one another, but it somehow came out flat. Perhaps they were all too drained. In any case, no one on either side could find the right words or the proper emotions for the coup de grace. So it all came out sounding like a sticks-and-stones jingle.

"Bad, bad, America's bad," the Iranians chanted in the blur and din of departure.

"Bad, bad America."

"I chimed in right with them," Commander Sharer recalled.

"Bad, bad Iran," he jeered back. "Bad, bad Iran."

There were 27 steps up the aircraft ramp. "I made it in about two leaps," Sharer said.

Hurried along, Kathryn Koob climbed the ramp, reached the top and took a last glance back at Iran and the Iranians. "I'm sure there were some among them who thought we should never have gone home," she said. "But I think that for most of them they were pretty glad to see us go."

Even as the hostages mounted the ramp, Jerry Miele had doubts about getting out. He was unsure they were leaving until he "got on the plane — that's the truth. There were so many of those false hopes that we just disregarded them till we were on the plane. Even then . . ."

Inside the aircraft, the Americans shouted greetings to one another — many had not seen some of the other hostages throughout the ordeal — and they hugged and kissed one another and began swapping tales of terror and adventure. "When we heard the plane engines kicking in, we knew we were going home," said Sergeant Persinger.

Later, there would be time to think and talk about the meaning of their experience, about President Carter's handling of the crisis and about the Shah, who, in a sense, had gotten them all into the mess.

Moorhead Kennedy regarded the Shah as "an awful man" and said the United States had shown bad judgment in its involvement with him. He did not criticize the President, however, and spelled out what appeared to be the continuing predicament of any American Administration:

"I didn't think you should negotiate with people who had seized an embassy. Maybe that means death for hostages. But you don't talk to terrorists. At least you don't for a while. But, of course, in the end you do."

Duane Gillette, the Navy petty officer, said: "There were times when I would have sacrificed myself gladly rather than humiliate the United States. If the United States had bent and met the demands of the Iranian militants, I would not have come home as proud and happy as I am."

As for President Carter, Gillette said that whatever mistakes might have been made, he respected the former President for having had the "courage" to go to Germany and "face us."

Charles Jones was less sanguine: "Carter came to Germany to explain to us what he was trying to do and what was on his mind at the time. He was a sincere man, but it was all above him."

Of the President's visit to the freed hostages, Donald Hohman said he would "always respect that man for what he did, to come and speak with the hostages when he didn't have to, and ask for our questions when he could have said, 'Look, President Reagan. It's your ballgame now. You take the answers and questions and put them together.' "

Instead, he said, President Carter "came to us and gave us honest answers, took it like a man. I'll always respect him for it. I hold him in the highest esteem."

Donald Sharer, the Navy commander, like many of the military men among the hostages, said that government policy was not his to make. "We realize that America could not let the lives of 50 people jeopardize the lives of 200 million others, and we talked about it quite a bit," he said, adding, "Every once in a while, we'd say, 'Well, God bless it, I wish they'd nuke this place.' "

Kathryn Koob said that she thought it had been "ill advised" to let the Shah into the United States in the first place. "All you had to do is watch the demonstrations and the millions who would march when Khomeini would call for a day of solidarity," she said. "There was — and I think still is — a strong base of Islamic support for this man."

In general, she said, she sympathized with the aims, if not the means, of the Iranian revolution. "I had no quarrel with the 24-year-old girl who sat with tears in her eyes and talked about the need for education for the young girls of Iran," she said, adding: "I think the Shah made a lot of mistakes. If he personally was not cruel, there was a great deal of cruelty done during his reign. I would like to see some sort of system set up so that leaders of countries are held accountable for their actions."

Now they tumbled into the airplane — still shocked that this time the hope of escape was not a false alarm, gathered together for the first time in their 444 days of captivity, stunned that it was ending — and it was time to trade stories and to exult that, at last, they were free.

"I got inside that airplane," Commander Sharer said, "and some of the Marines were already in there. I love those Marines and I started giving college yells and cheers like I was on a football field and scoring a touchdown, and we were happy from then on."

They were met inside the plane by Erik Lang, the Swiss ambassador, and his first secretary, Flavio Meroni, and there was some essential bookkeeping. On a sheet of hotel stationery, Meroni wrote the numbers 1 to 52 and asked each hostage to sign.

At the end, he looked at the list. There was a moment of panic. There was a blank line at Number 52.

Then it turned out that two hostages had signed at Number 40. All were safely aboard.

They looked out the windows and the runway lights suddenly flashed on. A full moon shone on the white peaks of the Alborz Mountains in the distance.

"We took any seats that were available," Robert Blucker remembered. "I sat down beside Jerry Plotkin and Duane Gillette. So I was back with the guy I started with, Jerry Plotkin."

At 8:55 P.M., the plane roared down the runway and was airborne. A few minutes later, unfastening their seatbelts, the hostages — now the former hostages — stood in the aisles to embrace and sob and talk, how they talked, on their way to Algiers.

Blucker said: "It was one stage of elation to walk into the plane, knowing it had nothing but civilized people on it. It was a second stage of elation to feel the plane actually taxiing and then to lift off. Everybody cheered. When the pilot announced the takeoff, there was another cheer."

Amid the jabber and joy, the Algerians served champagne and red wine. There were toasts — to freedom.

Blucker said, "The first thing I wanted to know was how people were treated and where they had been.

"I even smoked a cigar. I almost couldn't believe that. It was the first time I smoked in more than 20 years.

"I was going home. It was all over."

As the airplane climbed into the night, most of the former hostages had no inkling of the tumultous welcomes and intense celebrity that awaited them at home. They were emerging from captivity as innocents, soon to be stunned, even dazed, by their abrupt elevation to pedestals of heroism. They would have no voice in the nation's decision to make them heroes of a new American legend, and some would find the roles arduous and uncomfortable.

There would be a brief stopover in Algiers, where television cameras would begin recording their every move and remark; a three-day layover in Wiesbaden, where doctors and government debriefers would break into promised privacy, seeking to guide their transition back to "normal" life; an emotional reunion with their families at the United States Military Academy at West Point; a pomp-filled reception at the White House; a ticker-tape parade in New York City and, finally, farewells to one another and a fanning out to hometowns and loved ones. There would also be gifts from self-serving companies, offers from publishers, requests for product endorsements and other trappings of the commercial world to which they were returning.

But all of that lay ahead. For the moment, they were trying to cope with the strange feelings rippling through them.

In the air at last, the Americans, the walls between them gone, quickly began piecing together their common lives, filling in blanks, particularly the tantalizing ones of daily routine.

"Everybody was asking questions," Sergeant Sickmann said. "We'd recognize everybody's voices but we would ask questions, like, you know, 'What were you guys playing that night when I heard all that racket?' "

JANUARY 20, 1981

The source of the racket of rolled dice, the counted moves, the oohs and ahs, it turned out, was Parcheesi. And that strange game of flopping sounds? It was hostage basketball, played with rolled-up socks tossed toward a cardboard hoop.

A few of them did not yield to the moment until the Algerians turned on the cabin speakers to broadcast the pilot's conversation and let the control tower note the precise instant that the plane passed out of Iranian airspace and jurisdiction — from captivity to deliverance.

Some would grope for the words to describe the moment.

"The feeling of freedom," said Jerry Miele, "That's it. Freedom. You don't know what that is till you've come out and you are free. It changes your insides and you are alive again."

"It brought tears to the eyes," Duane Gillette said. "It was beautiful."

Their ordeal was over at last. For 444 days they had been captives of a nation that seemed determined to turn back to an ancient world. They had lived in conditions of primitive barbarism. They had been guarded by people who repudiated Western civilization and modern culture, the world that the Americans knew and loved. And now at last they were on their way home to their own land, their own people, their own time.

"When we got off the plane," said Rocky Sickmann, "we set our watches ahead 2,000 years."

PART II

Outside

1

Why Carter Admitted the Shah

By Terence Smith

When the evening packet of documents from the White House arrived at Camp David that Indian summer weekend, it included a memorandum from Secretary of State Cyrus R. Vance that required an immediate Presidential decision. Jimmy Carter could not know it at the time, but that decision would set in train an extraordinary series of events that would preoccupy the nation for the next 14½ months and profoundly affect his own future.

The issue posed by the memo on October 21, 1979, had been nagging the Administration for months: Should Mohammed Riza Pahlevi, the exiled Shah of Iran, be allowed to enter the United States? Despite the risks such a move would entail, especially for the skeleton crew of Americans manning the embassy in revolutionary Teheran, most of Carter's advisers were for it. The President himself had been adamantly opposed and had lost his temper more than once on the subject. But now a new and urgent development had changed the situation and Vance was on the telephone from Washington asking for a decision. Eighteen months later, in his first and only substantive interview on the Iranian crisis since leaving office, Jimmy Carter described the exchange.

"I was told that the Shah was desperately ill, at the point of death," he said quietly, gazing at the pine trees outside his home in Plains, Ga. "I was told that New York was the only medical facility that was capable of possibly saving his life and reminded that the Iranian officials had promised to protect our people in Iran. When all the circumstances were described to me, I agreed."

That point of decision has most often been explained as a spontaneous, compassionate response to a medical emergency. But, examined in the light of interviews with more than 50 people who played a part, it emerges as a much more complicated act. It reflected a calculated political gamble taken in response to high-pressure lobbying within and outside the Administration and with an eye on the upcoming Presidential campaign. And it led directly to the trauma of the following weeks and months: the seizure of the American hostages in Teheran, the shattering of relations between the United States and Iran, the altering of strategic realities in the oil-rich Persian Gulf.

The decision came after months of heated argument among top officials of the Administration and some of the nation's most influential private citizens. A high-powered, financial and political "old-boy network" — including David Rockefeller, who retired in April 1981 after long years as the chairman of the Chase Manhattan Bank; Henry A. Kissinger, Secretary of State for Presidents Nixon and Ford, and the lawyer-diplomat John J. McCloy — waged a campaign on behalf of the Shah's admission that was far more intensive than had previously been disclosed. Carter now concedes that he resented the campaign at the time and that it influenced several of his advisers.

Moreover, it was a decision based, in significant measure, on misinformation and misinterpretation. *The New York Times* learned, for example, of an important discrepancy between what Carter remembers being told about the Shah's medical state and the facts as recalled by the private physician who was the Administration's sole source of information about the Shah's condition. It was not medically necessary — as the President had been informed — to treat the Shah in the United States. And according to the Shah's doctor, his advice was that the monarch should be treated promptly, not that he was "at the point of death." Further, the Shah had successfully concealed the truth of his cancer from American intelligence for six years, even to the point of misleading American doctors. Knowledge of the seriousness of his condition and his limited probable life span might well have altered American policy toward Iran and, with it, the course of events.

It is possible that the militant students in Teheran might have found another excuse to seize the United States Embassy; certainly, they had tried before. But, as it turned out, the decision Carter made that Indian summer Sunday on the couch in his lodge at Camp David was the proximate cause of the takeover and all that followed.

The exile and final odyssey of the self-proclaimed Shahanshah ("King of Kings, Light of the Aryans and Vice Regent of God") began on January 16, 1979. Son of a commoner who had himself declared Shah, he had occupied the Peacock Throne for 37 years, a handsome, dark-eyed man who prided himself on his physical fitness and courage. He had staved off political disaster more than once during his rule, but now a revolution was tearing the ground from beneath him. He declared that he was leaving Iran for an extended "vacation."

The Shah's departure had been expected for weeks. President Carter had extended him a public invitation, and Sunnylands, the huge, well-guarded estate of the publisher Walter H. Annenberg in Rancho Mirage, Calif., had been prepared for the royal family.

But the Shah accepted another invitation — from his closest Middle Eastern ally, Egyptian President Anwar el-Sadat. On January 16, the Shah, his Empress, Farah Diba, and their entourage flew to Egypt, where they rested on an island in the upper Nile for six days. The royal family then moved on to Morocco as guests of King Hassan II, spending three weeks in a luxurious, palm-shaded palace in Marrakesh. The Shah took his family for long drives in the nearby snow-capped Atlas Mountains and played tennis. Periodically, the official invitation to come to the United States was renewed, but the Shah had been persuaded by his own advisers and by Sadat that the chances of a return to power would be greater if he remained in the Middle East, where he could follow events in Teheran more closely. In addition, a decision to settle in the United States would have underscored the popular image of him in Iran as an American puppet.

On February 1, the Ayatollah Ruhollah Khomeini enjoyed a triumphant homecoming from his exile in Paris, and he quickly started to lay the groundwork for his revolutionary government. On February 14, a mob overran the American Embassy. Nearly 100 Americans were taken hostage, in an episode much like the climactic takeover nine months later. But this time, in a move that gave the secular Iranian Government more credibility in Washington than it ultimately deserved, two senior ministers quickly negotiated the release of all the hostages.

These developments were helping to change Washington's attitude about admitting the Shah. The danger to Americans still in Iran had grown and would clearly be further increased if he were admitted. The Administration had begun to open contacts with the emerging revolutionary government, contacts that would be threatened by any new American overtures toward the Shah. Secretary Vance, in particular, was starting to feel the need for a change in policy, and Jimmy Carter tended to agree with him.

In the second week of March, the Shah moved to a palace in Rabat, the Moroccan capital. By that time, the Carter Administration was groping for a decorous way to let him know that the earlier invitation had been withdrawn. In search of an emissary to break the news gently, the State Department contacted two of the Shah's staunchest supporters: David Rockefeller and Henry Kissinger.

David Rockefeller's personal offices, 56 floors above Rockefeller Center, seem modest enough — until a visitor notices the French Impressionist originals on the walls. In an April 1981 interview, during which Rockefeller frequently consulted typewritten notes to refresh his memory, he said he had received "legal authorization" from the Shah's family to discuss, for the first time in any detail, his relationship and that of his bank with the Pahlevi family.

"I got a call on March 14, 1979," Rockefeller said, "from David Newsom [Carter's Undersecretary of State for Political Affairs]. Newsom said they had intelligence reports from Iran which suggested that, if the Shah were admitted to the United States, the American Embassy would be taken and it would be a threat to American lives. Therefore, the President wanted me to go and tell the Shah that it was not convenient for him to come to the United States at this time.

"I said I thought it was a mistake, that [the Shah] was a great friend of the United States and was seeking asylum and that it was in the American tradition to admit anybody under those circumstances, most particularly a friend. So I refused to do it."

WHY CARTER ADMITTED THE SHAH

In the months that followed, Rockefeller showed himself to be a true friend to the Shah. He and his staff helped to find the Shah a home in the Bahamas, to secure visas, to engineer his transportation by chartered jet, to facilitate his medical care. He also played a leading role in the campaign to persuade the Carter Administration to admit the Shah.

Today, Rockefeller charges that his motivations have been "monstrously distorted" by the press, pointing particularly to suggestions that he acted solely out of concern for Chase Manhattan's profits.

"Contrary to what has been said by a number of people," he insisted, "we have never been the [personal] bankers for the Shah or his family or the Pahlevi Foundation. There may have been small accounts of convenience, but they had no real significance." (The Pahlevi Foundation invested in real estate and business and distributed funds for the construction of hospitals and schools in Iran.)

On the other hand, Rockefeller did not deny that the financial relationship between Chase Manhattan and the Shah's Government was clearly significant. By 1975, for example, Chase had emerged as the principal syndicator for Iran's vast Eurodollar deposits. Some $2 billion in Iranian transactions were handled by Chase that year. Rockefeller emphasized, however, that the Shah's departure drastically changed that picture. As of January 1981, Chase's loans to and claims on Iran had dwindled to about $340 million, and clearly whatever help Rockefeller provided the Shah could only make matters worse with Khomeini's regime. But it was equally true that, had the Shah been restored to power during those early months, Chase's position would have been more enviable than ever.

David Rockefeller had been a longtime business acquaintance of the Shah, but his late brother Nelson, former Vice President and Governor of New York, had been a personal friend of the monarch for nearly two decades. By the end of 1978, Nelson Rockefeller had become alarmed about the Shah's eroding political position. "He wrote a personal, handwritten letter expressing his friendship and concern," David Rockefeller recalled, "which he sent to the Shah with Robert Armao."

Robert Francis Armao, then 30 years of age, had just been hired by Princess Ashraf Pahlevi, the Shah's twin sister and a longtime resident of New York City, to mount a public-relations campaign in the United

States in defense of the Shah's regime. A New York native with a dandy's taste for clothes, Armao had worked as a labor-relations aide to Nelson Rockefeller before starting his own public-relations firm.

Later, when the Shah's illnesses sapped his strength, Armao would grow ever more influential with the monarch and, in the process, engage in tempestuous arguments with senior officials of the Carter Administration. Armao contended that Carter aides repeatedly betrayed their promises to assist and protect the Shah; Jimmy Carter later described Armao as "a troublemaker who wouldn't tell the truth, who made damaging statements to the news media and, I think, caused the Shah a lot of grief."

Robert Armao delivered Nelson Rockefeller's letter to the Shah on the evening of January 9, 1979, in Niavaran Palace in Teheran. A few days later, Ardeshir Zahedi, the Shah's ambassador to Washington, visited Nelson Rockefeller in New York and asked his help in finding a temporary refuge for the Shah in the United States. Sunnylands, the California estate that had been prepared for the Pahlevis, no longer seemed safe, because there had been several West Coast protests against the Shah and his regime's human-rights violations. Nelson Rockefeller's staff located a suitable and secure substitute, a mansion on the grounds of Callaway Gardens, a resort in Georgia, but the Administration had other plans.

In mid-March, the State Department attempted again to find an influential emissary to tell the Shah he was no longer welcome in the United States. Now the target was Henry Kissinger, long a supporter of the Shah and protégé of the Rockefeller family, and once again the caller was David Newsom.

"I refused with some indignation," Kissinger said, recalling the telephone conversation. "I considered it a deeply wrong thing to do, a national dishonor, and I still do."

The Administration finally dispatched a C.I.A. agent to do the job. The agent, who had served in Iran and knew the Shah, met with the monarch in the palace in Rabat. According to Armao, the Shah told him that the agent began by stressing all the problems the royal family might encounter in the United States. "He talked," Armao said, "about lawsuits in American courts, the possibility that the Shah would be subpoenaed by Congressional committees and the security problems posed by the demonstrations."

Within days, the Shah received another jolt. King Hassan made it clear that the Shah's presence would be particularly awkward during the upcoming Islamic summit conference in Marrakesh. With his friend Nelson Rockefeller now dead, the Shah appealed to David Rockefeller for help in finding another refuge.

"We had to find a place very quickly," Rockefeller recalled. "I discussed it with Henry Kissinger and the idea of the Bahamas came up." The Bahamian Government agreed to provide a visa but insisted that the Shah go to the Resorts International complex on Paradise Island. David Rockefeller and some State Department officials believe that Lynden O. Pindling, the Bahamian Prime Minister, had a financial interest in Paradise Island operations and stood to benefit from the publicity that would inevitably accompany the Shah's arrival. However, Pindling insisted in an interview that he had no financial stake in the resort and that he had played no part in the decision.

The Shah and his family boarded a Royal Air Maroc 747 jetliner provided by King Hassan on March 30 and flew to the Bahamas. There they moved into the luxurious waterfront villa of James M. Crosby, chairman of the board of Resorts International, Inc. At the nearby Ocean Club, about 20 guests were forced out of their $250-per-day rooms to make way for the Shah's staff and security guards.

The State Department had adopted an official "hands-off" policy toward the Shah. But the Administration cared enough to want to keep tabs on him. Newsom frequently called Joseph V. Reed, David Rockefeller's executive assistant in New York, for progress reports. "They were very happy that we were making all the arrangements," David Rockefeller said with a trace of disgust in his voice, "but they wanted to know what was happening."

The Bahamas did not turn out to be a peaceful haven for the Shah. Security was difficult to establish in the midst of a popular resort. The royal family was hounded by newsmen, photographers, autograph hounds and hucksters of various persuasions. Moreover, the cost of the Shah's stay was astronomical, even for a man with a personal fortune conservatively estimated at $100 million. By the end of his 10 weeks in the Bahamas, his bill — including rooms and food for 26 guards flown in from the Wackenhut Corporation in Coral Gables — came to $1.7 million, an average of $24,000 a day.

Said David Rockefeller: "The Shah was taken for such a ride and so outrageously overcharged and treated in the Bahamas that he very quickly wanted to find an alternative place." Rockefeller explored the possibilities in Austria, while Kissinger approached contacts in Mexico.

Arriving in Vienna in April to attend a conference, Rockefeller sounded out Austrian Chancellor Bruno Kreisky. According to Rockefeller, Kreisky expressed some sympathy and said he would see what he could do. Independently, Arndt von Bohlen und Halbach, a principal heir to the Krupp iron and steel fortune and a flamboyant European playboy, wrote to the Shah offering him the use of Blühnbach, a family castle near Salzburg.

But it was not to be. Although Kreisky never formally said the Shah could not come to Austria, it became clear that the Shah's presence would have been difficult for the Chancellor politically, and the idea was dropped.

Meanwhile, Kissinger had been on the phone to an old friend in Mexico, a top aide to President José López Portillo. "He put it to the Presidente," Kissinger recalled, "and two or three weeks later I was informed that the Shah could come." The Mexican Foreign Ministry objected, however, on the ground that Mexico was being asked to take a risk that the United States itself was unprepared to take. "I had to make another phone call to get it back into the Presidente's hands," Kissinger said.

A six-month visa was granted, and just in time. On June 1, the Bahamian Government informed the Shah that he would have to leave when his visa expired 10 days hence. No official explanation was given, but the Shah later concluded that it was the result of American indifference to his plight and British hostility. Although he was a fatalistic man about such things, the Shah was growing bitter.

In Cuernavaca, the resort city 60 miles southwest of the Mexican capital, Robert Armao leased a vast, rose-colored, French-style villa with walled gardens sweeping down to a river. At $10,000 a month, the villa was a bargain compared with the Bahamian price. The estate was made ready within 48 hours, and on June 10, in a chartered aircraft, the royal family touched down on their fourth country of exile.

WHY CARTER ADMITTED THE SHAH

"For the first time since he left the Middle East," Armao said, "the Shah resumed something close to a normal life. He could play tennis, go into Mexico City for lunch or dinner." His visitors included Rockefeller and Kissinger on one occasion, former President Nixon on another. The Carter Administration, however, continued to shun him.

Meanwhile, in Washington, an intense struggle was under way within the Administration to rescind the decision to keep the Shah out. The sharpest conflict was between Vance and Zbigniew Brzezinski, the national security adviser. "It was my view from the beginning," Brzezinski said in an interview after the hostages were released, "that we should make it unambiguously clear that the Shah was welcome whenever he wanted to come. Our mistake was to ever let it become an issue in the first place."

On April 6, three days before David Rockefeller had an appointment to see the President, Kissinger called Brzezinski to renew his appeal for asylum for the Shah. "Brzezinski said he was in favor of this," Kissinger recalled, "but that I should talk to the President. So I called the President on April 7 and told him that I was behind whatever Rockefeller would raise with him [about the Shah]. I said I felt very strongly about this. He told me that he was not opposed to it, but that Cy Vance was violently opposed to it, and that I should take it up with Vance. He left me with the impression that this was a matter in which he could not overrule his Secretary of State." (Carter insists that, as of April, he was still personally dead-set against admitting the Shah.)

What made Kissinger's intervention particularly sensitive was the fact that it came just as the Administration was completing the second Strategic Arms Limitation Treaty talks with the Soviet Union and preparing for what it expected to be the biggest political battle of Carter's term. The President knew that Kissinger's position on SALT would influence the outcome of the ratification debate in the Senate. Both men say they never linked the two subjects in their discussions about the Shah, but explicit linkage was hardly necessary. "SALT," Hamilton Jordan, White House chief of staff, observed later, "was the background for all our discussions in those days."

David Rockefeller recalled that when he made that April 9 visit to the Oval Office, "I had some other matters I wanted to discuss with the

President, and as we stood up, at the end of the conversation, I told him of my concern that a friend of the United States should be treated in such a way and said I felt he should be admitted and we should take whatever steps were necessary to deal with the threats [to the Teheran embassy]. I didn't tell him how to deal with it, but I said it seemed to me that a great power such as ours should not submit to blackmail."

The President's reaction, Rockefeller recalled, was "stiff and formal." He added, "I got the impression the President didn't want to hear about it."

Carter's rebuff of Rockefeller's personal appeal led Henry Kissinger, as he later put it, "to go public." That same night, he tacked onto an unrelated speech he was giving at a Harvard Business School dinner in New York a phrase that would later haunt the Carter Administration. After all the years of alliance, Kissinger declared, it was morally wrong for the United States to treat the Shah "like a Flying Dutchman looking for a port of call." The "Flying Dutchman" reference turned up in newspaper editorials for months thereafter.

The main thrust of the campaign, however, continued to center on personal appeals to key decision makers. Kissinger confronted Vance over a private lunch in April, but to no avail. Rockefeller also spoke with Vance. Then in June, Brzezinski told Kissinger that Vice President Mondale, who had previously sided with Vance, was tilting in the other direction. Kissinger called Mondale to press the point, and gradually the Vice President came around and began urging the President to admit the Shah.

One participant in the Rockefeller-Kissinger behind-the-scenes campaign who was second to neither in his persistence and his passionate advocacy of the Shah's cause was John J. McCloy, the 86-year-old lawyer whose roster of important posts ranged from president of the World Bank to High Commissioner to Germany after World War II. McCloy had known the Shah for years and his New York law firm, Milbank, Tweed, Hadley & McCloy, represents the Pahlevi family in many legal matters. The firm also represents the Chase Manhattan Bank. McCloy, in fact, was a card-carrying member of the extraordinary "old-boy network" that was involved on both sides of the debate over the Shah. Thus, McCloy was a former chairman of the Chase Manhattan

Bank; Vance was a former chairman of the board of trustees of the Rockefeller Foundation; Kissinger once was director of special projects for the Rockefeller Brothers Fund and later became chairman of Chase's international advisory committee. Vance, Brzezinski and Rockefeller — not to mention Jimmy Carter and Walter Mondale — have been leading members of the Trilateral Commission, an international group formed to foster cooperation among the United States, Europe and Japan.

Using these connections, McCloy peppered top officials in the State Department and White House with letters. Cyrus Vance, in an interview in his 33d-floor law office overlooking New York Harbor, later observed with a wry smile, "John is a very prolific letter writer. The morning mail often contained something from him about the Shah."

Exactly how much the efforts of the old-boy network ultimately influenced the President's decision to admit the Shah is hard to gauge. "Not much," Carter replied somewhat defensively when asked months later. But he did admit that he resented the Rockefeller-Kissinger campaign when it was under way. "I don't have any criticism of them now, but at the time I did express my displeasure," he said.

Carter recalled a breakfast with his foreign-policy advisers in the late summer of 1979 when Mondale and Brzezinski were pressing him to change his mind. "I don't curse much," the former President said, "but this time I blew up. I said: 'Blank the Shah! I'm not going to welcome him here when he has other places to go where he'll be safe.' " (Recounting the story, Carter used the word "blank" rather than the four-letter word itself.)

But the effort to change the Administration's policy on the Shah was clearly having its political effects. As the summer passed, a number of influential Congressmen joined in. Senators Charles Percy, the Illinois Republican, and Claiborne Pell, the Rhode Island Democrat, began publicly urging the Shah's admittance and reinforcing their speeches with private entreaties to the White House and State Department. And all of this was catching Carter at a political low. His standing in the public-opinion polls had sunk to historic depths for a sitting President, and Edward M. Kennedy was preparing to challenge him for the Democratic nomination. The odds makers had Kennedy a 2-to-1 favorite.

As a political issue, the Shah cut both ways. If Carter allowed him in, it would enrage the liberal community that viewed the Shah as a murderous despot. Anti-Shah demonstrations were already endemic around the country. If Carter refused him admission, there would have been a furor on the right, where the Shah was seen as a long-standing ally.

The debates were already under way over who had "lost" Iran and why United States intelligence had failed to forecast Khomeini's revolution. Conservatives and that band of converted liberals known as neoconservatives felt strongly that abandoning the Shah in his hour of need would be read by other allies as another sign that America was untrustworthy. And if the Shah had died in Mexico City after being refused medical treatment in New York, there would have been an uproar. Kissinger later made it clear that he, for one, would have attacked Carter publicly for failing to help an old ally. Certainly Ronald Reagan — whom Carter had by this time, he says, identified as the likely Republican nominee — would have pounced. Carter conceded that the possibility of such a reaction was on his mind. "I can't deny that that may have been a factor," he said. "It probably was."

Carter's decision involved important foreign-policy considerations as well. Establishing relations with the new Iranian Government was a priority, as was the resumption of the interrupted oil flow to the West. There was also concern that the Khomeini Government might collapse and be followed by a regional splintering of the nation, a situation ready-made for exploitation by the Soviet Union.

Yet another factor in the decision was the President's understanding — or, rather, misunderstanding — of the political realities in revolutionary Iran. Carter and his aides put their faith in the promises of the secular leadership there, rather than recognizing that the religious leadership held the real power. They chose, for example, to believe that Mehdi Bazargan's Government would be willing and able to make good on its repeated promises to protect the United States Embassy — this in spite of repeated warnings from American diplomats that the admission of the Shah would make those promises unreliable.

One option that, curiously, was never seriously examined was the evacuation of embassy personnel prior to admitting the Shah. "We felt it was important to have representation on the ground in Iran," Hamilton

Jordan explained later. "We knew it was a risk, but we thought it was a reasonable risk. Obviously, in hindsight, we were wrong."

The first hint of the medical crisis that would tip the scales in favor of admitting the Shah was received by the Administration on August 10. It came in the form of an extraordinary personal letter to Carter from Princess Ashraf, the Shah's twin. Months later, in an interview in her Park Avenue triplex, the petite, fragile-looking, 61-year-old Princess said the letter had been written without the Shah's knowledge. "He was a very proud man," she said. "He would have been furious if he knew."

The letter began: "I am taking what may appear to be a great liberty in writing directly to you in regard to the increased difficulty and traumatic situation in which my brother, his wife and their son find themselves in their search for a relatively stable place where they could find some continuity in their family life." It went on to note "the quite noticeable impairment of his health in Mexico" and to urge that he be admitted for asylum immediately.

Eight days later, on August 18, the Princess received a reply from Warren Christopher, Deputy Secretary of State, "on behalf of the President, who is on vacation." The reply was polite but cool. Christopher stressed the Administration's efforts to "improve its relations with the new government" in Iran.

The Shah was sicker than his family knew. According to Princess Ashraf, only the doctors who treated the ruler and the Minister of Court, a confidential aide, were aware that the Shah had been suffering for six years from lymphoma — cancer of the lymph glands. He had been receiving chemotherapy from two French doctors who made periodic visits to Iran and later to Mexico. The Princess suspected that French intelligence had learned of the Shah's illness but that American intelligence had not. Jimmy Carter later confirmed this intelligence failure, which was a significant lapse. Among other things, earlier knowledge of the lymphoma would have made it clear that the Shah's days were numbered and that the United States needed to reconsider its policies and plan for an eventual successor. Such considerations might have led to an earlier and deeper study of the Iranian political situation.

In late September, Joseph Reed, David Rockefeller's assistant, asked Dr. Benjamin H. Kean, a tropical-disease specialist, to examine the Shah in Cuernavaca. Dr. Kean learned from Armao about the Shah's history of cancer. Arriving in Mexico, Dr. Kean also found that the Shah was suffering from advanced jaundice and fever. Unsure what else might be wrong, Dr. Kean recommended that the Shah undergo extensive tests to complete the diagnosis and proposed that it be done at New York Hospital-Cornell Medical Center or one of several other hospitals in the United States.

On October 18, Reed called Newsom with the startling news that the Shah had cancer in addition to his other problems. Within hours, the Shah's condition was discussed at a meeting of Carter and his senior foreign-policy advisers at the White House. In Brzezinski's notes of the meeting, there is the following quote from Carter: "We ought to make it clear that the Shah is welcome as long as the medical treatment is needed." Vance was directed to double-check the medical information and sound out the reaction of the Iranian Government to the Shah's being admitted, but the basic decision had been made.

Dr. Eben Dustin, the State Department medical officer at the time, consulted with Dr. Kean on the telephone and later held a casual discussion with the medical adviser to the United States Embassy in Mexico City. The State Department refused to release the memorandum containing Dr. Dustin's conclusions, and Dr. Dustin declined to be interviewed. But Carter's recollection of what he was told was that the medical equipment and treatment the Shah required were available only in New York and that the Shah was "at the point of death."

However, Dr. Kean contended in an interview later that that was not what he had told Dr. Dustin. His opinion at the time, Dr. Kean said, was that it would be preferable to have the Shah treated at New York Hospital or elsewhere in the United States, but that if necessary, it could be done in Mexico or virtually anywhere. Dr. Kean also said he told Dr. Dustin that the Shah had to be treated within "a few weeks," not necessarily within a few days. Thus, on two counts, Carter was apparently misinformed about what Dr. Kean had actually proposed.

In other circumstances, when a world leader has required such aid, medical specialists and elaborate equipment have been flown to him. But, because of the presumed urgency of the Shah's case, this option was never considered. For the same reason, according to Dr. Kean, Dr.

Dustin declined Dr. Kean's proposal that he go to Mexico to examine the Shah himself. No second opinion was sought.

The President's second order was that the prospect of the Shah's admittance to the United States be taken up with the Iranian Government. On October 21, L. Bruce Laingen, the embassy's chargé d'affaires, and Henry Precht, the man in charge of the State Department's task force on Iran, who was visiting Teheran, called on Prime Minister Mehdi Bazargan. Foreign Minister Ibrahim Yazdi was also present. The Iranians were informed that the Shah would probably be admitted to New York Hospital the next day.

The ministers were unhappy. Yazdi, Precht recalled later, did not believe that the Shah's ailments were so serious. The Iranians suggested that an Iranian doctor be sent to New York to verify the Shah's condition, but that was never pursued. Bazargan and Yazdi promised to provide protection for the United States Embassy, but, as Precht remembered the conversation, Yazdi issued a somber warning: "You're opening a Pandora's box with this."

On that same day, on the other side of the world, Jimmy Carter was relishing a political triumph. The day before, he had flown to Boston to speak at the dedication of the John F. Kennedy Library, and there, in the midst of Kennedy country, he had given one of the best speeches of his Presidency.

But now, relaxing on the couch in his lodge at Camp David, he opened the evening packet of documents from the White House. Included was the page-and-a-half memorandum from Secretary of State Vance, setting forth the gist of the medical and diplomatic discussions about the Shah and outlining the pros and cons. It contained a recommendation that, under the circumstances, the Shah should be admitted to the United States. Vance had come around. Carter made his decision, and the word was flashed to Cuernavaca.

The next night, shortly after 10 o'clock, a sleek Gulfstream II jet taxied to a remote corner of New York's La Guardia Airport. A five-car motorcade bore the Shah and his Empress into Manhattan. Hurried through a basement entrance, the Shah was whisked to the 17th floor of New York Hospital. The surroundings were familiar: the same two rooms he had occupied for a medical checkup during an official visit to

Harry S Truman in 1949 — the "good old days" of the Iranian-United States relationship.

Twenty-four hours later, the Shah underwent surgery for removal of his gall bladder and gall stones. Two days after that, he celebrated his 60th birthday recuperating in his hospital bed. He was still there nine days later, on November 4, when the student militants poured into the United States Embassy compound in Teheran and seized the hostages. The Americans, they said, would not be released until the Shah was returned to Iran to stand trial. Mohammed Riza Pahlevi's odyssey was not over — he would travel on to Texas and to Panama before he came full circle, returning to Egypt and his death in a Cairo hospital on July 27, 1980. But for the Americans at the embassy in Teheran, and for America, the ordeal had just begun.

2

The Shah's Health: A Political Gamble

By Lawrence K. Altman, M.D.

As princes have done since the beginning of kingdoms, the Shah of Iran, from the moment he learned he was seriously ill, chose to treat his illness as much as a matter of state as a medical problem. And from that point of decision by the Shah — a decision to gamble with his health for political ends — flowed a chain of events that dramatically reshaped recent American history and led, all too inevitably, to the 444 days of the hostage crisis.

The Shah indirectly detected his own cancer when, during a skiing trip in 1974, he felt a lump in the left upper portion of his abdomen. It turned out to be an enlarged spleen and led the French doctors Dr. Jean Bernard and Dr. Georges Flandrin to diagnose a form of cancer of the lymph system that resembled chronic lymphocytic leukemia and was called Waldenstrom's macroglobulinemia.

During the last five years of his reign, the Shah took an anticancer drug prescribed by the two French doctors who commuted frequently to Teheran to supervise his medical care. Yet, throughout his reign and well into his exile, the Shah kept his cancer secret even from his twin sister, Princess Ashraf, who said that she did not know of her brother's cancer until he had arrived in New York. And despite a vast United States intelligence network in Iran, American Government officials did not learn of the Shah's cancer until just a few days before he left Mexico to come to New York Hospital-Cornell Medical Center for emergency care on October 22, 1979.

In 1978, when the Shah's 87-year-old mother fell ill, he summoned three American cancer experts to diagnose her disease. She was found to have the same type of cancer that he had. The American doctors asked if other members of the family had cancer — a standard question in a medical history — and were told no; the Shah misled them by withholding the fact that he had cancer. In addition, his mother was not treated by his own French doctors, one of them later explained, because it would have jeopardized the secrecy of the Shah's condition.

It is unlikely that any of the physicians who treated the Shah knows his entire story.

His cancer was kept in check with chlorambucil from 1974 in Iran through his two months in Egypt, where he arrived on January 16, 1979, and during his two-week stay in Morocco. But shortly after he landed in the Bahamas on March 30, his odyssey took on a new dimension. He developed swollen lymph nodes on the left side of his neck, and Dr. Flandrin diagnosed a new — and usually fatal — form of cancer called Richter's syndrome.

Clearly the Shah had reached a critical stage in his medical care — his cancer was no longer responding to the chlorambucil, and he needed much stronger drugs and possibly radiation. At that point, most American doctors would have advised such a patient to enter a hospital for a variety of tests, and, depending on the circumstances, some would have recommended a splenectomy to determine the extent of the cancer and a new course of therapy. But the Shah was not admitted to a hospital.

Dr. Flandrin prescribed a combination of four anticancer drugs called MOPP, and the Shah's swollen lymph nodes and spleen shrank. The drugs also decreased the production of the blood-forming cells in his bone marrow to dangerously low levels, however, so the therapy was halted earlier than expected, after about five courses of treatment. By that time, the Shah was living in Mexico.

There, his skin began to turn deep yellow from jaundice; he had chills and fever, and from early August to late September, he lost about 20 pounds. Mexican doctors diagnosed malaria. Robert Armao, a protégé of Nelson Rockefeller, and Joseph V. Reed, an aide to David

THE SHAH'S HEALTH: A POLITICAL GAMBLE

Rockefeller, had both been sent to assist the Shah. Both were patients of Dr. Benjamin H. Kean, an internist at New York Hospital who specialized in malaria and tropical medicine. When the Shah's condition did not improve, they summoned him to Mexico to consult on the Shah's case.

Dr. Kean went to Cuernavaca on September 29, he said, and quickly determined that the Shah did not have malaria. But, without further laboratory tests usually performed in a hospital, he could not find the reason for the Shah's jaundice. Dr. Kean said that he knew the Shah had been treated for some time by French doctors, but he did not know for what. The jaundice led him to suspect cancer, but he could find no clues from a physical examination because, unknown to Dr. Kean at the time, the recent course of chemotherapy had shrunk any telltale lymph nodes. Despite his suspicions, however, Dr. Kean did not ask the Shah if he had ever been treated for cancer. And the information was not volunteered.

"I was not his physician," the American doctor said in explaining the omission of such crucial information. "I was a consultant, a specialist who knew a lot about malaria and jaundice. His physicians were his French physicians. With them he had no reserve."

The next day, Dr. Kean returned to New York. "I was perturbed about not knowing what was going on," Dr. Kean said. Then, he got a call from Armao. "He's worse," the Shah's aide told him. "And I learned he has cancer and has had it for a long time. Dr. Flandrin is here and will await your arrival to give you the history." Armao had already decided that the Shah should remain under Dr. Kean's care because he hoped to have the Shah admitted to New York Hospital and saw the American physician as his entrée.

When Dr. Kean returned to Cuernavaca on October 18, he said, "Dr. Flandrin handed me a thick document which outlined a several-year history of lymphoma."

Dr. Flandrin said he did not advise the Shah to go to New York Hospital but declined to disclose his recommendation. "I decided to leave, and after that Dr. Kean was in charge," Dr. Flandrin said.

"We were running out of time," recalled Dr. Kean, who told the Shah that his jaundice had to be relieved. "And no one doctor could take care of him."

The Shah asked where he could go for treatment, and Dr. Kean listed eight countries, including France, which had medical centers with adequate facilities. After each one the Shah shook his head. "It was clear he wasn't welcome," said Dr. Kean.

"We discussed Mexico at length," Dr. Kean said, adding that it was not chosen because of a variety of problems such as security, language differences and the belief that there was no team of experts "concentrated in one center as there was at New York Hospital." Dr. Kean said he knew that the sophisticated equipment needed for the Shah's diagnosis and treatment could be found in Mexico. Despite this fact, Armao contended shortly after the Shah arrived in New York that his employer had left Mexico because such equipment was not available there and that the Shah's doctors claimed that the particular radiation treatment he was undergoing was not available anywhere else in the world.

"That's nonsense," Dr. Kean said. But New York Hospital officials at the time did not refute the contention, upsetting many physicians elsewhere whose cancer patients were concerned that they were not receiving the best possible care.

When Dr. Kean returned to New York on October 19, he spoke with Dr. Eben H. Dustin, then the State Department's medical director, and outlined the Shah's medical problems. He informed him of the Shah's cancer and explained that his obstructive jaundice was being caused by either gallstones or cancer of the head of the pancreas. "After several weeks of this type of jaundice," Dr. Kean told Dr. Dustin, "action to relieve the obstruction must be prompt."

Dr. Dustin, who later was transferred to the United States Embassy in Vienna, declined to discuss his role in the Shah's case.

Dr. Jorge Cervantes, the senior medical adviser to the American Embassy in Mexico City, where he is also a surgeon at the American British Cowdray (A.B.C.) Hospital, said that he was attending a medical meeting in Washington around the time that Dr. Dustin learned of the Shah's condition. "Dr. Dustin asked me if the facilities existed in A.B.C. Hospital for the diagnosis and treatment of a patient with jaundice, and I said, 'Of course; we do it everyday,' " Dr. Cervantes recalled. "He then asked if we had a total-body CAT scanner. I said no — that they existed elsewhere in Mexico City — but that we could achieve the same results with other equipment, such as ultrasound." (A CAT scanner is a computer X-ray that shows cross-sections of the body; ultrasound is a diagnostic technique that relies on ultra-high-frequency sound waves that are bounced off the body's organs.)

U.S. Government officials conceded that the Shah could have been treated in Mexico, and that he was admitted to New York Hospital despite the fact that an extensive, independent examination was never conducted by the United States into his medical condition or the medical facilities available to him there. But many doctors contended even then that the necessary medical care was available in any of the world's developed countries.

Initially, according to Armao, the Shah did not want to come to the United States for medical care. "He yelled at me and Empress Farah," Armao said, "angry at the suggestion. He said, 'I'm not wanted there, and I'm not welcome. Forget it.' " But he eventually relented.

At New York Hospital, the Shah registered under the name of David D. Newsom, who was then Undersecretary of State for Political Affairs. David Newsom later said he never gave permission for the Shah to use his name and, in fact, did not even know it was being used until he read it in the newspaper, at which time the Shah's code name was changed.

Tests performed on the Shah during his first 24 hours at New York Hospital indicated that his jaundice was, in fact, the result of a blockage of his bile duct by gallstones, which itself can be a life-threatening condition. During a gall-bladder operation, the doctors also planned to remove several lymph nodes to determine more precisely the type of cancer as well as the extent of its spread. But, in addition, they wanted to answer some other troublesome questions, such as: What had caused the Shah's spleen to enlarge to about three times its normal size? And should they also remove the spleen for diagnostic and therapeutic purposes?

The day before the Shah's gall-bladder operation, his doctors agreed not to remove the spleen because of the added risks that the extra procedure would create in the face of infection from his gallstones. According to Dr. Hibbard E. Williams, then head of medicine at New York Hospital and now dean of the medical school at the University of California at Davis, the team reasoned that the spleen could be removed at a later date, if necessary.

Dr. Williams said he thought the Shah was so sick that he might have died during or after surgery. In addition, regarding the

Shah's cancer, he said: "My estimate, which I never told anyone else, was that he had only a year to live. He died 10 months later."

At the only news conference held by doctors at New York Hospital, Dr. Morton Coleman, the Shah's cancer specialist, emphasized his belief in "the potential for cure" in the Shah's case, citing a 50-50 chance for long-term survival. From a medical standpoint, he said, the Shah should stay in New York for intensive chemotherapy for at least six months and perhaps a year and a half. "Good medical practice," said Dr. Coleman, "dictates that you stay with your doctors."

Those comments had a strong impact on the revolutionaries in Iran. The medical reports were unsettling, according to Henry Precht, the senior Iranian task-force officer at the State Department, who was then in Iran, although, he said, the initial reaction of Ayatollah Ruhollah Khomeini and the Iranians was "exceptionally controlled."

"But one had the feeling that the Iranians, always suspicious, now sensed that they had indeed been duped," said Precht, "and that the Shah had come to the United States not for medical treatment but to set up counterrevolutionary headquarters."

The Iranians wanted their own doctors to examine him, but the Shah would not permit it. According to Newsom, the State Department then asked Dr. Kean and Dr. Williams to discuss the case with physicians selected by Iranian officials. But even that arrangement never worked out.

Meanwhile, Eamon Brennan, then vice president for public affairs of New York Hospital-Cornell Medical Center, urged his superiors to persuade the Shah and the State Department to allow thorough medical briefings to inform the public because of the international crisis. Mr. Brennan believed the public had a right to know the entire medical story to justify the Shah's admission to the United States, not just a few baffling facts. Mr. Brennan later resigned over the issue.

About a week after the gall-bladder operation, X-rays showed that a single gallstone had been left behind and was blocking the Shah's bile duct. Because of the limitations of medicine, even the best surgeons are unable to locate one or more remaining gallstones in a small percentage of such cases. "Finding the retained stone was a complete surprise," said Dr. Williams. "We thought we had it clean."

To deal with the complication, New York Hospital called on Dr. H. Joachim Burhenne of the University of British Columbia in Vancouver to come to New York and perform a stone-crushing technique he had developed, which saved such patients the increased risk of death from a second operation. The technique has been used in many hospitals since its development in 1972, but New York Hospital was not one of them. Dr. Burhenne performed the procedure on November 26.

After discovering the retained gallstone and considering three painful, cancerous lymph nodes in the left side of the Shah's neck, his doctors decided to postpone a multidrug chemotherapy program they had planned and to use radiation instead. Ten times, under tight security at hours ranging from 10 P.M. to 4 A.M., the Shah was wheeled quietly through the tunnel that connects New York Hospital and Memorial Sloan-Kettering Cancer Center. No one knew the time in advance. Each night, security agents determined a different route for the chief radiation therapist, Dr. Florence Chu, to follow from her home in New Jersey. As a result of the radiation treatments, the Shah's nodes shrank and his pain was relieved.

While the Shah was at New York Hospital, his family wondered if interferon, the natural substance that researchers are studying as a possible cancer treatment, might be the answer. They asked that Dr. Jordan U. Gutterman, an interferon expert at the M.D. Anderson Hospital and Tumor Institute in Houston, consult on the case. He did when, after 41 days at New York Hospital, the Shah was moved to Lackland Air Force Base. After examining the Shah at Lackland, Dr. Gutterman said, he determined that interferon was not the appropriate treatment.

At Lackland, the Shah's spleen again began to grow, causing his blood counts to drop. His New York and Air Force physicians met with his lawyers and Carter Administration officials to discuss further treatment. All of the doctors recommended that after a splenectomy, which carried with it perhaps a 15 percent risk of death, the Shah be treated with a combination of drugs. Then, Dr. Kean said, he went to see the Shah alone.

"Where can we do this?" the Shah asked. Dr. Kean answered, "Anyplace."

"Where's the best place to do it?" the Shah asked. Dr. Kean recommended the United States.

"No, I want to get out of the United States," the Shah said, adding, "They gave me chlorambucil when I had a big spleen five years ago."

"The drug isn't going to do much good now," Dr. Kean replied. "You need your spleen out and we can't give you intensive chemotherapy now because your blood counts are too low."

"Can they operate on me in Panama?" Dr. Kean said yes.

"Get me out. They think that my departure will help the hostages. They're wrong. But I will not stay in a place where I am not totally welcome."

But when the Shah left Texas for Panama a few hours later, no one foresaw the bitter feuds, only some of which became publicly known, that would develop among the Shah's doctors.

In a medical journal published in Panama, the Shah's Panamanian doctors wrote that the Shah said he wanted no surgeons from New York Hospital.

Dr. Kean denied that account: "The Shah left to me the choice of his surgeon." After he and the Panamanian medical team called on three American surgeons, all of whom declined, Dr. Kean asked Dr. Michael E. DeBakey, the Houston heart surgeon, who had wide experience as a general surgeon and had occasionally performed operations in foreign countries. Dr. DeBakey agreed to do the spleen operation in Panama.

Despite their own efforts to find an American surgeon, Panamanian doctors were upset by news reports in the United States that one of their own would not be doing the operation. They perceived it as a "campaign to discredit Panamanian medicine." When Dr. Kean and Dr. DeBakey arrived in Panama and went to the Paitilla Hospital to visit the Shah, they were turned back by security guards and were not permitted to examine him for several hours.

"My first reaction was to withdraw from the situation," said Dr. DeBakey, "because I thought that might relieve it. But I made it clear that I would not be an adviser. The only way I could participate was to have control of the operation. There could not be two surgeons."

The operation was postponed for about a week both for political reasons and because the Shah was recuperating from a respiratory infection. Dr. Jean P. Hester, a cancer specialist from M.D. Anderson Hospital in Houston, who was in Panama participating in the Shah's care, recalled that he asked her: "Isn't it dangerous for me to delay the surgery because of my low blood count?"

"I had no clear-cut answer," said Dr. Hester, who had not participated in the decision. "But I indicated that there would never be an optimal time and that there would probably be no substantial risk in waiting."

The Shah grew increasingly fearful, according to the medical-journal article, about being assassinated on the operating table. In addition, Iran had filed an extradition request which caused him further concern. On March 23, the Shah flew to Egypt, and five days later, Dr. DeBakey removed his spleen, which by then had grown to 10 times its normal size. From the operation, it was discovered that both his spleen and his liver were invaded by cancer. It was April before the Shah began to receive the multidrug chemotherapy treatment that had been outlined for him at New York Hospital five months earlier.

From the moment he left Iran on January 16, 1979, throughout his odyssey that ended with his death from a massive hemorrhage 18 months later, the Shah's political status remained more precious to him than his life. Despite his enormous wealth and power — perhaps because of those very factors — he was able to exercise extraordinary control over his own treatment, yet he received less coherent treatment than he might have gotten had he been an ordinary patient. Some experts conclude that his death came at a predictable point in the course of his disease — six to eight years after its diagnosis. Others suggest that with different treatment he might have lived for years, and some of the physicians who were intimately involved in the case debate several critical points in the Shah's medical care. In any case, it is probable that if the U.S. Government had known of his cancer from the beginning, history would have taken a very different turn.

3

How a Sit-in Turned Into a Siege

By John Kifner

The mountain village of Shemran sits in the foothills of the Alborz Mountains just above the smoggy sprawl of Teheran. Restaurants serving chello kebab, the Iranian national dish of pounded, grilled lamb and rice, cling to the sides of a gorge where a stream runs past a statue of a mountaineer, draped in ropes, pitons and climbing gear. From the village, narrow hiking trails, interspersed with terraced tea houses, run along the stream beds and up the brown, snow-capped mountains. On Fridays, the weekly holiday in Moslem lands, thousands of people, young and old, stroll the paths, seeking a brief refuge from life in the city. Before the revolution, the mountain paths served, too, as meeting places for the clandestine resistance to the Shah, where young people could gather unnoticed and make their plans in low voices.

On Friday, October 26, 1979, four days after the Shah had been admitted to New York Hospital-Cornell Medical Center, young revolutionaries again met along the mountain trails, this time openly. There were perhaps 80 people, members of the once-underground Islamic societies at several Teheran colleges, most of them from Polytechnic University. They were upset at several tendencies in the revolution and, particularly, at the Shah's being allowed to enter the United States. Nine days later, they would lead the takeover of the United States Embassy.

NO HIDING PLACE

"All the people said, there in the mountains, we must do something, we must make an action," one of the members of what would become known as the Students Following the Imam's Line recalled in a rare interview. "It was a matter of the prestige of our country; our honor was stained. We decided to make an action so that the cries of our oppressed people could reach all the world's ears, and through the problem of the Shah we wanted to show what America had done to the whole world with its international trickeries."

The decision was reached after prayers: A sit-in would be staged at the American Embassy. It was planned to last, at most, three to five days.

Set in motion by that meeting were events that would culminate in international upheaval. The students' decision would lead, far beyond its original intention, to the seizure of the American Embassy, the holding of American diplomats and other personnel hostage for 444 days and the intensification of political turmoil within Iran itself, and it would contribute in no small measure to the eventual downfall of a President of the United States.

The students were greeted with overwhelming and unexpected acceptance and enthusiasm for their sit-in by the Iranian people, though they regarded the Iranian Government as their opponent from the start. Their initial planning was careful and detailed, but events carried them forward in a way they could not fully control. The compelling forces of the country's past and present — the cataclysmic division between traditional clergy and more moderate, pro-West, but anti-Shah governing factions; the fierce and abiding hatred of the Shah — began directing the students as much as the students were directing these forces. And they could not turn back. It is not that no one was in control, not that there were no leaders. There were, in fact, key individuals with real influence, but it is apparent that the United States Government never really recognized who they were or how much influence they had.

Instead, it seems eminently fair to say, the United States was nearly always negotiating at the key points of the crisis with the wrong people. What results would have been achieved had it tried dealing with the Iranian clergy or even with student leaders themselves cannot be known, of course. The fact is that it did not, and so had no chance of succeeding.

176

HOW A SIT-IN TURNED INTO A SIEGE

What has come into sharper focus is a broad Iranian canvas whose detail, perspective and meaning American officials never sufficiently perceived or understood at the time of the crisis.

Once back from the mountains, the students immediately began formulating detailed tactics and individual assignments for the sit-in at the United States Embassy in Teheran. A central committee was put in overall charge, with subcommittees appointed for individual areas of responsibility. Though members of the Carter Administration would contend that the student group had been infiltrated by Marxist terrorists, the best evidence suggests that the students were what they said they were: young Islamic zealots. The student leaders met with Hojatolislam Ashgar Moussavi Khoeini. Khoeini, a militant young clergyman, became their adviser and, through them, he came to be an important figure in the months ahead, though he was virtually unrecognized by most United States Government officials. According to several sources, the students also notified Hojatolislam Ahmed Khomeini, the son and chief aide of the Ayatollah Ruhollah Khomeini, of their sit-in plans.

The previous week, the provisional government of Prime Minister Mehdi Bazargan had turned marching demonstrators away from the streets outside the American Embassy — to the relief of the Americans and creating, as it developed, false confidence. Now, more students were recruited at meetings of the Islamic societies at several universities in the city — Polytechnic, Teheran University, National University and the Industrial College. Most of them were told only a small part of the plan, only the roles that they themselves would play.

Maps of the 27-acre embassy compound and plans of the buildings were obtained. Armbands were made up, along with special protest signs, which would identify the members of the takeover group. A few days before the attack, several meetings were held in Teheran mosques and special identity cards were distributed. The women were to wear portraits of Ayatollah Khomeini pinned to the front of their all-encompassing black shawls, or chadors.

Burning in their minds was a speech that Ayatollah Khomeini, referred to as the Imam, or religious leader, had recently delivered from his headquarters in the holy city of Qum. "What do we need a relationship with America for?" he had asked. "Those who support the great powers like . . . the United States, which has given refuge to that corrupt germ, will be confronted in a different manner."

A little before 10:30 on the drizzly Sunday of November 4, some 450 students broke away from one of Teheran's frequent revolutionary demonstrations; this one was to commemorate Ayatollah Khomeini's exile 15 years before and to honor those who had died — the score of "martyrs," as they are always called — during the previous year's revolutionary protests at Teheran University. Now the students stormed down Takht-E-Jamshid Avenue and, with bolt-cutting shears, snipped through the chains holding the big iron gates in front of the American Embassy and swarmed into the manicured compound. Marine security guards, firing tear gas, in accordance with standing instructions, held them back for a time as the diplomats frantically tried to shred documents. But by midafternoon, the students had seized the buildings and rounded up the Americans along with 100 Iranians, most of them seeking visas to the United States. Several of the hostages remember being told not to worry, that it was merely a sit-in; others recall the students excitedly making calls from the embassy and recounting their adventures to their friends. A banner was strung up across the gates: "Khomeini struggles, Carter trembles." The occupation of the American Embassy in Iran had begun.

The students then began waiting. They wanted to see what their own government's reaction would be. "We were waiting to see if it would expel us or make problems," one participant recalled, "and immediately we gave speeches and made communiqués and had a press conference to explain why we had done what we did, saying that the reason was to protest against America's letting in the Shah."

"But we saw there was nothing from the government," a student, who gave his name as Akhbar, said. "And at that moment, we saw people coming, crowds coming. They were calling by telephone, sending messages of support. We realized our action was something great! Yes, something really great! It was like a bomb burst, and we realized then that we had to keep going." And the students were more than willing to do so.

Tens, hundreds of thousands of people began gathering outside the embassy, burning effigies of President Carter and chanting: "Margh Bar Amerika" — "Death to America." Crowds were bused in or summoned to demonstrations, and within days the scene became virtually institutionalized, with vendors selling boiled sugar beets, revolutionary tape cassettes, shoes and wool hats. And the students became, in those hours just after the takeover, a force much more powerful than they had ever dared hope.

"We realized," another student confirmed, "that the Iranian people were expecting something more than a sit-in. The people were saying, 'Bring the Shah back.' So the students made the decision that, if the United States didn't give back the Shah, they would put the hostages on trial. At that moment we started to say, 'We don't want any negotiations; we want the Shah back.' "

Pieces of the new reality swiftly fell into place. Ahmed Khomeini, the Imam's son, visited the seized compound. He congratulated the students and told them that Iran must break off all ties with the United States. A student sit-in had escalated to an international crisis.

Two days after the takeover, Prime Minister Bazargan's provisional government, undermined by nine months of battling with the dominant Islamic clergymen of the secret Revolutionary Council, collapsed. In retrospect, it seemed his fall had been ordained a few weeks after he had taken office when the Ayatollah scolded him for following the old ways to the extent that tea was still being served in the gold-rimmed imperial glasses. "You are weak, old man," the Ayatollah said.

The Students Following the Imam's Line became, aside from the Ayatollah himself, the most important political factor in Iran. And, for the next year, all of the Carter Administration's efforts to gain the release of the hostages would be doomed to failure. Any attempt at negotiation and a series of increasingly implausible behind-the-scenes "scenarios" would founder on two factors: the implacable, moral absolutism of Ayatollah Khomeini, who would brook no compromise on his demand that the Shah be returned for trial, and Iran's internal power struggle between Islamic traditionalist clergymen — who made use of the hostage issue and the students themselves — and the more secular political leaders.

Who were these Students Following the Imam's Line? Various intelligence agencies along with some syndicated columnists and members of the United States Government charged that they were not really students at all, but rather Communists and terrorists trained or directed by the Palestine Liberation Organization. But close observation and countless conversations with the students and other Iranians lead one to the conclusion that such was not the case — that, if anything, the reverse was so. These young zealots, far from being directed or motivated by outside forces, appear to have been acting primarily in response to their own national and religious instincts and traditions.

Each noon, they knelt in neat rows in the parking lot just inside the embassy gates, touching their foreheads to the ground in the direction of Mecca in the ritual prayer required of Moslems five times each day. The men and women prayed separately, men with sparse new beards in the religious fashion and olive combat jackets, women in the approved revolutionary garb of a coarse, thick scarf in dark gray, brown, blue or black covering the hair and pulled tightly down on the forehead, a dark, loose smocklike garment reaching the knees, blue jeans and imitation Adidas running shoes. They were in many ways the purest stream of this curious movement that was at once revolutionary and reactionary, that was at once leading the course of a nation and being led by it.

The core of the militant group came from Polytechnic University, a center of resistance to the Shah during the revolution; others had studied at several of the smaller universities around the city. In Iran, where university education was for many a new phenomenon, this had certain important sociological and political implications. The students at Polytechnic were likely to be among the first of their families to go on to higher education, most of them drawn from traditional families in the rural villages. The wealthiest families had long sent their children abroad to be educated; there were tens of thousands of them in the United States — the largest foreign-student group. Teheran University also attracted somewhat more sophisticated or well-to-do students; it was a stronghold of the leftist groups, the Marxist Fedayeen and the Mujahedeen, who combined Islamic religion with socialist principles (the Persian *fedayeen* means those devoting their lives to a cause; *mujahedeen*, those willing to fight for religious purposes). But it was primarily among those coming from traditional, religious backgrounds, encountering modernization for the first time, that the painful cultural clash exploded into the politics of Islamic revival.

The clash could be easily seen right from the start of the revolution.

180

HOW A SIT-IN TURNED INTO A SIEGE

In a typical instance, a petroleum engineer, though he had recently completed training in America, said that one of the first things that must be reformed in his country was its university system: Young men, he said, were forced to sit next to women whose hair was uncovered. At Teheran University, an American-educated radical professor told of the difficulties the students had with reading F. Scott Fitzgerald; for many students, it was a long, frightening distance from the rules of the Koran to Jay Gatsby and Daisy Buchanan. In science, the gap was even wider. One instructor remembered a student standing up in the middle of a discussion of photosynthesis and shouting, "You must not interfere with God's work!" But the students' traditionalism did not necessarily interfere with their scholarship. Some of the students who received the best grades at Polytechnic, recalled one former professor, were among the leaders of the takeover.

At the meeting in the mountains, participants said, the young militants talked heatedly about what they regarded as the Westernizing tendencies of Mehdi Bazargan and his associates. One of their concerns was that the Bazargan Government was moving toward rebuilding the old relationship with the United States. Indeed, the week before the embassy seizure, Bazargan had met briefly with Zbigniew Brzezinski, the United States national security adviser, during a conference in Algiers and discussed the possibility of resuming military spare-parts shipments. An important goal of the seizure was to embarrass the increasingly ineffective Bazargan Government; the students accused the Prime Minister of "sitting down at the table with the wolf." Another reason for mounting a demonstration, some said, was the fear that the "leftists" would gain a monopoly on anti-Americanism. By leftists, they meant the two youthful guerrilla groups which had battled the Shah, the Marxist Fedayeen and the Mujahedeen.

At one point after the takeover, the students called in sympathizers from universities around the country and demanded that all the Iranian universities be closed to purge them of Western thought. Days of bloody battles between fundamentalist street mobs and leftists followed. President Bani-Sadr tried at first to keep the universities open, but he swiftly backed down, marching to Teheran University at the head of a crowd declaring a "cultural revolution" in which the universities would be

181

closed pending "Islamicization." The militants were a reverse image of American campus radicals of the 1960's; they were rebelling not against traditionalist society, but in favor of a return to it. "It is not Western power we must fear," Ayatollah Khomeini said later, congratulating them, "it is Western ideas." The universities were still shut. Scores of the students volunteered for service in the war with Iraq, and a number were killed; others were sprinkled through government ministries or worked with the construction group attempting to repair war damage.

The Carter Administration seemed to miss the significance of the student-clergy movement, and it tended to view the militants in standard "red menace" terms. The White House press secretary, Jody Powell, told reporters fully two months after the takeover, that the militants were following "a rather radical and certainly a Marxist line," a remark greeted with some astonishment and amusement in Iran. "It's rather optimistic to say that," said a senior European diplomat fluent in Persian.

At the United States Embassy, where the phones were answered, "Nest of spies," a reporter was told none of the leaders were available to comment on Powell's analysis.

"They are all at prayers," it was explained.

"Whoever took religion seriously?" said one State Department official after the revolution. He was expressing surprise that a bearded old holy man could come out of nowhere to topple what had been seen as the strongest, most stable nation in the Middle East. The remark also revealed a certain lack of understanding of Iranian history.

Perhaps the single strongest political tradition in Iran for more than a century has been the religious opposition to foreign domination and economic exploitation — first by Russia and Britain, then by the United States. Islam recognizes no distinction between church and state. Shiite Islam, the minority branch followed by some 90 percent of Iranians, tracing its line of authority from the Prophet Mohammed through his son-in-law, Ali, is particularly political; it will recognize no true authority on earth until the Twelfth Imam, who was concealed in a cave as a child in the ninth century, returns as savior. Governments serve only in the stead of the Hidden Imam. In Iran, this attitude has expressed itself in successive dynasties as an almost adversary relationship between religion and authority; it is the obligation of the ulema, or Islamic scholars, to criticize and correct the government. The late Shah's father, Reza Shah, tried to crush the power of the clergy; the words of one of the leaders he had executed came back to haunt his son: "Our religion is our politics, our politics are our religion."

A series of uprisings led by the clergy against foreign economic domination began in 1872 when Baron Julius de Reuter, the founder of the news service, was granted a monopoly of mines, forests, railroads, banks, customs, canals and public works of every description that the British statesman Lord Curzon described as "the most complete and extraordinary surrender of the entire industrial resources of a kingdom into foreign hands that has ever been dreamed of, much less accomplished." The clergy succeeded in canceling the concession, as they did once again in 1891 during an uprising against a British tobacco monopoly. The 1891 rebellion presaged the Constitutional Revolt of 1906, in which a clergy-led movement imposed a Constitution on the Qajar dynasty. The first, brief overthrow of the Shah, in 1953, was backed by an important segment of the clergy.

It was in this tradition that the austere, implacable Ayatollah Ruhollah Khomeini grew from a symbol of resistance to charismatic political leader. A scholar in the holy city of Qum, he led his students in protest against the Shah's Westernizing "White Revolution" of 1963; soldiers stormed the theology school, killing a number of students. A key issue was called "capitulation," an agreement the Shah had made with the United States that Iranian courts would have no jurisdiction over American military and civilian advisers. Khomeini was sent into exile in Iraq, where he soon attracted dissident pilgrims. "You have extirpated the very roots of our independence," the Ayatollah thundered from Iraq. Khomeini's sermons were distributed on tape cassettes through a network of rebellious theology students and mullahs to mosques in every village and neighborhood. Even the revolution's style was religious, with its emphasis on long mourning processions and the Shiite obsession with martyrdom.

It is almost impossible to overestimate the extent to which the Shah was hated in Iran and the national emotion that led to his overthrow. Although regarded by successive American Presidents as a modernizer and a bulwark against Communism, the Shah and his circle were viewed by most Iranians with the revulsion reflected in the Persian poet

NO HIDING PLACE

Reza Barahani's book *The Crowned Cannibals*. The Shah's agricultural "reform" bankrupted small farmers, leaving them in shantytowns on the edges of cities; his industrialization benefited only a handful of Iranians and, above all, foreign companies; his attempts at Westernization broke down the old values but replaced them with little. His entourage was notoriously corrupt and ostentatiously decadent, and behind it all was the shadow of the police, the Savak, with its network of informers and hideous torture apparatus. As the French journalist Eric Rouleau observed: "The three favorite themes of the militant clergy — foreign domination, despotism, injustice — were precisely the evils suffered by the Iranian people under the reign of Mohammed Riza Shah."

And it is almost impossible to overestimate the extent to which the revolution was viewed as a dual victory — a victory not only over the Shah, but over the United States. For it was America, in the Iranian view, that supported and propped up the Shah, that took the oil, that profited from the enormous sales of arms and that helped train the Savak. The Shah, in the Iranian view, was a creature of the United States.

But, like each of the Iranian revolts of the past century, the revolution that overthrew the Pahlevi dynasty was made up of two contradictory factions joined against a common foe. The coalition consisted, on the one hand, of the clergy, the masses of the faithful and the traditional merchants of the bazaar, and, on the other, of the emerging class of Westernized but nationalist students, intellectuals, government servants and military men.

In the past, victories over foreign domination were short-lived; usually, the dominant foreign power aligned with Westernized domestic groups — often government servants or intellectuals who looked on the clergy as backward — restored some measure of the old order. The constitutional movement was thwarted when the British backed a coup by the Shah's father, at the time an officer of the cavalry regiment. Later, when he developed Nazi sympathies early in World War II, the British packed him off and installed his young son on the throne in 1941. After the Shah was deposed in 1953 and the new Prime Minister, Mohammed Mossadegh, attempted to nationalize the oil fields, a coup was organized by the United States Central Intelligence Agency, and the Shah was returned to power.

HOW A SIT-IN TURNED INTO A SIEGE

This Iranian history had the effect of creating a unique Persian character that is often startling to outsiders: xenophobic, devious, paranoid, and, by 1979, ready to believe, beyond all seeming bonds of logic, that everything was the result of an American plot.

"No negotiations — only returning the Shah," said the banner put up on the embassy gate.

After the students realized that the Iranian people were counting on them to bring about the Shah's return, they resolved to use the hostages to accomplish that goal. And, said one, they were opposed by the moderate government leaders, President Bani-Sadr and his Foreign Minister, Sadegh Ghotbzadeh. According to this student, "The government said you must release the hostages. But since the Imam said the United States must send the Shah back to Iran or we will put the hostages on trial, we said that too, because we were following the Imam's line. Still, Mr. Bani-Sadr and Sadegh Ghotbzadeh argued despite what the Imam had said. So of course we knew that, if Mr. Bani-Sadr wanted to secure custody of the hostages, it was only for releasing them. It was obvious. So we would never give them to the government. Everything we had the details of showed we shouldn't trust the government."

There was no shortage, however, of would-be mediators; they ranged from Yasir Arafat of the Palestine Liberation Organization, who actually succeeded in helping to get 13 blacks and women released within two weeks of the embassy takeover, to United States Representative George Hansen, Republican of Idaho. The early attempts at negotiations all sank on the rock of Ayatollah Khomeini's moral absolutism. "This is a war of Islam against blasphemy," he said. He dismissed the possibility of armed attack, saying that much of the population was "looking forward to martyrdom," and he brushed off the threat of economic sanctions: "We know how to fast."

The Ayatollah seemed to nurture a particular distaste for President Carter; it was Carter who had toasted the Shah as an "island of stability," Carter who had sent what was seen as a congratulatory message after the Shah's soldiers machine-gunned unarmed demonstrators in the Jaleh Square massacre and Carter who had sent tear-gas and riot-control gear as the protests mounted.

But even some who liked their politics dramatic were startled at the students' zeal and intractability. "These people are really crazy," a Palestinian involved in an early mediation attempt said, lighting a cigarette with the three remaining fingers of his right hand. "Whoever heard of stealing an embassy in your own country?"

In the end, the Iranians released the hostages when they got ready to; all of the American strategy seemed irrelevant.

The two crucial events of the summer of 1980 appeared to have tipped the scales toward release: the death of the Shah and the political crushing of President Abolhassan Bani-Sadr.

The Shah's death removed the question of returning him to Iran for trial as an issue; since this had been the initial and repeated demand of Ayatollah Khomeini, the release of the hostages might otherwise have been impossible. More important in terms of the internal political power struggle — which was largely played out with the hostages as pawns — the Islamic fundamentalists appeared to have bested Bani-Sadr and his liberals. Ayatollah Beheshti, by interpreting the constitution to suit his political aims, had forced the President to accept the Islamic Republican Party's man, Mohammed Ali Rajai, as Prime Minister. The President was reduced to a mere figurehead.

Too, despite the unceasing rhetoric, there seemed to be a growing realization that the holding of the hostages was isolating Iran in the world, ultimately harming the revolution. Envoys sent abroad to tell Iran's story were peppered with questions about the hostages, and frustrated when no one was interested anymore in their tales of the Shah's tortures. The invasion of the oil-rich Khuzistan Province on the gulf strengthened this feeling, for now the isolation — and the difficulty getting weapons and spare parts — was downright dangerous.

Once committed to negotiating the release, the Iranians, particularly Deputy Prime Minister Behzad Nabavi, pressed on though there were still three months of complex maneuverings. Indeed, the roles became almost reversed as the liberals quietly took note of the financial losses — mainly when they paid off all Iran's debts the traditionalists were running up — and the disparity between the original terms and the final settlement. They hoped to use the hostage issue against the clerics as it had been used against them.

But it was too late for Bani-Sadr, who would be dismissed by Ayatollah Khomeini in June 1981 and, along with westernized liberals associated with him, driven into exile. From his refuge in France, Bani-Sadr would continue his opposition to the cleric-dominated government in Teheran with a curious blend of appeals for moderation and calls for the death of his enemies, some of whom were later assassinated.

4

Putting the
Hostages' Lives First

By Terence Smith

Dawn was still hours away on November 4, 1979, when the telephone rang in McLean, Va., beside the bed of Harold H. Saunders, the Assistant Secretary of State for Near Eastern Affairs. A duty officer in the State Department operations center was on the line. He hurriedly explained that the United States Embassy in Teheran was under attack and that he had Elizabeth Ann Swift, the embassy's political officer, waiting on another wire. The call was patched through, and Saunders, sitting on the edge of his bed, heard an eyewitness account of the takeover.

"It looks serious," Elizabeth Swift said, describing how the mob had clambered over the wall and entered the embassy compound. For more than two hours, the tall, bespectacled Saunders stayed on the line. "I told her to do the obvious things," he recalled, "like destroying the plates the consular people use to issue visas. But, mostly, I just listened."

Meanwhile, calls were going out to other key Administration officials. Presidential aide Hamilton Jordan was spending the night in a friend's plush weekend home on Maryland's eastern shore. In an interview months later, he remembered having two immediate reactions, one right after the other: "The first was, 'My God, this could mean war.' The second was, 'What will this do to the campaign?'" Secretary of State

NO HIDING PLACE

Cyrus R. Vance dressed quickly and headed for his office; there he encountered Arnold Raphel, his lanky, laconic special assistant, at the elevator. Vance, employing a line that had become their routine greeting at such off-hours emergencies, muttered: "We have to stop meeting like this."

Jimmy Carter was at Camp David, where he spent so many of his weekends as President, when the call came. In an interview in Plains after leaving office, Carter remembered that he had experienced, almost immediately, a nightmare vision that would haunt him for months to come. "I could picture the revolutionaries keeping the 72 hostages, or whatever the number was at the time, in the compound," Carter said, "and assassinating one of them every morning at sunrise until the Shah was returned to Iran or until we agreed to some other act in response to their blackmail. It's still a very vivid memory to me."

At 5:15 A.M., still on the phone to Teheran, Harold Saunders heard Elizabeth Swift report that the staff of the American Embassy had no choice but to surrender. "We're going down now," she said, setting down the receiver in the office on the top floor of the chancery. As Saunders recalls it, "The line stayed open for a few minutes and then went dead." The countdown had begun.

When Cyrus Vance arrived at his office on that chill November dawn, he recalled, "My first impulse was to get in touch with Bazargan and Yazdi and demand that they make good on their promise to protect our people." The Carter Administration's confidence in Prime Minister Mehdi Bazargan and Foreign Minister Ibrahim Yazdi had led to the decision to admit the Shah in the first place. Now, in the early hours of the hostage crisis, the White House was still looking to the secular leadership for help.

In fact, L. Bruce Laingen, the embassy's chargé d'affaires, was in Yazdi's office at that very moment, demanding the release of the captives. Yazdi, a medical doctor who had become a naturalized American during a decade as student and teacher at Baylor University, in Waco, Tex., offered breezy assurances that the takeover was no more serious than a sit-in at an American college campus in the 1960's. It would be over in a matter of days, he said. Instead, it was the Bazargan-Yazdi Government that was over in a matter of days. A prime objective of the

Islamic militants who engineered the embassy action had been the ouster of the secular, Western-leaning ministers. That objective was achieved within 48 hours.

In Washington, on the day of the takeover, the White House secretly asked the Joint Chiefs of Staff to determine whether an immediate rescue attempt could be mounted. Pentagon planners did come up with such a scheme, but the military leadership concluded that it was not realistic in the short run.

Another move, an immediate show of American military force near Iran, was considered that first day in a brief telephone conversation between Zbigniew Brzezinski, the President's national security adviser, and Defense Secretary Harold Brown. An aircraft carrier group en route from the Far East to the East African port of Mombasa could have been diverted into Iranian waters. "We decided against it," Brzezinski said in an interview, "for fear of giving the kidnappers an excuse to kill their hostages."

The two men did not, however, give up on the idea of a military response. On Thursday of that first week, Brzezinski recalls, he convened in his office the first in a series of high-level, secret meetings of what came to be known as the "military committee." Its confidentiality was such that the group's meetings did not even appear on the daily schedules of the participants, who included Brown, Gen. David C. Jones, the Chairman of the Joint Chiefs, and Stansfield Turner, the Director of Central Intelligence.

The military committee, which met two or three times a week, also laid the plans for the rescue effort that was finally launched the following April. Among those the group consulted was H. Ross Perot, the flamboyant Dallas millionaire, who, 10 months earlier, had employed former Green Beret officers in a successful raid that freed two of his Electronic Data Systems Corporation employees from a Teheran jail. "Perot gave us some useful information," Brzezinski recalled later, "but the two rescue efforts were of such different magnitude that very little of it applied."

Disappointed in its initial hopes that the crisis would pass with the help of Bazargan and Yazdi and convinced that neither a military move nor a rescue attempt was immediately desirable, the White House decided on a two-track strategy to exert pressure on Iran. The first track was diplomatic, including an effort to isolate Iran in the world community. The second was economic, with sanctions aimed at undermining whatever financial stability remained after the revolution. The goal was to convince Iran's leaders that it was in their own interest to let the hostages go.

Groping for diplomatic pressure points, the Administration sent cables to scores of governments and individuals, asking them to intercede. The governments ranged from close European allies of the United States to militant Arab supporters of Khomeini's revolution, including Syria and Algeria. The President, himself, contacted between 25 and 30 world leaders directly, including Soviet leader Leonid I. Brezhnev. In the interview after he left office, Carter described these personal contacts: "Those were private messages from me to the leaders themselves, worded individually, depending on whether they were Moslem or Christian or atheist."

Before the diplomatic drama was ended, it would include an exotic cast of characters. One such was Archbishop Hilarion Capucci, a Syrian Orthodox clergyman who had once been imprisoned by the Israelis on arms smuggling charges. Capucci visited Teheran at least twice during the months after the embassy takeover and was among the few foreigners allowed to see and talk to some of the hostages. He later escorted the bodies of the American soldiers killed in the unsuccessful April 1980 raid back to the West.

In another unlikely episode, unreported at the time, a group of Iranian clerics approached the State Department in late January with an extraordinary offer: In exchange for $20 million to be placed in an escrow account in an Italian bank, these mullahs said they would mobilize Iranian public opinion in favor of freeing the hostages. They included a guarantee that, if the hostages were not released within 20 days, the money would revert to the United States. The State Department dismissed the proposition as unworkable.

Other emissaries at various stages of the crisis would include an Egyptian editor, the Director General of UNESCO and the former Prime Minister of the Sudan.

One of the early intermediaries was the P.L.O.'s Yasir Arafat, whose organization had close ideological ties with the Iranian revolutionaries and had trained some of their guerrillas. But there was a problem: The American Government has an agreement with Israel, dating back to 1975, not to have any contact with the P.L.O. In fact, however, the Central Intelligence Agency has for several years maintained and occasionally used a little-publicized, so-called "back-channel" line of communications with P.L.O. headquarters in Beirut. It has been helpful, for example, in assuring the safety of Americans and American diplomats in the Lebanese capital, where the P.L.O. controls sectors of the city. Israel has known of these contacts since they began and officially looks the other way. The "back channel" to Beirut was employed within a week of the embassy seizure to ask Arafat to use his influence with Khomeini.

Meanwhile, acting on his own initiative, Representative Paul Findley, the Illinois Republican who has long championed Palestinian causes, telephoned an Arafat aide and urged that the P.L.O. leader lend a hand. The aide called back and said that Arafat had agreed. "There was no quid pro quo," Findley recalled in an interview, "but Arafat wanted me to advise the Administration of two things. First, that he would pay a political price in the Arab world for his efforts and, second, given the complications, he was not at all sure of success."

Bruno Kreisky, the Chancellor of Austria, also perceived Arafat as the ideal go-between. Kreisky urged that President Carter make a public appeal to Arafat. Such an appeal, Kreisky argued, would constitute a de facto recognition of the P.L.O.'s role in Middle Eastern affairs, which would be all the inducement the Palestinian leader would need. But the Carter Administration finally preferred the secret "back channel" to a public action that could antagonize Israel and its American supporters.

Eventually, Arafat sent a message to Khomeini urging the release of the hostages. Two senior P.L.O. officials were dispatched to Teheran, where they met with the Revolutionary Council. Vance and other former government officials now believe that Arafat's intercession was instrumental in securing the release of 13 women and black hostages on November 19-20. Thereafter, the Arafat-Khomeini relationship apparently deteriorated, and there is no evidence of any further impact upon the hostage situation by the Palestinian leader.

Meanwhile, a series of secret meetings was under way in a very different setting — the second-floor sitting room of Kurt Waldheim, Secretary General of the United Nations. It was there, overlooking a manicured private garden on Manhattan's East River, that the United States and Iran first exchanged their respective conditions for a resolution of the crisis. As it turned out, the package Iran finally accepted more than a year later was remarkably similar to the conditions first outlined by Cyrus Vance in Waldheim's elegantly furnished Sutton Place townhouse.

Because of the sensitivity and importance of these negotiations, Vance handled them personally — and he went to extraordinary lengths to keep his participation secret. During the month of November, he spent most weekdays at his desk in the State Department, drafting and redrafting the American position. Then, on Saturday afternoons, his limousine would bear him away from the office, ostensibly headed for home, but in fact en route to Andrews Air Force Base in suburban Maryland. There, he would board an Air Force Jetstar for the 40-minute flight to La Guardia Airport and the meeting with Waldheim.

The two diplomats were a matched pair, both in their early 60's, tall, formal, soft-spoken. By mid-November, they had progressed far enough to inspire Abholhassan Bani-Sadr, then the Iranian Foreign Minister, to dispatch a personal envoy, Ahmad Salmatian, to New York, with Iran's latest demands. They included three main conditions for the release of the captives: the return of the Shah's wealth, an American pledge against interference in Iran's internal affairs and an international forum in which Iran could air its grievances against the Shah and the United States. In private, at least, the Iranians were no longer demanding the extradition of the Shah, who was recuperating in New York Hospital.

Vance was anxious to meet face to face with Salmatian, but that was not part of the Iranian's mandate from Bani-Sadr. Instead, they engaged in the diplomatic dance known as "proximity talks," passing papers back and forth through Waldheim. Bani-Sadr, himself, was due in New York on November 29 to attend a Security Council meeting on the crisis. And Vance and his aides had high hopes of reaching a settlement with the Iranian Foreign Minister that would lead to the early release of the hostages.

On November 27, however, Khomeini denounced the upcoming Security Council meeting as "made to order" for the purposes of the

United States. The next day he summarily removed Bani-Sadr from his post and replaced him with Ghotbzadeh, who canceled the New York trip. The Vance-Waldheim negotiations came to an abrupt end.

By this stage of the crisis, Khomeini had no intention of letting the hostages go. As symbols of the Iranian defiance of the United States in particular and of Western ways in general, the American captives had become pawns in Iran's internal political struggles.

In addition to diplomatic initiatives, the Carter Administration had determined to apply economic pressure to bring the Iranian revolutionary Government around. Ten days after the embassy takeover, the United States froze the estimated $6 billion in Iranian assets on deposit in American banks. The decision had been put off for several days out of fear that other countries — Saudi Arabia, for example — would view the move as a precedent that endangered international banking understandings. If these nations had reacted by withdrawing their huge deposits in American banks, it could have caused a run on the dollar and a collapse of the banking system. Lloyd N. Cutler, the urbane, silver-haired Washington lawyer who had become White House counsel, remembered: "It seemed a very real fear at the time. We had some terrific arguments in the Administration about whether we were about to cause the 'Crash of '79.' "

On the morning of November 14, however, Bani-Sadr announced in Teheran that Iran was going to withdraw all its assets from American banks that day. This inexplicable warning reached Washington at about 5 A.M., giving Carter time to sign the freeze order before the banks opened. G. William Miller, then Treasury Secretary, got on the telephone to the Saudi Finance Minister and assured him that the freeze was an act of financial self-defense, designed to protect the dollar, and not a matter of political retaliation. The Saudis and other nations accepted the distinction and made no effort to transfer their funds to another currency, and the dollar held firm.

The Carter Administration reinforced the freeze with an embargo on American trade with Iran. Purchases of Iranian oil were suspended. But, in a country that had earned billions of dollars from its oil exports, it would take months before the pinch was felt.

November 20, 1979, was a day of reckoning and reappraisal. Frustrated by the failure of his initial diplomatic efforts, alarmed by Khomeini's public threat to put the hostages on trial for espionage, President Carter called his chief advisers to Camp David for a thorough review. They considered contingency plans drawn up by the Pentagon. According to participants, those options included a naval blockade of Iran, mining of Iranian harbors, seizure of the oil depots on Kharg Island and a punitive bombing of the huge refinery at Abadan.

The plans were all militarily feasible, but none held out the promise of freedom for the hostages. Jody Powell, Carter's press secretary, remembered asking: "If we seize Kharg Island, then what? We have Kharg Island, and they have the hostages." Hamilton Jordan recalls, "There were a number of things we could have done to satisfy the nation's desire for action, but most of them would have endangered the lives of the hostages rather than freed them."

Yet there was also a consensus among those at the meeting that some action was necessary if Washington was to arrest the drift in Teheran toward trials that might well end with executions of some or all of the American captives. That same day, a blunt message was dispatched to Teheran via Swiss diplomatic channels: Mistreatment of the hostages would lead to the mining or blockade of Iranian harbors. Publicly, the White House issued a statement that raised, for the first time, the possibility of using military force to free the hostages. In Iran, talk of trials quickly subsided and the treatment of the captives improved.

Many months later, private citizen Jimmy Carter sat in his home in Plains, playing with his grandchildren, and recalled that decision — the closest, he said, he had come to using military force against Iran other than the ill-fated rescue attempt. "We made plans — detailed plans — for those military actions to be implemented if the occasion demanded it," Carter said, "but I never came close to ordering that kind of military action, absent the death or serious injury to our hostages."

There were times, such as this, during the crisis when Washington took a tough stance. But, in the view of most of those interviewed by *The New York Times*, President Carter had reached a fundamental decision within a few days of the embassy takeover, a decision that generally guided the Administration's handling of the matter during the following 14½ months. By his actions and statements, Carter made it clear to Iran and the rest of the world that the lives of the hostages were his first order of priority.

Carter later insisted that he never made such a decision, at least not in those terms. "I never placed the hostages' lives first," he said, heatedly and somewhat defensively. "I always — and you can check back on my public statements — said that there were two considerations that were not mutually exclusive. One was to protect the honor and integrity of our nation, and the other was to protect the lives of the hostages." As it turned out, he added, he never had to choose between the two.

Perhaps. Yet President Carter met repeatedly with the families of the hostages and prayed publicly with them at the National Cathedral. He confessed to reporters that virtually his every waking moment was spent worrying about the fate of the captives. On December 7, he emerged from a meeting with the families at the State Department and vowed publicly that, as long as the captives were not put on trial or harmed, "I am not going to take any military action that would cause bloodshed or arouse the unstable captors of our hostages to attack or punish them."

As Cyrus Vance and other Administration officials recall it, this emphasis on saving the lives of the hostages was spontaneous and guided the President's actions from the first moments of the crisis.

At the same time, it was good politics. It may, in fact, have been the only option for a President about to declare his candidacy for a second term. Film of the hostages and emotionally charged interviews with their families were dominating the television newscasts, personalizing the captives for millions of viewers. Early polls showed that most Americans, angry as they were, opposed military action lest it endanger the hostages.

The public rallied to Carter's side. Senator Edward M. Kennedy learned to his sorrow how sensitive the issue was when he criticized the Shah — and by implication Carter's decision to admit him — and was attacked from all sides for playing politics with the safety of the hostages. The President himself seemed to be capitalizing on the situation when he withdrew from a scheduled debate with Kennedy in Iowa (a debate Carter's pollster had decided would not be to his advantage) and announced that he would forgo campaigning until the hostages were free. Kennedy cried foul at this "Rose Garden strategy," but Carter continued climbing in the polls.

In the opinion of some analysts, Carter's emphasis on the hostages' safety tended to undercut America's negotiating position. The Iranians knew they need have no fear of American military retaliation so long as the hostages were alive and captive.

On the other hand, Jody Powell said that the President and most of his advisers felt at the beginning of the crisis that the national honor could best be protected by protecting the lives of the hostages. "But we all realized," he added, "that, at some point, the issue of their safety and our larger national interests might conflict."

One person who soon thought the conflict already posed a problem was Henry Kissinger. Two weeks after the embassy takeover, in a controversial speech to a meeting of Republican Governors in Austin, Tex., Kissinger argued passionately for "a reassertion of American will," and an end to a policy of "self-abasement" in dealing with the Iranian regime. "I think it is crucial," he said, "for the United States to remember the question of national honor."

Another kind of "national honor" that Kissinger and others were concerned about was the nation's standing among its allies and enemies around the world. Four years earlier, the United States had incurred some 70 casualties in freeing the 39 crewmen of the Mayaguez, an American freighter seized by Cambodia, and most Americans surveyed at the time felt the cost was justified. That act embodied a particular kind of national honor or national pride — of the "don't-tread-on-me" variety. By appearing impotent in the face of provocation by a band of student militants in Teheran, Kissinger said later, the Carter Administration undercut America's image elsewhere around the world.

In any event, however, the Carter Administration's central devotion to the safety of the hostages was clear, and it set the parameters for the months of negotiations that followed.

While the President and his aides were convening in Camp David on that chill November 20, the Shah of Iran was still recuperating from his gallstone operation in New York Hospital. The man whose admission to the United States had sparked the crisis remained in this country, an obstacle to any negotiated release of the hostages. And he had not been forgotten by the "old-boy network" of high-powered financiers and diplomats that had lobbied for his admission.

On November 5, the day after the embassy was seized, David Rockefeller, a leader of the network, had taken up his telephone, called the White House and asked Susan Clough, Carter's secretary, to put him through to the President. There were at least two unusual aspects to the call: David Rockefeller does not customarily do his own dialing, and those accustomed to dealing with the White House know that Presidents are not likely to be immediately available, even to a Rockefeller. Nonplussed, Carter's secretary refused Rockefeller's request and then called him back to make sure the call was genuine.

When Rockefeller finally got through, he recalled in an interview, "I expressed my shock at what had happened." Rockefeller went on, he said, to tell the President that "the problem of handling the Shah's arrangements had become too big for any one citizen to handle. I said it was time for the government to take responsibility for him and asked the President to send an emissary to see the Shah and his people."

Henry Kissinger and lawyer-diplomat John J. McCloy, strong supporters of the Shah, reinforced this appeal with calls to senior State Department and White House officials. Public controversy over the network's involvement with the Shah had intensified. One Congressman even suggested that the United States should keep the Shah and send David Rockefeller to Iran to stand trial.

The appeals of the "old-boy network" notwithstanding, the Administration continued to avoid official contact with the Shah. Then, on November 29, Mexico suddenly announced that the Shah would not be allowed to resume his exile in that country, reversing a personal promise given him by President José López Portillo. In an interview in Mexico City, Jorge Castenada, the Foreign Minister, explained: "It was simply not in Mexico's interest to have the Shah return after the hostages had been taken. It would have put us in an extremely difficult position, seemingly allied with the Shah against the will of the Iranian people."

With the Shah scheduled to leave the hospital in three days, and no refuge outside the country available to him, the Administration stepped in. "We had decided," Hamilton Jordan recalled, "that nothing was going to move with the hostages until we got the Shah out of the country." Lloyd Cutler flew to New York and met secretly with the Shah in his hospital room. Cutler nominated Paraguay and South Africa as possible destinations. The Empress Farah rejected both — the first had inadequate medical facilities, and the second was where the Shah's father had died in exile 35 years before.

On December 2, an Air Force jet flew the Shah and his entourage to temporary quarters at Lackland Air Force Base in Texas. Then the Administration learned that Panama was willing to accept the Shah. Hamilton Jordan, who had developed a close relationship with General Omar Torrijos, the Panamanian leader, during negotiations on the Panama Canal treaties a year earlier, flew to Panama City to confirm the offer and then to Lackland, where he persuaded the Shah to accept it. Jordan made a second trip to Panama on December 13 to select a suitable house for the Shah on Contadora Island, off Panama City, and he returned to Lackland with a handwritten note for the Shah from Torrijos that began: "You and your family will be welcome." Torrijos concluded by saying: "I feel instinctively that we will establish a solid friendship." It was a most gracious invitation, but the Shah's stay in Panama would hardly be peaceful.

The next day, Cutler and Jordan met with the Shah. The understanding they reached was known informally as the Lackland Agreement. Recalling it later, Carter said, "Our commitment to the Shah basically was that, if he needed medical attention which could uniquely be provided in our country, we would let him come back in." The United States also promised to provide the Shah with secure international telephone communications on Contadora Island, helicopter transportation to Panama City and full use of the facilities at Gorgas Hospital, the American military installation there.

On December 15, hours before the Shah's departure from Lackland and the United States, he received a call from Jimmy Carter, who wished him well and reiterated the main points of the Lackland Agreement. It was the first time the two men had spoken since New Year's Eve, 1977, in Teheran, where Carter had publicly praised the Shah's nation as "an island of stability."

Thus, the situation that had led to the embassy takeover no longer existed: The Shah was gone. But, by this point, the crisis had assumed a political life of its own in Teheran. The Shah's physical presence in the United States was no longer the issue.

Omar Torrijos was waiting at the airport in Panama City when the Shah and his much diminished entourage arrived. "Imagine that," he observed ruefully to a friend, "2,500 years of the Persian empire reduced to 10 people and two dogs."

The Shah had not been in Panama 10 days before the Iranian Government moved against him. Two men, hired by Ghotbzadeh, arrived to present Panamanian authorities with a formal request for the Shah's extradition to Iran. In an unlikely turnabout, the two became the Carter Administration's principal conduit to Teheran over the next two months.

They were an improbable pair of emissaries. Christian Bourguet was a bearded, intense, left-wing French lawyer. Hector Villalón was a fast-talking Argentine who had dealt in everything from Cuban cigars to Middle East oil. Convinced that they represented a pipeline to the power center in Teheran, Torrijos alerted his friend Jordan and urged him to meet with them. As Jordan recalled, "There was a big question in the White House whether I should see these guys. We didn't know much about them. But after two months in which we'd tried everything else, they seemed to be live fish on the line."

Accompanied by Harold Saunders, Jordan took the supersonic Concorde to London on January 18. It was the first of many secret negotiating trips the 35-year-old Presidential aide would make over the coming months, most of them on weekends when his absence from the White House would not be noted. Jordan and Saunders traveled under assumed names when they flew on commercial aircraft, and Jordan carried a disguise consisting of tinted glasses and a dark mustache. He says he never used it, but he did once try on the disguise in the family quarters of the White House, to the great amusement of the Carters. He also delighted in showing acquaintances a Polaroid picture of himself in the getup, which made him look vaguely like an overfed South American revolutionary.

On that first negotiating trip, Jordan and Saunders talked with Bourguet and Villalón for more than 12 hours in the London home of an American diplomat. The idea that emerged from the meeting and was honed at subsequent encounters in Washington, Bern and Paris was the establishment of a United Nations Commission that could serve as a forum for airing Iran's grievances against the Shah and as a vehicle for the release of the American hostages.

During the London session, Bourguet and Villalón stressed to Jordan how much the Iranians despised the Shah, the degree to which they felt abused by the United States and the necessity to find some face-saving compromise. The Presidential aide returned to Washington, as he later said, convinced that the United States would have to "find some way to create the right political climate in Iran in which the release of the hostages would be possible."

Jordan set forth these thoughts in a 15-page memo to Carter. The President read it, wrote "interesting idea" in the margin and directed his aide to set up a meeting with Vice President Mondale, Vance, Brzezinski and other top foreign-policy advisers to discuss a new American approach.

The result was a six-point modified position in which the United States said for the first time that it was prepared to work out, in advance, detailed plans for a forum to hear Iran's grievances, to release its frozen assets and to resume the shipment of military spare parts. The new position, with its more conciliatory tone, was transmitted to Teheran in late January, but it evoked no enthusiasm. The hostages were too valuable to Khomeini's internal political maneuvering to give up.

Fresh from a visit to Teheran, Bourguet and Villalón arrived in Washington on January 25 for a second round of talks. They went immediately to the White House and plunged into two days of intensive meetings with Jordan and Saunders in Jordan's large and airy corner office in the West Wing. To establish their credentials as insiders with the ruling forces in Teheran, the two emissaries brought with them a tape recording of the tumultuous meeting earlier that month between Waldheim and the members of the Revolutionary Council. The argument had centered on the establishment of a United Nations Commission to hear Iran's grievances.

The United States had indicated as early as the first month of the crisis that it was willing to agree to the creation of such a commission, but only *after* the release of the hostages. Now Bourguet and Villalón brought a new idea from Ghotbzadeh: If the United States would agree to the establishment of the commission *before* the hostages were released, Iran would permit the commissioners to meet with the hostages in the embassy compound. This prospect was attractive to the Americans, who were concerned at that point about how the hostages were being treated and were uncertain, in fact, whether all were still alive. There had been no outside visitors since Christmas.

Ghotbzadeh's scheme embodied an exquisitely Persian ruse. If it had worked, it would have brought about the transfer of the hostages from the control of the student militants to the government of the newly elected President, Bani-Sadr. If the U.N. commissioners visited the embassy compound, Ghotbzadeh believed, they would discover how poorly the hostages were being treated. He was convinced that Khomeini would denounce such mistreatment as un-Islamic and authorize the transfer of the captives to the government. Their release would, theoretically, follow shortly thereafter.

For the next two days, Jordan and Saunders and the two emissaries worked intensively on a plan to bring the U.N. Commission into being. Bourguet and Villalón then took the fruits of that weekend's labor back to Teheran to discuss it with Ghotbzadeh and Bani-Sadr, who basically endorsed the scheme and gave the emissaries letters authorizing them to negotiate on the government's behalf.

The scenario was further refined at a third secret meeting between Jordan and Saunders and the two emissaries in the ornate Bellevue Palace Hotel in Bern, Switzerland, on February 9-10, when they worked 16 hours a day and broke only for meals. The negotiators added another twist to the scenario, whereby the publication of the U.N. Commission's report would be held up until the hostages had been released. The report, which presumably would include documentation of abuses under the Shah, was eagerly awaited by the leaders of the revolution.

According to this script, a copy of which was obtained by *The New York Times*, the commission would hear testimony of alleged past crimes, visit the hostages, prepare a report and meet with the Revolutionary Council. Once the hostages had been transferred from the control of the students, the commission was to return to New York and submit its findings to Waldheim. Three days later, the hostages were to be released and allowed to leave Iran. One hour after their departure,

Waldheim was to release the commission's report and two previously prepared statements from the governments. The Iranians would "admit the moral wrong of holding hostages, express regret and promise to respect international law." The Americans would "express understanding and regret for the grievances of the Iranian people, including the widespread perception of U.S. intervention in Iran's internal affairs."

Jordan and Saunders returned to Washington from Bern in high excitement; a solution seemed genuinely within grasp. All that was needed was Teheran's agreement to the final details.

Jordan received that assurance in dramatic fashion the following weekend in Paris. Having flown there for another encounter with Bourguet and Villalón, he met face to face for the first time with Sadegh Ghotbzadeh. The Iranian confirmed that, not only did he and Bani-Sadr and the Revolutionary Council agree to the scenario, but the Ayatollah Khomeini endorsed it as well.

The Jordan-Ghotbzadeh meeting in Paris was a landmark in the crisis, the first high-level contact between the governments since the hostages had been seized three months earlier. At that encounter, Ghotbzadeh pleaded with Jordan not to disclose the fact that they had met. It would cost him his life, he said, if his opponents in Teheran learned of it.

The White House, accordingly, denied press reports about the meeting at the time, and the participants have never acknowledged it since. Jordan would not talk about it. "There were a lot of trips I took and meetings I held that I will never be able to discuss," he said in an interview in his apartment in Atlanta after leaving office. "I gave my word."

Other former top officials, however, confirmed the meeting in talks with *The New York Times.* "It was terribly significant at the time," observed Warren Christopher, the former Deputy Secretary of State who would play a major role in later negotiations. "It was the first and only meeting between officials of the two governments for the first 10 months of the crisis."

The initial steps of the scenario were played out according to the script. The five-member U. N. Commission actually was formed and, after some delays, flew to Teheran on February 23. But the Ayatollah Khomeini departed from the script, announcing publicly that the fate of the hostages would have to be decided by the still-to-be-elected Parliament. Subsequently, he called upon the students to prevent the commission from seeing the hostages until its report had been published. That would have deprived the commission of its last bargaining chip, and the Ayatollah's condition was thus unacceptable.

On March 10, the U.N. Commission met with the Revolutionary Council for a showdown. Despite frantic, last-minute telephone calls between Teheran, United Nations headquarters in New York and Hamilton Jordan's office in Washington, the commission members felt they had reached an impasse and gave up. The scenario had failed, at least for the moment.

The next day, Jordan and Saunders flew to Bern for another rendezvous with Bourguet and Villalón, who flew in from Teheran. Although the Americans were profoundly depressed, the two emissaries were optimistic that the scenario could be put back on track. After 36 hours of intensive drafting, they came up with yet another variation.

Before this version could be set in motion, however, a new development in Panama threatened to derail it. Since the turn of the year, Iran had been pressing to have the Shah sent home. Panama and Iran have no extradition treaty, and Panamanian law forbids extradition for political offenses in cases where the death penalty might be involved. Nonetheless, the Panamanians had played along with the Iranian request. Their strategy was to use the theoretical possibility of the Shah's extradition as a lever to persuade the Iranians to release the hostages. Thus Iran was encouraged to file a formal extradition request within 60 days, and the Panamanians implied that they would place the Shah under arrest once those papers were received.

Privately, Omar Torrijos, the Panamanian leader, sought to reassure the Shah that he would never be sent back to Iran. But he did mention casually to the monarch that he might have to be placed under a technical house arrest, as required by Panamanian law once an extradition proceeding is under way. The Shah, according to his aides, began to get nervous.

Up to that point, Torrijos had been a gracious host. On at least one occasion, according to sources in Panama City, the Generalissimo's hospitality had included a night on the town for the monarch at a suite in the El Panama Hilton, away from the Empress Farah and his security aides.

But now relations between the Shah's staff and the Panamanian authorities had reached the breaking point. Robert Armao, the Shah's chief aide de camp, was convinced that the Panamanians were tapping the Shah's phones. Moreover, as Armao recalls, the price was high: The Shah's expenditures totaled some $500,000 for the first 10 weeks of his stay, including large cash tips allegedly solicited by Panamanian security officials.

Complaints about these abuses reached the White House, but Jimmy Carter, for one, had little sympathy. "I felt the Shah had adequate financial resources," Carter said dryly in the interview in Plains. "That wasn't my responsibility, and I had very little interest in it."

In March, the Shah's health took a sharp turn for the worse. His spleen had become painfully enlarged and had to be removed. But his American and Panamanian doctors had fallen into protracted argument about where and when he should have the operation. There were bruised feelings on both sides of this "medical soap opera," as the Shah once called it, and the monarch began to fear it would cost him his life.

Concerned about his health and faced with the prospect of extradition proceedings that were to begin formally on March 24, the Shah began to consider alternative sites for his operation and recuperation. One possibility was Egypt, where he had a standing invitation; another was returning to the United States under the terms of the agreement worked out three months earlier at Lackland Air Force base.

When the White House heard that the Shah was considering a move, it became alarmed. "We were certain," Hamilton Jordan recalled later, "that if the Shah exercised his right to come back to the United States, some of the hostages would be killed. We had real warnings to that effect." Even a move by the Shah to Egypt seemed likely to upset the hostage negotiations, since the Iranians might read it as an American plot to return him to power. Jordan and Lloyd Cutler flew to Panama to try to unsnarl the dispute among the Shah's doctors and to persuade the monarch to have his operation in Panama.

On that same day, March 21, Princess Ashraf, the Shah's twin sister, once again intervened with the President, seeking permission for her brother's operation in the United States. A courier arrived at the White House with an emotional, two-page letter in which she begged Carter "not to turn your back on this dying man whom you once called friend and ally."

Carter replied that very afternoon in a brief, handwritten note which, inexplicably, said that the Shah could have his spleen operation in Houston — precisely the option Cutler was trying that same evening in Panama to convince the Shah to forgo. Carter's motive in this is not clear; he may have been merely trying to reassure the Princess.

In a four-hour meeting with the Shah and Empress Farah that evening in Panama, Cutler said that the United States would honor its commitment under the Lackland Agreement. He added, however, that if the Shah wanted to have his operation in the United States, the monarch would have to make his return as "nonpolitical" as possible — by abdicating his throne. "We didn't think he would do that," Cutler said later.

The Shah looked at Cutler and, after a brief consultation with his wife, shook his head. "He said that he was an old man," Cutler recalled, "and that abdication wouldn't matter to him, but that he would never give up his son's right to the throne."

In the course of the night, President Carter telephoned Anwar el-Sadat and discussed the prospect of the Shah's return to Egypt. "Carter satisfied himself that it would not cause too much internal domestic trouble for Sadat," Cutler said.

On March 23, one day before the deadline for the filing of the extradition brief that could have led to the Shah's detention, the King of Kings and his entourage boarded a chartered aircraft for the flight to Egypt. Feverish, weakened by his illness, the Shah had only four months to live.

On the telephone from Teheran, Ghotbzadeh pleaded with Torrijos to hold the Shah in Panama. If that was done, he promised, the hostages would be transferred to the control of the government and subsequently released. Torrijos decided it was a hollow promise and made no effort to interfere. The Shah's plane took off at 1:45 P.M.

The prospects for an end to the hostage crisis had never been darker, and Carter's political fortunes were similarly bleak. The public, which had supported his handling of the crisis in the early months, was having second thoughts. And the pressures on him to take some kind of action — almost any action — were beginning to build. Then, on March 25, the Carter campaign received a political scare: Kennedy scored a startling, upset victory in the New York primary.

Just what effect these political setbacks played in the decision is uncertain, but four days later, Carter sent a tough message to Bani-Sadr. It warned that if the hostages were not transferred to the control of the Iranian Government within 48 hours, Washington would impose harsh new sanctions on Iran and on Iranian citizens in the United States. And, once again, tough talk produced results.

Bani-Sadr made the warning public and took the issue to the Revolutionary Council. For the first time, the council voted, on March 31, to assume control of the hostages from the militants — as Carter had demanded and as called for in the Jordan-Saunders scenario. In return, the United States was expected to recognize the role of the Parliament in the hostage crisis and to refrain from any propaganda or military action against Iran. Bani-Sadr was to make the proposition official in a speech the next day, April 1, at 4 A.M. Washington time. The United States accepted the package.

Carter and his top advisers gathered before dawn. "I was convinced we had an agreement," Carter recalled in the interview. "We were all in the Oval Office, sometime after 4 A.M., listening for the transcript of the speech. The key phrases came through from Iran indicating that Bani-Sadr had concluded the deal as outlined — through Hamilton's efforts."

At 7:20 A.M., an elated President called in reporters and television cameras to describe Bani-Sadr's speech as "a positive basis" for a negotiated solution and to announce that he would delay the imposition of the sanctions he had threatened three days earlier. It was the morning of the crucial Wisconsin primary, an opportunity to recoup the previous week's loss, and the polls were just opening when Carter broke the news.

The President romped to victory in Wisconsin, but his early-morning broadcast produced a backlash. Kennedy and others accused Carter of cynically timing his broadcast to affect the vote. And the President's elation over the seeming diplomatic breakthrough proved premature. Bani-Sadr, confronted by continued opposition to the hostage transfer among the clerics on the Revolutionary Council, lost his nerve.

PUTTING THE HOSTAGES' LIVES FIRST

"In my judgment," Carter said, "Bani-Sadr got frightened about the political consequences of releasing the hostages and changed his position and said he had to have a unanimous vote in the Revolutionary Council. He fumbled around and tried for that, and the whole deal fell through.

"I think Khomeini had made a decision at that time to let the hostages go. It was a transient phase, because later, when the situation deteriorated, Khomeini reversed himself, and the crisis dragged on. But I have always believed that, at that moment, Khomeini was willing to stand aloof and let the hostages be released."

Many Iranian specialists dispute Carter's reading of Khomeini at this crucial stage. They tend to feel that the Ayatollah did not in fact favor the Bani-Sadr plan, that the furthest he went was to withhold his disapproval until he had measured the degree of opposition.

Within a week, the President's hopes had so soured that he severed diplomatic relations with Iran and imposed the threatened sanctions. A few days later, feeling that he had exhausted his diplomatic and economic options, he gave the go-ahead for the attempt to rescue the captives.

On April 28, three days after the mission failed, Cyrus Vance resigned his post as Secretary of State. Vance had never believed such a scheme could work. He was convinced it would kill more hostages than it would save. In fact, he told friends at the time that, based on his own service in the Pentagon in the 1960's, the Joint Chiefs' estimate of about 15 probable casualties among the hostages was likely to be short by half.

During the interview in Plains, Carter for the first time expressed publicly his resentment of Vance's resignation. "I was surprised," he said, "and I was disappointed. I had expected that Vance would back my decision just as he and other leaders in my Administration had on numerous occasions when there was a dissenting voice."

Following the debacle of the rescue attempt, any movement on the negotiation front seemed out of the question, at least for several months. The President, now in the final stages of his primary campaign against Kennedy, abandoned the Rose Garden and returned to the hustings. He deliberately shifted the hostage issue to the back burner, adopting the low-key strategy that several European allies had been urging from the outset. The crisis in Iran became a dark backdrop to that summer's political conventions and the start of the fall campaign.

The breakthrough that ultimately led to the return of the hostages had nothing to do with secret messages and elaborate scenarios; it had everything to do with a timetable set by Khomeini and the Iranian clerics. They had won control of the newly elected Parliament and, with it, responsibility for the hostages. They had no further use for the 52 pawns, and Western economic and political sanctions were taking their toll. It was time to get rid of the captives.

On September 9, a German diplomat in Washington entered the elegant, seventh-floor office of Edmund S. Muskie, who had succeeded Vance as Secretary of State. He reported that a close associate of Khomeini wanted to meet urgently in Bonn with a senior representative of the United States Government to work out conditions for the release of the hostages. The message was that simple.

As Warren Christopher remembered it, Muskie and the other officials in the office could hardly believe their ears. After all those months of trying to reach someone who could speak with authority for the new rulers of Iran, an apparently authentic representative of the true center of power in Teheran had come forward. If he was genuine, as the Germans believed him to be, a solution could not be far off.

Muskie and Christopher immediately called Carter with the news and later that evening went over to discuss it at the White House. Carter listened and, according to Christopher, told him: "Chris, I want you to handle this yourself." Within 24 hours, the Deputy Secretary had assembled a team of specialists and begun work on the position he would outline a week later to Sadegh Tabatabai, the man he would meet in Bonn. Tabatabai was well-connected politically and personally to Khomeini. Moreover, he demonstrated his authenticity to the Americans by conveying the essence of Khomeini's conditions for the release of the hostages three days before the Ayatollah made them public in a speech. For the first time, there was no mention of the earlier demands for ransom or for an apology from the United States.

Yet it would be more than four months before the hostages were finally freed. On several occasions, success would seem to be within the President's grasp, only to slip away. Some of the key moments of decision during those final months help illuminate the hostage episode as a whole:

SEPTEMBER 1980. In a West German Government villa outside Bonn, Christopher met secretly with Tabatabai — a dapper, 40-year-old Iranian who served as a press attaché in Germany and was married to a German woman. In his lawyerly, matter-of-fact fashion, Christopher outlined how far the United States would go to meet Khomeini's conditions. Tabatabai said that the American position sounded reasonable and that he would return to Iran on September 22 to clear it with Khomeini. First, Tabatabai had speaking engagements in Germany. On September 22, Iraq attacked Iran. Teheran's airport was closed, and Tabatabai's return was put off for nearly a week. By the time he reached Iran, the war had pushed the hostage question aside, at least temporarily.

OCTOBER. Mohammed Ali Rajai, the Iranian Prime Minister chosen by the Parliament in August, arrived in New York to plead his country's case before the Security Council. Although Rajai refused to meet American officials during his visit, virtually every other foreign official he encountered in New York — including the permanent representatives of Algeria and four other Moslem nations — urged him to release the hostages. American officials were convinced that Rajai and the leaders in Teheran were surprised and concerned by the degree of Iran's diplomatic isolation.

NOVEMBER. Two days before the United States election, the Iranian Parliament adopted the conditions outlined by Khomeini for the release of the hostages and asked Algeria to serve as a mediator. Jimmy Carter received word of the move at 4 A.M. in a hotel room in Chicago where he had been campaigning. After a dawn flight to Washington, he stepped down from a helicopter onto the South Lawn. Brzezinski handed him a copy of the full Parliament text. As Carter strode across the lawn toward the Oval Office, he hastily scanned the document and realized to his dismay that there was no way the crisis could be resolved before the election. ("Until that time," Carter would later recall, "I had hoped that we could reach an agreement in principle, with details to be worked out later, that would have permitted the hostage release before November 4. In hindsight, of course, that was unrealistic.")

The President could score a few points — by announcing, for example, that a solution was at hand. But he resisted the temptation and went on television with a subdued statement describing the conditions as "a positive basis" and pledging that the United States would continue negotiations without regard to the election.

DECEMBER. Negotiations all but collapsed when Iran stunned Washington with a demand for $24 billion to cover what it claimed was the total of its frozen assets and the property taken by the Shah and his family — a larger sum than had previously figured in the negotiations.

In a crucial decision, the Administration decided to ignore the $24 billion figure and press ahead with negotiations. No figures were mentioned in the American response, but talks continued. The American reply included an innovative idea devised by Warren Christopher, that the final agreement should be in the form of a declaration by the Algerian Government, signed by Iran and the United States. This was aimed at relieving the Iranian concern about dealing directly with "the great Satan," and established the form that would lead to the solution a month later.

JANUARY. After Iran had reduced its demand to $9.5 billion, Christopher and his team flew to Algiers for the final negotiating push. For 13 days, he and a group of diplomats and bankers worked day and night with Mohammed Ben Yahia, the Algerian Foreign Minister, to complete one of the most complex international agreements in recent history. Carter was extravagant in his praise for Christopher's tireless performance. Christopher, in turn, lauded another man: Ulric S. Haynes Jr., the American ambassador to Algeria, whose role received little attention. "Haynes sensitized me," Christopher said, "to the Algerians' acute concern about their role as a mediator and their image with Iran and the third world."

Christopher and his team of diplomats were soon joined in Algiers by a group of lawyers and bankers who had been negotiating on their own since the previous June with the Central Bank of Iran. Their talks had laid an important groundwork for the eventual financial solution. Equally important was the Iranian decision on January 16 to pay off the entire $3.67 billion in outstanding loans with Western banks, rather than simply bring them up to date.

The final documents were signed in Algiers. Missing were most of the early Iranian demands — the establishment, for example, of an international body to hear Teheran's grievances or anything approaching

212

an American apology. Under the agreement, the hostages were freed and the United States released nearly $8 billion worth of Iranian assets that had been frozen in this country. About $5.1 billion of this amount was set aside to pay off Iran's debts to American and European banks, and the rest was recovered by Iran.

Champagne was broken out at the White House and, before dawn on January 20, Carter offered a simple toast in the Oval Office. "To freedom," he said. But it was not until about 12:35 P.M. that day that Jimmy Carter received word that the hostages had been freed and their plane had cleared Iranian air space. His limousine was en route to Andrews Air Force base for the flight home to Georgia. Ronald Reagan had been President for about 35 minutes.

Looking back, Carter's aides agreed that the new President had in fact played a significant role in the hostage release. Reagan's sharp public condemnations of the student militants in Iran as "barbarians" and "kidnappers" made it obvious to Khomeini that he could not expect a better deal — if any deal at all — once Reagan took office.

The President-elect's remarks were not cleared in advance with the outgoing Administration, but the Carter officials quickly perceived their potential value in the ongoing negotiations. Warren Christopher made it clear in his talks with the Algerians, for the benefit of the Iranians, that his authority ended January 20. A new Administration, with different priorities, would take over at that time — and it would not be bound by any terms short of a final agreement. To underscore the deadline, Christopher openly had his Air Force jetliner readied in advance for departure from Algiers at noon, Washington time, on January 20.

Indeed, Carter officials felt it was vital that the negotiations be completed by Inauguration Day. Lloyd Cutler, the White House counsel, said later that, had the Reagan Administration made good on its plan to freeze the talks after taking office, "the hostages probably would have been put on trial, and we would have been in the soup." Iran would most likely have responded by putting the hostages on trial, he said, and the United States would have gone ahead with a contingency plan to blockade Iran or mine its harbors.

The Carter Administration's handling of the crisis was criticized on several counts. Reagan's foreign-policy advisers charged that

Carter was not tough enough at the outset and had failed to maintain a consistent approach. They argued that Carter's refusal to campaign, his emotional emphasis upon the hostages — almost to the exclusion of other foreign-policy issues — had merely served to convince the Iranians of the enormous value the United States placed on the prize they had seized. Khomeini was free to raise the negotiating stakes at will.

Some political officers and Iranian specialists in the State Department felt the same way. In fact, in March 1980, after the United Nations Commission had quit Teheran, several of them prepared a memorandum to Vance recommending an alternative strategy. The thrust of their argument, as one of the authors later described it: "We should do and say nothing about the hostages publicly, but advise Iranians in private that we are going to tighten the screws on them, politically and economically, and come down hard if they do anything to harm the hostages." By the time the memorandum reached Vance, however, Carter had already authorized the rescue attempt, and a low-key approach was no longer possible.

Jimmy Carter had second thoughts of his own. "I've thought about it a lot," he said. "The first few weeks, or even months, I neither did anything nor had to do anything to keep the issue of burning importance in the minds of the American public. But later, when the press was excluded from Iran, I think the issue would have died down a lot more if I had decided to ignore the fate of the hostages or if I had decided just to stop any statements on the subject. That may have been the best approach."

He paused for a moment, reflecting on what he had said. "But," he continued, as though arguing with himself, "if that had happened, what would the Iranians have done to the hostages to revive the issue? That was always a concern to me."

Carter said he thought both sides had learned bitter lessons from the experience. "Iran suffered horribly," he said. "They became vulnerable and, I think, precipitated the Iraqi invasion." For the United States, it was vivid proof that "there are limits, even on our nation's great strength," he said quietly, his voice trailing off. "It's the same kind of impotence that a powerful person feels when his child is kidnapped."

Terence Smith was assisted in the reporting of this chapter by Bernard D. Nossiter, The Times's U.N. bureau chief, and Paul Lewis, in the Paris bureau.

5

Going the
Military Route

By Drew Middleton

After five months of fruitless negotiations to free the American hostages, Jimmy Carter decided to interrupt the diplomatic approach in favor of direct action. On April 11, 1980, at a meeting of the National Security Council in the White House, the President took the decision to "lance the boil" of American frustration, as National Security Adviser Zbigniew Brzezinski put it, with a daring rescue raid on the United States Embassy compound in Teheran *(see map following page 219).*

The meeting was held a day after Secretary of State Cyrus R. Vance, the principal objector to a rescue raid, left Washington for a vacation at Hobe Sound, Fla. Vance, whose Foreign Service personnel constituted a majority of the hostages, was not informed of the meeting before his departure.

For months, a hard-nosed Pentagon view had held that the seizure of the hostages had been an act of war and that the United States was justified in adopting a military response. The imminent start of Iran's dust-storm season, which could hamper vital helicopter operations for months to come, quickened the decision-making process. The raid came two weeks later.

At 7:30 P.M., Iranian time, on April 24, eight Navy RH-53D Sea Stallion helicopters whirled up from the flight deck of the aircraft carrier Nimitz, deployed in the Arabian Sea off the coast of Iran, and headed for the Great Iranian Salt Desert. Their first stop, a refueling and rendezvous point code-named Desert One, was five hours' flying time away.

As the helicopters departed, six Air Force C-130 Hercules tactical air transports, one modified as a tanker, took off from a base at an undisclosed location to join the choppers in the desert. An advance party of American agents had been infiltrated into Iran to aid the raiders. Secrecy was so tight that no ally of the United States had been informed of the rescue operation.

The C-130's, which have a maximum range of about 2,100 miles, could have come from an American base in Turkey, or from a base serving an American missile testing range in Crete, or possibly from one of the American-leased airfields in southern Egypt. But given the need for secrecy, it seems likely that they took off from a second aircraft carrier in the Arabian Sea or the Indian Ocean.

About 80 miles into Iranian airspace, one of the helicopters was forced down by rotor-blade trouble and landed in the desert. Its crewmen removed code books and secret papers, abandoned their craft and were picked up by another chopper that continued on to Desert One.

Halfway to the rendezvous point, the remaining seven helicopters flew into a dust storm, which had not been seen or forecast by military meteorologists. Such storms appear with regularity and great force in that part of Iran in the spring. After flying through the storm without difficulty, however, the helicopters ran into a second, larger storm — a howling, swirling dust cloud 200 miles wide and 6,000 feet high. To avoid radar detection, the helicopters had to fly low, and to conserve fuel they did not try to fly around the storm. And as they groped their way through the storm, a second mishap occurred: the navigation and flight instruments on one of the seven remaining helicopters failed, probably as a result of the dust. From all indications, none of the helicopters on the mission had dust filters, which should have been standard equipment. The pilot, weighing the deteriorating weather and the diminishing chances of a safe flight to Desert One, decided on his own authority to return to the Nimitz. He did so unaware of the first copter's failure.

The six remaining helicopters flew on to Desert One, an airstrip in central Iran that had formerly been used by Savak, the Shah's secret police force, and was known to American military authorities. The choppers arrived at intervals that put them 50 to 85 minutes behind schedule. Waiting for them were the six C-130's, which apparently had not encountered any difficulties en route.

Sometime after the rendezvous, three civilian vehicles — a bus carrying a driver and 43 passengers, mostly elderly people and children, a small fuel truck and a pickup truck — came down a nearby road. None of the drivers halted on signal, so an American road-watch team fired warning shots. The bus stopped and its driver and passengers were detained, but the fuel truck caught fire after its engine block was struck by one of the warning bullets. Its driver jumped out and ran to the pickup truck, which escaped in the turmoil.

Col. Charlie Beckwith, the Army officer in command of the ground rescue team, assumed that the two men had been smugglers and would not raise an alarm, so no attempt was made to pursue the pickup truck, though shots were fired at its tires.

Meanwhile, a third chopper broke down. It had sustained a partial hydraulic failure in flight, was judged unsafe and scratched from the mission by the helicopter unit's commander, Air Force Col. James Kyle. This left the helicopter force at five, one below the minimum decreed by operational planners.

Colonel Kyle, the on-site commander at Desert One, consulted Colonel Beckwith, who recommended that the mission be aborted. Colonel Kyle then reported by radio to the operation's joint task force command in Washington, which relayed word to President Carter through Defense Secretary Harold Brown. It was 3:15 A.M., Iran time, on April 25 when the President gave the order to cancel the mission.

Despite their disappointment, the prevailing view among the troopers as they prepared to withdraw from Desert One was that it was only a temporary setback and that they could try again. But that was not to be.

As one of the helicopters changed position to allow a second to refuel for the flight back to the Nimitz, it collided with a C-130. Both aircraft burst into flames. Shell casings and burning ammunition from the C-130 peppered the other helicopters.

The dust storm may have been partly to blame. "We had all this dust coming down from the [helicopter's] rotors and all our dust comes right at them from our engines," said Joseph J. Beyers 3d, an Air Force staff sergeant who was a radio operator aboard the C-130 that was hit. Beyers said the helicopter hit the C-130 because "there was just too much dust and stuff flying around."

Apparently, he said, the helicopter pilot couldn't see where he was going. "He turned away from where he was going [and] that's when he hit us," he said. As the crash occurred, the navigator "opened that escape hatch and something blew and the escape hatch came down and hit me on the head and knocked me down the steps. Either that, or the oxygen blew up."

Eventually, Beyers crawled to the crew door. "They said they saw me stand up . . . and then it looked as though I was catapulted out," he said. Someone picked him up, he said, "like a loaf of bread." Beyers suffered extensive burns on his hands, arms and buttocks.

Another crew member told of a knife edge of panic at the scene, but Colonel Beckwith, a Vietnam war veteran with a daring combat record, pulled things together, shouting orders and assessing the damages and casualties.

Eight crewmen died in the crash — three in the helicopter, five in the C-130. Their bodies were left behind. The decision to do so was made in part because of the urgent need to get out before the explosion's flames, visible for miles, were spotted by the Iranian police or army. Even if it had been possible to douse the flames quickly, crewmen said, it would have taken too much time to let the aircraft cool sufficiently to make it safe to recover the bodies.

After releasing the bus driver and his Iranian passengers, the 200-man American task force left Desert One at about 4 A.M., almost four hours after its first contingents had arrived. Left behind aboard the abandoned helicopters in the quick getaway were numerous classified materials, including personnel lists, planning papers and alternative escape routes.

At 1 A.M., Washington time, on April 25, President Carter went on television to announce that an attempt to rescue the hostages had failed. Later, military men would detail the operation in a series of post-mortems as among the most humiliating and tragic of their careers.

"It was the biggest failure of my life," said Colonel Beckwith, who was subsequently assigned to producing training manuals at Fort Bragg,

N.C. "I cried for the eight men we lost. I'll carry that load on my shoulders for the rest of my life."

Planning and training for the rescue raid had begun shortly after the hostages had been seized in the embassy takeover the previous November 4. Originally, Army and Air Force teams were involved. Much later, Navy and Marine Corps personnel were included.

From the start, military sources said, command and control of the operation were somewhat tenuous and fragile at intermediate and lower levels. Further complications arose because each service had its own training methods and interpretations of tactical doctrine.

The number of helicopters to be used in the raid was a critical issue. The official thinking was never disclosed, but as few as four may have been proposed and some officers said that as many as 25 might have been deployed. President Carter accepted the relatively small number of eight, a figure believed put forward by the Joint Chiefs of Staff, apparently because he wished to present the mission to the world as "humanitarian," and not an act of war against Iran.

Training proceeded through the early months of 1980. A scale model of the embassy compound was constructed for the raiders to practice in. Helicopter and C-130 practice flights were made over mountain and desert terrain in Utah and Nevada. There were also practice runs in aerial refueling and other operations.

By the time President Carter sat down to preside at the April 11 meeting, the principal participants — Vice President Walter Mondale; Gen. David C. Jones, Chairman of the Joint Chiefs of Staff; Adm. Stansfield Turner, Director of Central Intelligence, and White House aides Hamilton Jordan and Jody Powell — had become persuaded of the raid's necessity and its chances of success.

Many highly qualified senior military officers were convinced that total casualties among the hostages and their rescuers would not exceed 18 killed or wounded. Other military experts questioned that figure, however.

Brzezinski and Secretary of Defense Harold Brown, who were also present at the White House meeting, were the plan's leading proponents. Secretary of State Vance was the principal opponent, but he was not at the meeting. Filling in for Vance was Deputy Secretary of State

IF THE RESCUE PLAN HADN'T FAILED

The attempt to free the American hostages in April 1980 was a bold and highly complex air-land-sea operation. As indicated on this map, if the plan had not been aborted at Desert One, the action would have shifted to the American Embassy compound in Teheran (inset). New details of this critical phase of the operation, and the planned airlift to freedom, are given in the chronology below.

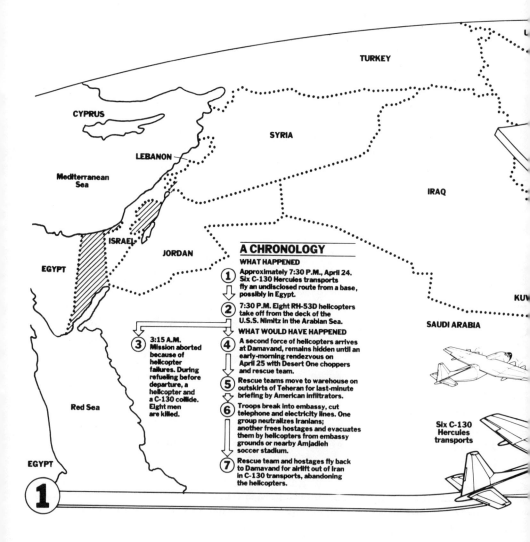

TURKEY

CYPRUS

SYRIA

LEBANON

Mediterranean
Sea

IRAQ

ISRAEL

JORDAN

EGYPT

A CHRONOLOGY

WHAT HAPPENED

(1) Approximately 7:30 P.M., April 24. Six C-130 Hercules transports fly an undisclosed route from a base, possibly in Egypt.

(2) 7:30 P.M. Eight RH-53D helicopters take off from the deck of the U.S.S. Nimitz in the Arabian Sea.

WHAT WOULD HAVE HAPPENED

(3) 3:15 A.M. Mission aborted because of helicopter failures. During refueling before departure, a helicopter and a C-130 collide. Eight men are killed.

(4) A second force of helicopters arrives at Damavand, remains hidden until an early-morning rendezvous on April 25 with Desert One choppers and rescue team.

(5) Rescue teams move to warehouse on outskirts of Teheran for last-minute briefing by American infiltrators.

(6) Troops break into embassy, cut telephone and electricity lines. One group neutralizes Iranians; another frees hostages and evacuates them by helicopters from embassy grounds or nearby Amjadieh soccer stadium.

(7) Rescue team and hostages fly back to Damavand for airlift out of Iran in C-130 transports, abandoning the helicopters.

KUW

SAUDI ARABIA

Red Sea

EGYPT

Six C-130
Hercules
transports

(1)

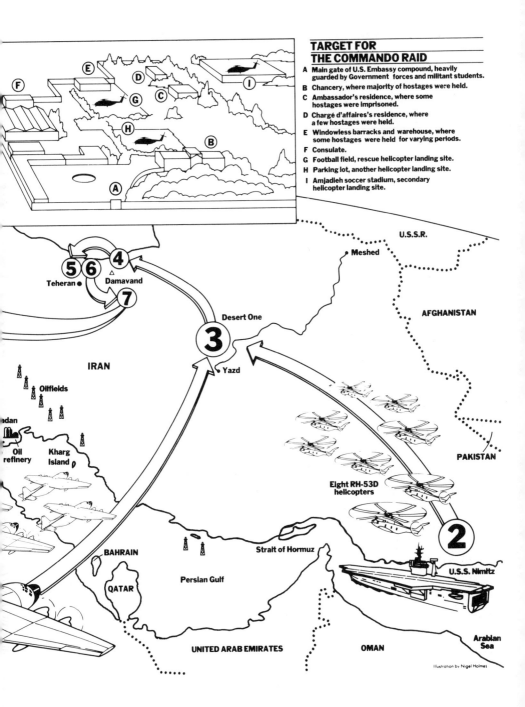

TARGET FOR THE COMMANDO RAID

A Main gate of U.S. Embassy compound, heavily guarded by Government forces and militant students.

B Chancery, where majority of hostages were held.

C Ambassador's residence, where some hostages were imprisoned.

D Chargé d'affaires's residence, where a few hostages were held.

E Windowless barracks and warehouse, where some hostages were held for varying periods.

F Consulate.

G Football field, rescue helicopter landing site.

H Parking lot, another helicopter landing site.

I Amjadieh soccer stadium, secondary helicopter landing site.

U.S.S.R.

Meshed

AFGHANISTAN

Teheran ● Damavand

Desert One

IRAN

Yazd

Oilfields

adan

Oil refinery

Kharg Island

Eight RH-53D helicopters

PAKISTAN

BAHRAIN

Strait of Hormuz

U.S.S. Nimitz

QATAR

Persian Gulf

UNITED ARAB EMIRATES

OMAN

Arabian Sea

Illustration by Nigel Holmes

Warren Christopher, who became the chief American negotiator in resolving the crisis months later.

Because of tight operational security, Christopher had not been told of plans for the raid. He emerged from the White House meeting with the impression that, though his boss had opposed a rescue raid, Vance had preferred it to the politically volatile option of a military attack on Iran. Such an attack had been in the wings in recent weeks.

There had been growing apprehensions that the Iranians might take drastic steps, such as selected executions, against the hostages. So a plan of punitive military measures had been worked out. It included a naval blockade; the bombing of Kharg Island, the site of Iran's main oil-export facility, and air strikes on the huge refinery at Abadan, which produces most of Iran's fuel.

Under the impression that Vance, who was taking his first time off in months, had given his tacit, if reluctant, approval to the plan, Christopher decided not to disturb him with word of the decision to go ahead. Vance learned of the decision only on April 14, after his return to Washington.

At a private meeting with Carter in the Oval Office the following Saturday, April 21, Vance repeated his objections, stressing the likelihood that some hostages would be killed and suggesting that the raid might invite Soviet intervention. That Monday, three days before the April 24 raid, Vance told Carter that he could not support the plan and felt he had to resign. He said he would hold off doing so until after the raid, and that until then, he would remain publicly silent.

Had the raid not ended in death and destruction in the desert, plans had called for a second force of helicopters carrying Special Forces troopers to land at a site near Damavand, a small town in the mountains about 50 miles northeast of Teheran. Rescue teams from the Desert One and Damavand forces were to have moved into Teheran in trucks provided by C.I.A. agents infiltrated into Iran earlier. The trucks bore Iranian Army markings and license plates.

The first stop for the rescue teams was to have been a warehouse on the outskirts of Teheran. There, the troops would have been briefed on conditions in the embassy by secret agents who had been monitoring the compound closely and with remarkable accuracy for some time. The number of guards, the kind of weapons they had and their probable off-duty locations all were known.

In addition, the State Department had provided the rescue teams with detailed blueprints of every building in the compound so that they would know the precise location of all telephone and electric lines and where to sever them to cut communications.

One rescue group was to have neutralized guards with nonlethal gas and percussion grenades, while another collected the hostages and led them to a football field and a parking lot inside the compound. There, helicopters would be waiting to evacuate them. A simultaneous effort would be undertaken to free the three hostages held in the Iranian Foreign Ministry.

If the rescue helicopters were prevented by enemy fire from landing in the compound, they would put down at Amjadieh Soccer Stadium, just to the east. If necessary, the hostages and their rescuers would fight their way to the stadium to be picked up. No one underestimated the difficulties of such a fight. The noise of the attack was expected to bring Iranian reinforcements quickly. Speed was essential.

The plan was to fly the hostages and rescuers to Damavand, where the helicopters would be abandoned. Then, the Americans would be airlifted out of Iran in C-130 transports.

Though the plan fell apart in the desert, one small touch of success did attend the mission. The agents who had been infiltrated into Iran to assist the raiders were all able to slip out of the country by April 29. Confidential reports from foreign intelligence services indicated, however, that some Iranians who had helped were not so fortunate.

What went wrong? Why did the Carter Administration and the Joint Chiefs of Staff send in only eight helicopters? Was operational security too tight? Why was sensitive intelligence material left in the aircraft abandoned in the desert?

The government's official evaluation was made in a report issued by the Special Operations Review Group, which was appointed by President Carter. The group — described by a senior Air Force general as "about as experienced a bunch as you could assemble: very fair, no axes to grind" — was headed by Adm. James L. Holloway 3d, a former Chief of Naval Operations.

The other members were Lieut. Gen. Samuel V. Wilson, a retired Army officer and former deputy director of the C.I.A. and director of the Defense Intelligence Agency; Air Force Lt. Gen. Leroy J. Manor, who commanded a joint task force that attempted to rescue prisoners from North Vietnam; Maj. Gen. James C. Smith, Army Deputy Chief of Staff for Operations; Maj. Gen. John L. Piotrowski of the Tactical Air Command and Maj. Gen. Alfred M. Gray, a Marine Corps veteran experienced in amphibious operations.

Their report — a short declassified version of which was released a month after the mission — criticized some facets of the rescue plan but was not notable for sharply worded judgments.

In general, it called the plan for the desert rendezvous "soft" in various respects: There were insufficient rehearsals. There was not enough coordination among the armed services. Personnel with "critical functions" were not known to everyone in the mission. Command and control were lax at middle and lower echelons.

And it cited numerous specific problems: There were no messengers in case radios were knocked out. The rendezvous site was too near a busy highway. Communications between Air Force weathermen and operation planners had been poor. Some classified material left in the desert should have been destroyed.

Some military officials gave a harsher view. There were problems right from the start, they said, over what they called an obsession with security by the armed services. Some officers said it had been unrealistic to try to maintain total secrecy in a large group of men throughout a training period that extended over many months, and that the effort to do so had tied the services up in knots.

A former intelligence officer said: "This is an open society. You start to train 15 or 20 helicopter crews and you widen the risk area. You think the Russians don't watch every major base and exercise area in this country? Maybe you can be reasonably sure that 20 servicemen will keep their mouths shut about what they're doing. You double that number and you quadruple the risk. Too many operations have been blown by some smart aleck talking big to show how important he is."

The report by the President's group conceded that "many things, which, in the opinion of the review group, could have been done to enhance success, were not done because of the strict [security] considerations."

Among other things, it cited a lack of sufficient combined exercises by the various armed services. "As complex and difficult as the Desert One scenario was, it had not been fully rehearsed. A training exercise . . . conducted on 13-14 April with two C-130's and four helicopters was used to validate the Desert One concept," it said.

Some officers were critical of the operation's conception and execution, but declined to be specific for fear that talking too much about the Desert One affair could imperil the success of future similar missions.

The same tight security invested in the raid also cloaked a reported training program for a second raid. NBC-TV said that planning for a second attempt began almost immediately after the failure at Desert One, despite the fact that the Iranians had announced they were moving the hostages out of the embassy to a number of other sites in an attempt to frustrate another rescue operation. In July 1980, a chopper being used in the training for a second raid crashed in Monticello, Utah. A mechanic, J. Stuart Schatte, was killed and six other crewmen were injured.

The President's review group, evaluating the raid, said that command and control of the operation were excellent at higher echelons, but were more tenuous and fragile at the intermediate levels and that further down the command structure, "relationships were less defined and not as well understood."

Although the Desert One rendezvous was "feasible," the report said, the risks of compromise on a nearby road between Yazd, a city of 100,000, and Meshed, a city of 500,000, "were high." Many people traveled the road by night because it was too hot during the day. However, the report noted, "no suitable alternative" was available in a relatively remote location.

The report said the failure to destroy classified personnel lists, planning papers and alternative escape routes aboard the helicopters left at Desert One had had no impact on the mission's outcome. But it "resulted in possible enemy exploitation of sensitive material."

Another problem, some officers said, was the decision late in the planning to expand the original Army-Air Force team to include the Navy and the Marine Corps. "On the basis of my experience," said a former Pentagon official, "each service would want a piece of the action, and simply settling who was to do what . . . would be a major problem."

Military criticism of the aborted rescue, however, focused most strongly on the key question of why the helicopter force was so small. Yitzhak Rabin, Israel's former Prime Minister and Army Chief of Staff, voiced the feelings of many in asking, "America doesn't have enough helicopters?"

Defenders of limited air support contended that additional aircraft would have risked discovery by hostile radar. Opponents of this view said the C.I.A. had supplied detailed information about radar sites along Iran's borders and contended that a larger number of helicopters could have avoided detection.

The U.S.S. Nimitz could have carried additional choppers, but did not do so, some experts said, because to make room for them it might have had to divest itself of combat aircraft needed for protection in a dangerous region.

The fuel available at Desert One, an Army officer said, would have sufficed to refuel at least 10 helicopters and, with relatively minor adjustments in loadings, could have refueled up to 15, allowing for a backup force if the first wave of choppers encountered trouble.

Incredible though it may seem in retrospect, the first estimate of the number of helicopters required for the mission was four. The number the President settled on was eight, but, as some military officers wondered, why not 12 or 15? A few civilian experts suggested that 25 could have been deployed without undue risk.

These experts said that breakdowns should have been anticipated, for there were many potential problems: One was the length of the flight to Desert One, over 500 miles. There was also the probability of desert dust storms, and the known vulnerability of helicopters to such harsh conditions.

The report said that more helicopters "would have reduced the risk" of failure. An "unconstrained planner," it said, would have asked for 10 helicopters under Joint Task Force Combat rules, 11 under a "most likely case scenario," based, apparently, on the breakdown of one or more choppers, and 12 if the record of earlier, roughly comparable operations had been consulted.

It is not known whether the mission's planners ever actually asked for more than eight helicopters. The Chairman of the Joint Chiefs of Staff, General Jones, did say the services were "not denied anything by anybody." But that begs the question of whether more helicopters had been sought by the Pentagon.

In general, the report of the Presidential review group said the concept of a small, clandestine operation was "sound" and "capable of execution," and that a larger, overt attempt "would probably have resulted in the death of the hostages before they could be reached."

President Carter, in a subsequent interview, said virtually the same thing. "I thought it was a good rescue plan," he said. "It was the best we could evolve."

But to some military experts, there was a sense that those who planned and executed the raid had "gone by the book," and that the book, as snappy and stiff as a plebe's salute, made no provision for unorthodox responses to the unexpected, real-life snafus that always happen.

6

For America,
a Painful Reawakening

By Steven R. Weisman

For 14½ months, it was a nightmare that preoccupied the nation, shook its confidence and filled its people with frustration. And yet it is almost hard now to remember, much less recapture, the frenzy and emotion the crisis brought forth. It is as if the catharsis of the event has temporarily overwhelmed our ability to consider its impact.

More than anything else, Americans encountered in Iran a symbol of their impotence. A nation yearning to believe in itself again, after Vietnam and Watergate, instead became enmeshed in a struggle with an ancient religious culture whose record of misunderstanding and hostility with the West dates from ancient times.

The hostage crisis illuminated the extent to which the United States could prove itself unable to protect its vital strategic and economic interests, as well as its citizens. It will be remembered further as a lesson in the limitations of force, since an invasion or blockade might have thrown the United States into a confrontation with the Islamic world, strained relations with its allies, jeopardized the West's oil supply, invited Soviet intervention and threatened the lives of the hostages themselves.

But the spectacle of American failure in Iran will long haunt Americans, especially because it was driven home by yet another blow to their self-assurance. For a society that believes almost religiously in technology, the breakdown of three helicopters in a desert dust storm was a bitter setback. Fifteen years ago, the American military failure in Vietnam had spoken of the futility of trying to stop a revolution by force. On the sands of Dasht-e-Kavir Desert, the failure spoke of courage undermined by poor maintenance and planning.

If President Carter had gotten the hostages out, he might well have won re-election. If, on the other hand, he had failed where he succeeded — in negotiating an end to the hostage crisis before leaving office — he would have left his successor with a set of dismal choices that would have changed the character of Ronald Reagan's Presidency.

Historically, however, the Iran crisis is likely to have some less hypothetical effects. Just as the Vietnam War led to new restrictions on a President's ability to commit the United States overseas, the hostage crisis will likely give the President fresh latitude to respond to acts of terrorists. A President in the years ahead may find the nation once again held hostage but less willing to endure 444 days of mostly fruitless negotiations to extricate itself. Americans are likely to demand a policy that falls between the tough, punitive bombing pursued by President Nixon in Vietnam, and the milder, more conciliatory approach of President Carter.

Also, Iran provided Americans a look into the abyss of hatred for America abroad that is going to make it more difficult, especially on an emotional level, for the nation to do future business with the Third World. The hostage crisis reawakened the United States to an old reality: that its good intentions are not enough; that the world is a complex place, even if its complexities are reduced each night to a grotesque television drama — a screeching collision of two cultures fated to misunderstand the righteous indignation and callousness of each other.

Having stared into the face of what it regarded as the embodiment of "evil," America is now probably more likely than ever to assert, free of guilt, the "virtue" of its own self-interest around the globe. The United States could therefore become more distrustful of the demands of the people whose cultures it does not readily understand.

It will be the task of historians to sort out the contradictions of our behavior during the crisis. They are likely to find it odd, for instance, that a nation willing to lose 57,000 lives in Vietnam later became so ob-

228

sessed with saving the lives of a few score men and women that it restrained its response. Historians will also have to account for the fact that what might well have been an occasion for humiliation blossomed instead into a cause for celebration. The hostages returned home to a heroes' welcome made poignant by the simple but awesome heroism of people who did little more than survive with grace and dignity.

In the years ahead, it probably will become clear that America's communal obsession with the fate of the captives helped produce the nation's ineffectual response to their plight. Many experts already believe that a policy of ignoring or de-emphasizing the sense of crisis might have caused the Iranians to lose interest in holding the Americans captive. In any case, the emotional reaction will tell historians much about what kind of nation America was as it headed into the 1980's.

In terms of American attitudes, the Iran crisis never produced a permanent consensus for any course of action — military, diplomatic or economic — to free the hostages. But, according to Daniel Yankelovich and Larry Kaagan, two public-opinion specialists writing in *Foreign Affairs* magazine, 65 percent of the public agreed that the incident, and the way it was handled, decreased American prestige, while 80 percent felt the situation had "brought the American people together and helped unify the nation."

Moreover, Mr. Yankelovich and Mr. Kaagan found that the crisis reinforced changes in attitudes that had already begun. America's renewed interest in building up its military capacity was proceeding well before the hostage crisis, and it probably received its biggest boost in 1979 from the Soviet intervention in Afghanistan in late December, nearly two months after the Americans were seized. Whereas only one out of every nine Americans favored an increase in defense spending at the beginning of the decade, three out of four favored this course by the end of 1980.

As for military moves to free the hostages, surveys of American attitudes can be misleading. In the early part of the crisis, the polls showed that Americans favored "holding off for now" on a military response. By April, after the collapse of a hopeful series of negotiations, it appeared that they were ready to support such a response, and when the raid occurred at the end of that month, most Americans not only backed

229

it but suggested that it should have come sooner. In general, the public appeared to be "far more aggressive and oriented toward risky action than most press or leadership commentators," wrote Mr. Yankelovich and Mr. Kaagan.

But experts on public opinion know also that American attitudes are unpredictable, volatile and, in the end, pragmatic. If a military solution to a future hostage situation were to destroy American lives in a futile attempt to assert American self-righteousness, Americans would no doubt rise up in protest. Indeed, the fateful and fatal landing at Desert One seemed to dampen subsequent demands for action. Even so, support for President Carter's handling of the crisis continued to fall from its peak of nearly 80 percent in the first weeks to 29 percent by the end of June.

After the seizure of the United States Embassy in Teheran on November 4, 1979, President Carter faced a limited set of choices: The use of force might have backfired; for months there was no government with which the United States could negotiate, given the chaos that gripped postrevolutionary Iran. But the difficulty of the choices hardly served to temper the nation's emotional response.

There seem to have been four factors in the release of the emotional torrent. First, the Americans seized were for the most part civilians whose families we grew to know and whose fate we worried about because of a natural sense of kinship with identifiable victims. Second, their captivity offered the American people an unaccustomed opportunity to unite and play the role of aggrieved party in an otherwise ambiguous situation. Third, the national fixation was at least in part a product of the actions of President Carter. And fourth, it was a product of the attention of the news media. Each of these factors needs to be examined if one is to understand the meaning of the American reaction to the events in Iran.

The feeling of kinship is perhaps easiest to comprehend, because it is what came through in the tears of happiness that brought the hostages home. "We knew the victims as individuals," said David Riesman, the Harvard sociologist. "The hostage crisis was similar to a situation in which a community is turned upside down after someone falls into a well or a mine shaft. The victims were like us, and we were able to identify with them."

FOR AMERICA, A PAINFUL REAWAKENING

More subtle than this phenomenon, perhaps, was the self-righteousness that fueled the rage of Americans and sent our diplomats into the World Court and the more amorphous "court of international opinion" in a vain attempt to isolate the Iranians by showing how just was our cause. Rarely does a modern nation have the chance to portray its problems legitimately in a black-and-white context. The American view of Iranians as evil found its echo with nations around the globe who also have a stake in preventing terrorism from poisoning the conduct of international diplomacy and who agreed that the American grievance was real.

But having seen that its cause was right, what purpose was served by the nation becoming mesmerized by its grievance against Iran? Richard Sennett, the New York University sociologist, argued that such an attitude was counterproductive. "The crisis became a symbolic confrontation in which a realistic judgment of the stakes gave way to an exercise in mass hysteria, in which we pursued the thing that yielded the greatest psychic and emotional benefits," he said. "Whereas probably the moment we had said to the Iranians that these people aren't worth it to us, they would have been freed."

Mr. Sennett's assertion is, of course, debatable. Mr. Sennett agreed that it is virtually impossible to imagine any President writing off the hostages, effectively declaring them martyrs in advance, particularly after the news media began their coverage of the captivity.

Certainly, President Carter and his advisers assert in retrospect that they had little choice but to keep the lives of the hostages in mind, balancing their safety against the dictates of the nation's honor, and of demands for potentially disastrous military response. Mr. Carter sought to show the world the importance he attached to the hostages as individuals as his way of preventing their being put on trial or even executed. The President also felt the need to sell to the American people a policy of military restraint that he had settled on for practical reasons.

But the fact is that it also served Mr. Carter's political purposes in his fight for re-election to dwell on the lives of the men and women in Iran, to be seen "acting Presidential" as he visited with their families and kept dim the lights of the White House Christmas tree. Whatever his motives, it seems certain that the American people followed his lead in becoming obsessed with the fate of the hostages.

231

NO HIDING PLACE

The fourth and final factor whipping up American emotions, the behavior of the news media, may be the most complicated.

Despite the drumbeat of Walter Cronkite's nightly countdown and, on another channel, the expanded news of "America Held Hostage," television's coverage of the crisis was at least as much a product of the nation's obsession as it was an instigator; the network news shows all experienced surges in their ratings when the hostage situation came to a boil. But it is also true that when the camera crews were kicked out of Iran, American interest waned. When they were there, demonstrations took place on cue as the cameras whirred, so that each night Americans were absorbed in the spectacle of marching masses, screaming their unintelligible slogans. Surely this presented a distorted picture of the lives of the Iranians, the complexities of their sentiments toward the United States and the painstaking, frustrating task confronting American diplomats. But for most Americans, these demonstrators remained the commanding image of Iran throughout the hostage ordeal.

"Television played it like a soap opera, and made it the greatest soap opera of the year," complained George W. Ball, former Undersecretary of State and onetime adviser on Iran to President Carter, in an interview before the release of the hostages. Referring to the seizure by North Korea of 83 crew members aboard an intelligence ship, Mr. Ball said, "In 1968, when the Pueblo hostages were taken, it was not made into one of the great events of our time. It's true, they were naval personnel, but they were in much worse shape, because they were tortured, and they were kept for nearly a year. Television has played this situation up so that it has become the central issue of American policy, which I think is absurd."

Television executives argue, in response, that the United States Government set the tone from the outset of the hostage drama. "If the Government had nothing public to say, except that it would run things as if no crisis existed and we will negotiate quietly until they're released, the media would not have been able to do anything with the Iran story," says Jeff Gralnick, executive producer of ABC's "World News Tonight."

The news media have been adding drama to events of the day, of course, since the graphic revolution of the 19th century first allowed newspapers to print photographs. The ability of the press to whip up domestic furor about events overseas was classically demonstrated during the Spanish-American War. The question facing the country today is whether the dramatics have taken over, and what sort of relationship there is between reality and the events portrayed on the news each night.

It is important, in recounting the extremes of American emotionalism during the Iran crisis, to remember that certain excesses were avoided. There has been no ugly binge of recriminations over "Who lost Iran?" Although Americans displayed some vindictive feelings toward Iranian nationals in the United States, and Mr. Carter tried to expel many of them, there was no repetition of the brutal treatment of Japanese-Americans that occurred on the West Coast during World War II. There were no rampages of lynch mobs, and during the negotiations there seemed to be a widely shared recognition that Iran was due some concessions. Although the deal to free the hostages was criticized in many quarters, it was allowed to stand, and there have been few cries of retaliation. "What good would just revenge do and what form would that take?" asked President Reagan at his first news conference. "I don't think revenge is worthy of us. On the other hand, I don't think we act as if this never happened."

The hostage drama encompassed two final elements, the rise and fall of Jimmy Carter himself and the culmination of American misunderstanding of Iran itself.

For Mr. Carter, the Middle East became the region of his greatest triumphs and failures. Having succeeded in bringing peace between Israel and Egypt and moving the United States away from its dependence on imported oil, he nonetheless met his destiny in a vendetta with an Iranian regime that saw fit to rebuke him personally by releasing the hostages minutes after he left office. And no one will ever know for sure how much their release was speeded by some comments from Ronald Reagan, calling the Iranians "barbarians" and "common criminals" and suggesting that they might find it tougher to negotiate with *him*.

In a sense, the 444-day hostage crisis encapsulated the arc of Mr. Carter's popularity, with a politically triumphant strategy used skillfully, and sometimes shamelessly, at the outset against his election opponents. In the end, though, it insured that the voters would punish him on

Election Day, November 4, 1980 — one year after the hostages had been seized — for having failed to get them out.

Iran also encompassed the uncertainties of Mr. Carter's foreign policy, which began with a promise to free us of our "inordinate fear" of world Communism and ended high on the battle stations of a renewed cold war. Mr. Carter sought to restore morality by emphasizing human rights, but his policy evidently sent mixed signals to the Shah and shook his faith in our resolve to back him up. In the end, with Iran, Mr. Carter was left to assert a different kind of morality — that of the victim.

The hostage crisis in Iran may not have been what drove Jimmy Carter from office, but it seemed to epitomize the forces that did. And a President who had risen to office because of his mastery of symbolism, achieving its height in his walk down Pennsylvania Avenue on Inauguration Day, met his fate in large measure because Iran had become a symbol of what Americans had come to dislike about their country — its seeming inability to get control of events and serve as the master of its fate.

Yet another image comes to mind when one thinks of Jimmy Carter and Iran — the glittering dinner December 31, 1977, with the Shah and Empress Farah in Teheran, where the President turned to his hosts and declared: "Iran, because of the great leadership of the Shah, is an island of stability in one of the more troubled areas of the world." The President took no note, that New Year's eve, of the anti-Shah demonstrations that had led to still more arrests of Iranian dissidents earlier in the day.

Here was a foreshadowing of American misperception of Iran, although in fairness Mr. Carter was at this moment serving simply as its vessel. How could the United States have evolved from its role as a savior of modern Iran in the ashes of World War II — when President Franklin D. Roosevelt pressed both Joseph Stalin and Winston Churchill to assure its independence as a nation — into a country denounced as a "great Satan," if not without a vast quantity of delusion?

In his book, *Paved With Good Intentions*, Barry Rubin, a Fellow at the Center for Strategic and International Studies at Georgetown University, recounts how, from the beginning, the United States — in its zeal to establish the Shah as its ally in the Persian Gulf — had failed to understand three basic concepts dating from ancient Persian history: the importance to the people that their ruler be religiously pious, a quality more important even than his being democratic or nationalistic; the fact that from the beginning, Iran had never fully succeeded in accommodating the competing claims of secular and religious authority and the fact that throughout Iranian history swirled a tradition of xenophobia and distrust of foreigners.

And so the United States had failed to see how the Shah's modernization program had menaced an ancient religious culture and failed to see — in part because it looked away — the savagery of his domestic persecutions. There was also the failure to learn anything about the elements in Iranian society that had grown weary of the Pahlevi regime.

Public opinion surveys showed later that most Americans blamed the Shah for sowing the seeds of his own downfall, but it took the hostage crisis to drive the point home. Meanwhile, the earlier American failures simply presaged others to come: the willingness to accept assurances from a shaky government that the American Embassy would be protected if the Shah were allowed into the United States; the insistent belief that Iran's secular leaders were capable of concluding a deal to free the hostages; the failure to comprehend how little Iran's religious clerics cared about their country's image in the world, and how the logic favoring release of the hostages was destined to be undermined by internal political disputes.

For its own reasons, America had cast its lot with the Shah of Iran, and perhaps history showed no other course of action for the nation to take. During the hostage crisis, the news media often seemed to mirror the confusion rather than to clarify it, which is understandable in times of turbulence. Now that the hostage crisis is over, though, it is still not clear what lessons the United States has learned. President Reagan has said that the hostages should have been declared "prisoners of war" and that next time the United States will follow a policy of "swift retribution" against terrorists. But how will such a policy be executed?

Already there is talk, in fact, that Iran has become the focus of a sort of selective amnesia that characterized Vietnam. Americans who initially celebrated the end of the hostage crisis later seemed to want to forget it. But this does not mean that it will have no deep effects on the nation's psyche, only that those effects will have to be measured in the light of future developments.

It seems certain that the hostage crisis taught Americans once again that the world is a violent place, filled with people who don't love them after all — a reminder likely to propel the nation to assert its interests with less of a desire to be loved. But only in the years ahead will it become apparent whether the United States has overcome its tendency to alternate between self-flagellation and euphoria and awakened from the Iranian nightmare clear-eyed enough to react rationally to events overseas, without necessarily banishing emotions that in this case brought unity of purpose and, in due time, a sense of joy to the American people.

PART III

The People

Profiles:

The Hostages

Repeatedly, glimpses of the hostages had flickered across television screens. Repeatedly, reporters had interviewed their families in America, their wives and children, their parents.

The impressions of who they were, this disparate group that had become the focus of the nation's attention, inevitably remained blurred as individuals in it were in, then out of, the spotlight.

But, as the nation prepared to welcome them home, its attention focused again on them and their families. Here are brief sketches of the 52 as they were about to be freed:

Thomas Leo Ahern Jr. . . . 48 years old, of Falls Church, Va. . . . listed as narcotics control coordinator on embassy staff . . . one of the Americans accused by Iranian militants of being a spy . . . on December 6, 1979, militants displayed documents, including a forged Belgian passport, a set of instructions detailing the cover to be used, and a set of immigration stamps, all allegedly his . . . 20 years with State Department . . . arrived in Teheran in May 1979 . . . journalism degree from University of Notre Dame, 1954 . . . Army Counter-Intelligence Corps, 1954-60 . . . security officer in Laos embassy in 1960's . . . wife, Gisela; one daughter.

NO HIDING PLACE

Clair Cortland Barnes . . . 35, of Falls Church, Va. . . . a communications expert assigned to the United States Embassy in Teheran.

William E. Belk . . . 44, of West Columbia, S.C. . . . communications and records officer . . . arrived in Iran October 1, 1979 . . . joined State Department in 1974 . . . tours of duty in Thailand, Belgium and the Congo . . . born in Winnsboro, S.C., but grew up in Seattle . . . served two years in the Air Force and 20 years in the Marine Corps . . . wife, Angela; two sons.

Robert Olof Blucker . . . 53 . . . economics officer specializing in oil matters . . . joined Foreign Service in 1957, with assignments in Washington, Buenos Aires, Bonn, Berlin, Lagos and Tripoli . . . speaks German and Spanish . . . volunteered for Iran duty while in Berlin . . . in Teheran one week before embassy was seized . . . worked for Texaco 1954-57 . . . served in Navy 1946-47 and 1951-52 . . . single . . . native of North Little Rock, Ark., where he attended high school . . . bachelor of science degree, chemical engineering, University of Wisconsin, 1954.

Donald Cooke . . . 25, of Memphis . . . vice consul at embassy . . . on first Foreign Service tour . . . joined Foreign Service in November 1978 and was sent to Teheran as vice consul July 1979 . . . single . . . parents, Susan and Ernst F. Cooke . . . born on Long Island but grew up in Cleveland, where he graduated from St. Joseph's High School . . . studied pre-law at Case Western Reserve University for two years, then transferred to Ohio State University, graduating in 1976 with geology degree . . . graduate study in economics at University of Baltimore.

William J. Daugherty . . . 33, whose widowed mother lived in Ossining, N.Y. . . . no official State Department designation . . . attended Tulsa Central High School in Oklahoma, 1963-64, before switching to Oklahoma Military Academy in Claremore, now Claremore Junior College . . . attended Oklahoma State University . . . enlisted in Marines and trained to be pilot . . . later joined State Department . . . arrived at embassy in August 1979 . . . Iranian militants asserted on December 2, 1979, that he admitted being an agent for C.I.A.

PROFILES: THE HOSTAGES

Robert A. Englemann ... 34, of Hurst, Tex. ... lieutenant commander in Navy, whose work as attaché involved sale of surplus Iranian military equipment to other countries, according to relatives ... one week from end of Iran tour when taken hostage ... native of Pasadena, Calif. ... father, Ardo, a retired Air Force major ... psychology graduate, State University of New York at Stony Brook, L.I., 1968 ... sea duty aboard submarines and oiler ... Navy assignments in New York and Philadelphia, where he was involved in sale of arms to Iran while Shah was in power ... single.

Sgt. William Gallegos ... 22-year-old embassy guard of Pueblo, Colo. ... enlisted in the Marine Corps in 1977 and served tour in Okinawa ... sent to Teheran in July 1979 after attending embassy-protection training school in Quantico, Va. ... first hostage interviewed by American correspondents, on NBC News December 10, 1979, five weeks after crisis began ... promoted from corporal while captive ... single ... oldest of four children of Richard and Theresa Gallegos ... grew up in Mexican-American neighborhood of Pueblo, on football and track teams at Pueblo East High School.

Bruce W. German ... 44, of Rockville, Md. ... embassy budget officer ... lived in the Washington area for 19 years before being sent to Teheran five weeks before takeover on what was to be an 18-month assignment ... wife, Margarite; two sons, one daughter.

Duane L. Gillette ... 24, of Columbia, Pa. ... Navy communications and intelligence specialist ... graduated from Hempfield (Pa.) High School ... joined Navy in 1975 ... transferred from Malta to Teheran in July 1979 ... single ... youngest of three children of Ivan and Alberta Gillette.

Alan Bruce Golacinski ... 30, of Silver Spring, Md. ... born in Austria ... a civilian whose title at the embassy was regional security officer ... had been in Teheran four months before the takeover ... single ... became engaged to Jennifer Ross of Miami just before he left for Teheran ... 1972 graduate of University of Maryland with bachelor's degree in criminology ... joined State Department, December 1973 ... tours of

241

duty in Argentina, Chile and Morocco . . . the eldest of five children in "close-knit" family . . . father was an Air Force officer who died when Alan was 16 . . . mother, Pearl, one of several relatives who visited European leaders in efforts to win captives' freedom . . . raised in Morocco, Spain and the United States . . . fluent in Spanish and French.

John Earl Graves . . . 53, of Reston, Va. . . . embassy public affairs officer . . . family was first to break publicly with Carter Administration, issuing an appeal March 4, 1980, that called on United States to apologize to Iran for American actions there . . . master of arts degree, University of Michigan, 1952 . . . joined United States Information Agency (now International Communications Agency) in 1962 . . . served in Vietnam, Zaire, Cameroon, Togo and Madagascar . . . received meritorious service award for duty in the Congo in 1964 . . . promoted to Foreign Service senior inspector in 1973 . . . served in Navy, 1945-46 . . . teacher in United States, 1952-59, and overseas, 1959-62 . . . wife, Bonnie; six grown children.

Warrant Officer Joseph M. Hall . . . 31, who lists Elyria, Ohio, as home . . . assigned to embassy by Army as military attaché . . . arrived in Teheran in August 1979 . . . born in Oklahoma but grew up in Bend, Ore., where he graduated from high school in 1967 . . . enlisted in Army in 1968 . . . has served in Jacksonville, Fla.; Washington, D.C.; Greece and Indonesia . . . wife, Cheri, staying in Washington suburb . . . before takeover, she had been with him on overseas assignments for nine years . . . parents, Zane and Dorothy Hall, live in Little Falls, Minn.

Sgt. Kevin Jay Hermening . . . at 21 the youngest hostage . . . an embassy guard on his first assignment after graduating from Marine Corps Quantico security school in August 1979 . . . Barbara Timm, his mother, visited him in April in Iran although United States Government tried to discourage her from going . . . father, Richard Hermening, of Cudahy, Wis. . . . eldest of five children . . . born in Milwaukee . . . grew up in Oak Creek, Wis., where he graduated from high school in 1977 and joined Marines that year . . . served in Okinawa for 13 months before going to Iran . . . Boy Scout and clarinet player . . . star of the embassy baseball team . . . single.

PROFILES: THE HOSTAGES

Donald R. Hohman ... 38, of West Sacramento, Calif. ... Army medic with rank of Specialist 6 ... re-enlisted in Army six years ago after leaving the service for a year ... transferred from West Germany to the Teheran embassy in August 1979 ... German-born wife, Anna; two sons, two daughters ... attended James Marshall High School in Sacramento.

Col. Leland James Holland ... 53, of Fairfax, Va. ... an Army attaché ... arrived in Teheran in June 1978 for what was to be a three-year tour ... in military intelligence ... served two tours of duty in Army in Vietnam and other tours in West Germany and Italy ... born in Shullsburg, Wis. ... grew up in Scales Mound, Ill., where he graduated from high school in 1945 ... drafted in World War II ... entered seminary in Dubuque, Iowa, in 1949 but left to re-enlist in the Army in 1952 ... family had lived in Iran ... wife, Mary Anne; six children.

Michael Howland ... 34, of Alexandria, Va. ... a member of the embassy security unit who was with L. Bruce Laingen, the chargé d'affaires, and Victor L. Tomseth, senior political officer, in Iranian Foreign Ministry when the embassy was seized.

Charles A. Jones Jr. ... 40, of Detroit ... communications specialist and teletype operator ... went to Teheran from Israel ... only black hostage not released in November 1979 ... previously assigned to posts in Egypt, West Germany, the Congo and France ... born in Memphis in 1940 and his family moved to Detroit when he was 2 ... graduated from high school in 1957 and joined Air Force ... left Air Force in 1962, became an apprentice draftsman and later joined Foreign Service ... wife, Mattie; four daughters.

Malcolm Kalp ... 42, of Fairfax, Va. ... duties at embassy unknown ... accused by Iranian militants of being a C.I.A. agent ... served in Vietnam ... wife, Cheryl; one son.

Moorhead Cowell Kennedy Jr. ... 50, of Washington, D.C. ... a native of New York ... economic and commercial officer and the third-ranking diplomat in embassy ... went to Iran in September 1979 ... an

Islamic law scholar and economics expert . . . attended Groton School and earned B.A. from Princeton, 1952, and law degree from Harvard, 1959 . . . served in Army, 1952-54 . . . worked for the Federal Government, 1954-55 . . . joined State Department in 1959 as an intelligence research specialist . . . previous Foreign Service duty in Middle East . . . speaks Arabic and French . . . posted to Yemen, 1960; Athens, 1962-65; and Beirut, 1965-69 . . . returned to Washington in 1969 to direct office of investment affairs . . . spent a year at War College, 1974-75 . . . commercial consul in Chile in 1975-78 . . . posted to Beirut, 1978-79 . . . wife, Louisa, was co-director and spokesman for the Family Liaison Action Group and led some hostages' relatives on European mission . . . four sons . . . parents, Moorhead Sr. and Anna Kennedy of New York City . . . hobbies sailing, mountain climbing and reading.

William Francis Keough Jr. . . . 50 . . . head of American School in Islamabad, Pakistan . . . was visiting embassy when it was seized . . . went to Iran to collect student records from private, 4,000-student American School in Teheran, of which he had been superintendent, but which was closed after fall of the Shah . . . native of Waltham, Mass. . . . graduate of Boston College . . . former school superintendent in Bedford, Mass.; Burlington, Vt.; and Huntington, L.I. . . . wife, Katherine; two daughters, one son.

Cpl. Steven William Kirtley . . . 22 . . . of Marine Corps, native of Little Rock, Ark. . . . embassy security guard . . . stationed in Teheran since June 1979 . . . single . . . father, Troy, a disabled World War II Army veteran, two of four brothers in Army and one of three sisters in Air Force . . . attended high school in Little Rock.

Kathryn L. Koob . . . 42, of Fairfax, Va. . . . cultural officer in International Communication Agency . . . was director of Iran-America Society, which ran educational and cultural exchange program until it was closed in the Iranian revolution . . . one of two women held throughout the crisis . . . went to Teheran in July 1979 . . . was seized at society's offices and taken to embassy compound to be held with other hostages . . . native of Jesup, Iowa . . . grew up on a farm, one of six daughters of Harold and Elsie Koob . . . teaching degree, 1962, Wartburg College, a Lutheran school in Waverly, Iowa . . . teacher of speech and drama at Newton, Iowa, 1962-68 . . . master's degree, University of Denver, 1969, when she joined United States Information Agency . . . posted to Ivory Coast, Upper Volta, Rumania, Nigeria and Zambia.

Frederick Lee Kupke . . . 34, of Francesville, Ind. . . . an embassy communications officer and electronics specialist . . . part Kiowa Indian . . . born in Meers area of southwestern Oklahoma and attended a Comanche County elementary school . . . attended Cameron University in Lawton, Okla., before joining State Department . . . previously assigned in the Sinai . . . volunteered for duty in Teheran . . . tour in Iran was to have ended November 5, 1979, the day after embassy takeover . . . single . . . son of Arthur and Eleanor Kupke.

Lowell Bruce Laingen . . . 58, of Bethesda, Md. . . . chargé d'affaires and the top United States diplomat in Iran after exile of Shah . . . was at Iranian Foreign Ministry when embassy compound was overrun and was held at ministry until after Christmas 1980 . . . native of Minnesota . . . State Department employee since 1949, serving as vice consul in Hamburg in 1951, political officer in Teheran in 1953, ambassador to Malta, 1976-78, Deputy Assistant Secretary of State for European Affairs, 1973-76, Deputy Assistant Secretary of State for Near Eastern and South Asian Affairs, 1971-73, deputy chief of mission in Afghanistan, 1968-71, and tours in Pakistan, West Germany and Washington as Greece desk officer in 1950's . . . lieutenant junior grade in Navy in World War II . . . saw action in the Philippines. . . . wife, Penelope; three sons . . . B.A. in political science, St. Olaf College, 1947; M.A., University of Minnesota, 1949 . . . studied history, economics and international relations.

Steven M. Lauterbach . . . 29 . . . embassy administrative officer, maintenance . . . in Teheran since April 1979 . . . native of Dayton, Ohio . . . graduated from Chaminade High School in Dayton . . . received bachelor's degree from Bowling Green State University and master's from University of Michigan . . . was a librarian in Fresno, Calif., before joining the State Department in 1978 . . . served in Washington before going to Iran . . . single.

NO HIDING PLACE

Gary Earl Lee ... 37, of Falls Church, Va. ... administrative officer ... went to Iran in spring of 1979 ... coordinated logistics for Presidential visits to the Middle East and for "shuttle diplomacy" carried out by Henry A. Kissinger when he was Secretary of State ... had State Department assignments in Bombay, Madras, Muscat, Damascus and Yemen ... born in New York City and lived as a child in India, where his father, the Rev. Earl Lee, was a missionary ... speaks Hindi and other languages ... joined State Department in 1971 after working for financial corporation ... B.A., Youngstown State University, 1970 ... married, one daughter.

Sgt. Paul Edward Lewis ... 23, of Homer, Ill. ... Marine guard arrived one day before takeover ... graduated in 1975 from Homer High School, where he was on the football and baseball teams and was homecoming king ... enlisted in Marines in 1977 ... served in Budapest before transfer to Teheran ... single ... parents, Gloran and Phillip Lewis ... eldest of four children.

John William Limbert Jr. ... 37, of Washington, D.C. ... political officer assigned to Teheran in summer of 1979 ... joined State Department in June 1973 ... Peace Corps volunteer in Iran, 1964-66 and instructor at Pahlavi University, 1969-72 ... wife, Parvaneh, an Iranian; two children ... bachelor's and master's degrees in Middle East history, 1964 and 1971, from Harvard.

Sgt. James Michael Lopez ... 22, of Globe, Ariz. ... Marine guard was assigned to duty in Iran one month before takeover ... graduated in 1976 from Globe High School, where he played football and played trumpet in school band ... attended Mesa Community College ... enlisted in Marines April 1977, was top recruit in class ... two brothers, one a Marine, and two sisters ... single ... parents, Jesse and Mary.

Sgt. John D. McKeel Jr. ... 27, of Balch Springs, Tex. ... Marine guard ... attended high school in Dallas suburb of Mesquite ... signed up for a second tour of duty in summer of 1979 and attended school for foreign embassy guards, arriving in Teheran little more than a week before takeover.

246

PROFILES: THE HOSTAGES

Michael John Metrinko . . . 34, of Olyphant, Pa. . . . embassy political officer . . . in Iran since 1977 . . . had been United States consul in Tabriz, and was held hostage in his consulate by anti-Shah demonstrators for five days in February 1979, after which the consulate was closed and he moved to Teheran . . . born and reared in Olyphant, near Scranton . . . B.S., Georgetown University, 1968 . . . joined Peace Corps in 1968 and served in Turkey and Iran . . . joined State Department in June 1974 and served in Syria, Greece and Iran . . . fluent in Arabic, Turkish and Persian . . . single . . . two brothers.

Jerry J. Miele . . . 42, of Mount Pleasant, Pa. . . . communications officer . . . joined State Department 18 years earlier . . . assigned to Teheran in March 1979 . . . graduate of Hurst High School in Mount Pleasant . . . served in Navy . . . single . . . mother in Mt. Pleasant, about 30 miles southeast of Pittsburgh.

Staff Sgt. Michael E. Moeller . . . 31 . . . head of Marine guard unit at embassy since July 1979 . . . directed shredding of classified material . . . born in Loup City, Neb. . . . nine years in Marines . . . posted to Iran after two years at American Embassy in Islamabad, Pakistan . . . met his wife, Elisa, when he was training Marines at Camp Pendleton and she was working in the post exchange . . . two daughters.

Bert C. Moore . . . 45, of Mount Vernon, Ohio . . . volunteered for post of embassy administrative consul and was posted to Teheran in July 1979 . . . Iranian militants accused him of being a member of intelligence unit at embassy . . . in Foreign Service since May 1961 . . . formerly stationed in Canada, Rhodesia, Washington, Zaire and France, where he worked for the Organization for Economic Cooperation and Development . . . B.S., Ohio State University, 1957, and master's in public administration, Syracuse University, 1972 . . . wife, Marjorie; one daughter, three sons.

Richard H. Morefield . . . 51, of San Diego . . . consul general in Teheran since arriving in July 1979 . . . joined State Department in 1956 . . . consular tours in Colombia, Oslo, Montevideo and Bogotá . . . served in Army, 1951-53, promoted to first lieutenant . . . wife, Dorothea; one daughter, four sons ... fifth son was shot in Alexandria, Va., in 1976 in a robbery at a restaurant where he worked ... bachelor of science degree, University of San Francisco, 1951, and master's degree, University of California, 1956.

Capt. Paul M. Needham Jr. ... 30 ... Air Force logistics officer ... from Bellevue, Neb. ... former wife and two sons in Wayne Township, near Dayton, Ohio ... on temporary assignment from the International Logistics Center at Wright-Patterson Air Force Base, Dayton, to give assistance to Iranian Air Force.

Robert C. Ode ... at 65, the oldest hostage ... retired from Foreign Service, September 30, 1975, with more than 34 years of service ... occasionally called up on temporary assignment ... on October 3, 1979, sent to Teheran for 45-day tour of duty as special consular official ... previous State Department assignments in Poland, Britain, Iceland, Canada, West Germany, Switzerland, Italy and Liberia ... in Navy in World War II ... worked in sales for a chemical company ... sent letters to newspapers, relatives and the White House, describing conditions in the captured embassy and called for "prompt action to free us from this terrible situation" ... wife, Rita, moved from Falls Church, Va., to a retirement home the couple had chosen in Sun City West, Ariz.

Sgt. Gregory A. Persinger ... celebrated 23d birthday on Christmas Day, 1980 ... from Seaford, Del. ... joined Marines in 1976 ... volunteered to be Marine guard when re-enlisting and was assigned to embassy in August 1979 ... single ... three brothers, one sister.

Jerry Plotkin ... 47, of Sherman Oaks, Calif. ... private businessman on his first trip outside the United States ... arrived in Teheran in October 1979, "seeking business opportunities," according to his lawyer, Steven Klein ... was visiting embassy when it was seized ... born in New York City, lived in California for 18 years ... a distributor of notions and household items until mid-1979, when Mr. Plotkin established his own business to recruit for jobs abroad, according to his lawyer ... wife, Deborah; no children.

PROFILES: THE HOSTAGES

Master Sgt. Regis Ragan . . . 38, of Johnstown, Pa. . . . had been a guard at embassy since 1974 . . . previously served in the Army in West Germany and Vietnam, where he won Bronze Star and other decorations . . . son of Mrs. Martin J. Ragan.

Lieut. Col. David Roeder . . . 41, of Alexandria, Va. . . . deputy Air Force attaché . . . in Teheran a week and at his post only three days when embassy seized . . . 19 years in Air Force . . . flew more than 100 combat missions in Vietnam . . . Iranian militants called him a "war criminal" because of his Vietnam missions . . . wife, Susan; one son, one daughter . . . grew up in Whitefish Bay, Wis., where his father was an assistant high school principal . . . Eagle Scout and football player in high school . . . was in Reserve Officer Training Corps at DePauw University in Greencastle, Ind. . . . graduated from DePauw in 1961.

Barry Rosen . . . 36, of Brooklyn . . . press attaché . . . lived in Iran in 1960's while in Peace Corps, returned in November 1978 . . . referred to by militants as "a famous spy and plotter" . . . wife, Barbara, was among four relatives of hostages who visited European leaders in April 1980 . . . son and daughter.

William Blackburn Royer Jr. . . . 49, of West University Place, near Houston, Tex.. . . . a teacher who worked in Middle East since 1963 . . . was sent to Iran in September 1979 as director of the Iran-America Society . . . seized at the society offices and taken to embassy by the militants . . . had served in education administration and cultural posts in Saudi Arabia and Morocco for United States Information Agency, which he joined in 1967, and its successor, International Communications Agency . . . served in Navy, 1951-55 . . . single . . . B.A., University of Texas, 1961 . . . spent next two years managing the bookstore there.

Col. Thomas E. Schaefer . . . 50, of Tacoma, Wash. . . . Air Force attaché at embassy . . . born in Rochester, N.Y. . . . a bomber pilot in Vietnam . . . vice wing commander of the Fifth Bombing Wing at Minot Air Force Base in North Dakota . . . joined Air Force 30 years ago and is a graduate of Squadron Officer School, Air Command and Staff College and Air War College . . . commissioned as a second lieutenant in June

1953 . . . served with the Strategic Air Command throughout the country . . . B.S. in business administration, Lehigh University, 1953, and master's in public administration from George Washington University . . . attended high school in Pennsylvania . . . assigned to Iran in 1978 for three-year tour . . . wife, Anita, in Falls Church, Va.; two sons.

Col. Charles Wesly Scott . . . 48, of Stone Mountain, Ga. . . . Army officer assigned to Teheran as a military attaché in 1979 . . . on second tour of duty in Iran when embassy was seized . . . had been an Army attaché in first tour, 1965-66 . . . served in Vietnam and as commander of an infantry battalion with the First Infantry Division, Fort Riley, Kan., 1971-73, and with the Defense Intelligence Agency . . . named readiness coordinator for the Army Reserve in 1977, and was chief of Plans Division with the Army Forces Command, Fort McPherson, Atlanta . . . holds Silver Star, Bronze Star with oak leaf cluster . . . B.A., Benedictine College, in Atchison, Kan., 1969 . . . wife, Elizabeth Kelley Scott; one son, one daughter.

Cmdr. Donald A. Sharer . . . about 40 . . . Navy pilot of Chesapeake, Va. . . . duties at embassy unknown . . . in Iran since April 1979 . . . grew up in Plainfield, Ind., a suburb of Indianapolis, and was captain of Plainfield High School football team and president of the senior class . . . graduated from Indiana University in 1963 with a bachelor of science degree in management and administration . . . wife, Frances, in Chesapeake, Va.

Sgt. Rodney Virgil Sickmann . . . 23, of Krakow, Mo. . . . guard at embassy . . . assigned to Teheran in October 1979 . . . joined Marines three years earlier and served in Okinawa and on aircraft carriers in Mediterranean before volunteering for guard duty . . . a high school football star . . . known as "Rocky" . . . single.

Staff Sgt. Joseph Subic Jr. . . . 23, of Redford Township, Mich. . . . military policeman . . . formerly of Bowling Green, Ohio . . . joined Army at 17 after leaving school . . . single . . . father, a machinist, a retired Army sergeant.

PROFILES: THE HOSTAGES

Elizabeth Ann Swift ... 40, of Washington, D.C. ... chief of embassy's political section ... accused by captors of taking part in intelligence work ... believed to be ranking official in the embassy at time of takeover ... one of two women detained after others were released ... born in Washington, where her mother, Helen, resides ... joined Foreign Service in 1963, with assignments in Philippines, Washington and Indonesia, where she was one of the few Americans to speak the language ... also served with the State Department's Congressional relations team ... single ... graduate of Radcliffe, 1962.

Victor Lloyd Tomseth ... 39, native of Springfield, Ore. ... senior political officer ... originally held at the Foreign Ministry with L. Bruce Laingen, the chargé d'affaires, and Michael Howland, a security officer ... had served in the consulate in Shiraz, Iran, before it was closed ... joined Foreign Service in 1967 and served 1968-71 in Thailand, where he met his wife, Wallapa, in Bangkok, where she grew up ... posted to Iran in 1975 ... served in Nepal with Peace Corps ... fluent in Nepalese, Thai and Persian ... one son, one daughter ... 1959 graduate of Springfield High School ... bachelor's degree in history from University of Oregon, 1963, and M.A., University of Michigan, 1966.

Phillip R. Ward ... 40, of Culpepper, Va., administrative officer ... accused by militants of taking part in intelligence work ... joined the State Department in 1972, and worked as a telecommunications technician in Manila ... wife, Connie; one son.

251

CHRONOLOGY

January 16, 1979 — The Shah of Iran, Mohammed Riza Pahlevi, leaves Iran for Egypt, accompanied by his wife, Empress Farah Diba. Iran has been torn by rioting and political unrest for months, and the move is seen by the world as one into exile for the leader. He does not admit this in his departing speech, however. Having recently appointed a new civilian government headed by his longtime political enemy, Shaphur Bakhtiar, the Shah says: "I hope the government will be able to make amends for the past and also succeed in laying the foundation for the future."

January 22, 1979 — The Shah and Empress fly from Egypt to Marrakesh, Morocco, at the reportedly reluctant invitation of King Hassan II. In Washington, Ambassador Ardeshir Zahedi of Iran announces that the Shah will delay a planned visit to the United States. Mr. Zahedi says that despite an official "welcome signal" he is convinced that the United States does not want the Shah to visit.

January 23, 1979 — Sources in Cairo say the Shah has accepted an invitation from Egyptian President Anwar el-Sadat, to take up residence in Cairo after his visit to Morocco.

January 27, 1979 — The Shah receives a private message from Secretary of State Cyrus Vance telling him he is still welcome to come to the United States.

January 31, 1979 — Ayatollah Ruhollah Khomeini, the Shah's bitterest political enemy, returns triumphantly to Iran from exile in France. He begins the process of dismantling the Shah's government and transforming Iran into an "Islamic Republic."

February 14, 1979 — A mob storms the U.S. Embassy in Teheran and takes about a hundred Americans there hostage. Within a few hours, however, two senior ministers of the Ayatollah Khomeini's new government persuade the mob to release the hostages and leave the embassy compound.

February 15, 1979 — The Shah and his family leave Marrakesh for a stay in a government guest house in Rabat, Morocco. the Moroccan Government announces on this same day that it will recognize the new Iranian Government set up by Ayatollah Khomeini.

February 22, 1979 — President Sadat renews his offer of Egyptian asylum for the former Shah.

March 6, 1979 — The former Shah says, in an interview for ABC television, that he has no intention of abdicating the Iranian throne.

The new Iranian Government says it will try the Shah in absentia for crimes he committed during his reign.

March 14, 1979 — David D. Newsom, the American Undersecretary of State for Political Affairs, contacts David Rockefeller, one of the former Shah's most influential American friends, to tell him that the Carter Administration feels it might be dangerous to admit the former ruler to the United States at this time.

Around this time, Mr. Newsom also calls former Secretary of State Henry Kissinger, another friend of the former Shah, to ask him to dissuade the Shah from visiting the United States. Dr. Kissinger refuses the request.

March 29, 1979 — A U.S. Government official says that the Carter Administration is willing to help the former Shah find a place of refuge, and that he is still welcome to come to the United States despite the problems his presence might create.

March 30, 1979 — The former Shah and his family fly from Morocco to the Bahamas for an extended stay at the Paradise Island home of James Crosby, chairman of the board of Resorts International. This visit was quickly arranged by David Rockefeller and his aide Robert Armao after Moroccan leaders indicated they would like the exiled Shah to leave their country.

April 6, 1979 — Henry Kissinger calls National Security Adviser Zbigniew Brzezinski to press for American asylum for the former Shah. Mr. Brzezinski says he agrees with Dr. Kissinger's request and suggests that Dr. Kissinger speak to President Carter.

April 7, 1979 — Dr. Kissinger calls President Carter, who says he is not opposed to the idea of giving the Shah asylum, but that Secretary of State Vance believes it might be dangerous.

April 9, 1979 — David Rockefeller visits President Carter to press the asylum issue. He later says the President's reaction was "stiff and formal."

Henry Kissinger says in a speech that the United States must stop treating the exiled Shah like "a flying Dutchman looking for a port of call."

Soon after this, Dr. Kissinger and Mr. Rockefeller begin trying to arrange alternative refuge for the former Shah. Dr. Kissinger speaks to President José López Portillo of Mexico, and Mr. Rockefeller to Chancellor Bruno Kreisky of Austria.

May 13, 1979 — The head of Iran's Revolutionary Court says that the former Shah and his family are considered to be under death sentences and that anyone who assassinates them would be considered to be "carrying out the people's verdict."

May 17, 1979 — Engelad Birang, a newspaper in Qum, Iran, offers an all-expenses-paid pilgrimage to Mecca to anyone who murders the former Shah.

May 25, 1979 — President Sadat reiterates his offer of asylum for the exiled royal family.

May 31, 1979 — Airport officials in Nassau, the Bahamas, report that the former Shah and Empress left secretly for Costa Rica on May 30. Costa Rican officials deny any knowledge of their presence. However, police guards at the house of James Crosby on Paradise Island say the former Shah will leave the Bahamas on June 1 for an undisclosed destination, and that his children flew to California on May 26.

June 1, 1979 — The government of Mexico announces it has authorized the former Shah to visit Mexico on a tourist visa valid for three months.

June 10, 1979 — The former Shah and Empress fly from the Bahamas to Mexico City.

June 11, 1979 — State Department officials disclose that both the State Department and Henry Kissinger have asked Mexico to allow the Shah to visit.

June 13, 1979 — In Cuernavaca, Mexico, where he is staying in a guarded mansion, the former Shah holds his first full-scale news conference since leaving Iran, and says he is leaving it "to Providence" whether or not he escapes assassination or ever returns to Iran. He says also that Iran is "destroying itself."

June 16, 1979 — Iran announces it has dispatched an "assassination squad" to Mexico to kill the former Shah.

June 27, 1979 — An Iranian official and some Mexican newspapers report that the former Shah has been wounded in an unsuccessful assassination attempt. This is denied by a spokesman for the former ruler.

July 13, 1979 — Former President Richard M. Nixon visits the Shah in Mexico.

July 20, 1979 — Representatives of the Shah are reported to be looking at a New York City townhouse or a Connecticut estate for the former Shah in anticipation of his eventual move to the United States.

The State Department says again that the entry of the former Shah into the United States at this time would present a threat to the security of Americans living in Iran.

August 10, 1979 — President Carter receives a letter from Ashraf Pahlevi, twin sister of the former Shah, asking that her brother be allowed to enter the United States and mentioning "the quite noticeable impairment of his health in Mexico."

August 18, 1979 — Ashraf Pahlevi receives a letter from Deputy Secretary of State Warren Christopher in response to her letter to the President. The letter stresses the efforts of the Carter Administration to reach better relations with the new Iranian regime, but says "serious and sympathetic consideration" is being given to the idea of eventual American asylum for the former Shah.

September 29, 1979 — A serious deterioration in the health of the former Shah, who has lost 20 pounds and become jaundiced, leads Robert Armao and Joseph Reed, two aides to David Rockefeller who have been serving the Shah in exile, to call Dr. Benjamin H. Kean to Mexico to examine the former ruler. Dr. Kean, a specialist in malaria and tropical disease, looks at the former ruler, but is not told that he has been under treatment for cancer for the past six years.

October 16, 1979 — On a second visit to Mexico to examine the former Shah, Dr. Kean is told of the Shah's medical condition and history. He and the exiled ruler discuss possible places of treatment.

Joseph Reed calls David Newsom and tells him the former Shah has cancer of the lymph system, and that Dr. Kean has proposed that he be admitted to the New York Hospital-Cornell Medical Center for full treatment.

In light of this news, President Carter discusses the situation with his top foreign-policy advisers. He asks Cyrus Vance to double-check the medical information and sound out the current Iranian regime about allowing the former Shah into the United States, but says that if the former Shah's medical condition warrants it he will have to be allowed to enter the United States on humanitarian grounds.

October 21, 1979 — President Carter receives a memorandum from Cyrus Vance confirming the reports of the former Shah's condition. On reading this, he makes the decision to allow the former ruler to enter the United States for treatment.

Bruce Laingen, American chargé d'affaires in Iran, and Henry Precht, the State Department's Iranian desk officer, inform the Iranian Government that the former Shah will be flown to the United States the next day. The Iranian officials express dissatisfaction with the news but say they will see to it that the U.S. Embassy is protected.

October 22, 1979 — The former Shah is flown secretly to New York City for treatment and tests at the New York Hospital-Cornell Medical Center.

October 26, 1979 — Dr. Hibbard E. Williams, chief physician at New York Hospital-Cornell Medical Center, says that the former Shah might have to stay at the hospital for as long as a year.

A group of about 80 Iranian students gathers in the mountains near Teheran and plans to take over the U.S. Embassy in Teheran in protest of what they see as a scheme to allow the former Shah exile in the United States.

November 1, 1979 — Zbigniew Brzezinski, in Algiers for Algerian Independence Day celebrations, meets with Iranian Prime Minister Mehdi Bazargan and Foreign Minister Ibrahim Yazdi. The three men hold a tense discussion about the former Shah's presence in New York.

November 4, 1979 — Iranian students storm the U.S. Embassy in Teheran, seize its occupants as hostages, and vow to stay there until the former Shah is returned to Iran to stand trial.

November 5, 1979 — Religious leaders in Iran voice support for the seizure of the embassy and call for the severance of ties with the United States.

November 6, 1979 — Militants holding the hostages vow to kill them if the United States attempts a military rescue.

Mehdi Bazargan, Prime Minister of Iran, resigns because of the powerlessness of the civilian government there.

November 9, 1979 — The U.S. Government stops a shipment of $300 million worth of military spare parts to Iran.

The United Nations Security Council calls on the militants to release the hostages.

November 10, 1979 — Abolhassan Bani-Sadr is named Foreign Minister of Iran. He voices support for the takeover of the U.S. Embassy.

November 12, 1979 — President Carter orders an immediate cutoff of oil imports from Iran. Iranian Oil Minister Ali Akbar Moinfar says that the Iranian Revolutionary Council had already decided to halt oil shipments to the United States.

November 13, 1979 — The Justice Department orders a crackdown on Iranian students in the United States.

November 14, 1979 — President Carter orders the freezing of all Iranian assets in American banks after an Iranian attempt to withdraw its funds from American banks and their overseas branches.

November 17, 1979 — Ayatollah Khomeini orders the release of women and blacks being held at the U.S. Embassy in Teheran. He says Islam holds women in high regard, and that blacks are oppressed in America.

CHRONOLOGY

November 18, 1979 — Three hostages — two blacks and a woman — are released from captivity.

Ayatollah Khomeini says that unless the Shah is returned to Iran for trial, the American hostages will be tried as spies.

November 20, 1979 — Ten more hostages — four white women and six black men — are released from captivity. Two white women and a black man remain in captivity, presumably because they are suspected of having been spies.

November 22, 1979 — Five non-American hostages are released from the U.S. Embassy in Teheran.

Ayatollah Khomeini endorses the students' threat to kill the hostages if the United States attempts a military rescue mission.

November 23, 1979 — Foreign Minister Abolhassan Bani-Sadr announces that Iran will repudiate all foreign debts, estimated at $15 billion, but later shows journalists a list of debts, some of which he says will be honored and some not.

November 28, 1979 — Abolhassan Bani-Sadr is ousted as Foreign Minister of Iran. Sadegh Ghotbzadeh, director of state television and a longtime intimate of Ayatollah Khomeini, is named to the post.

November 29, 1979 — The government of Mexico, which had previously said it would welcome the former Shah back, announces it will not allow the former Shah to return there.

White House counsel Lloyd Cutler flies secretly to New York City to speak with the former Shah and Empress about alternative asylum arrangments.

The United States petitions the International Court of Justice at The Hague for an urgent hearing and a speedy judgment that Iran must free the American hostages immediately.

December 2, 1979 — The former Shah is flown from New York City to Wilford Hall, the major U.S. Air Force medical facility, in San Antonio, Tex. This marks the first time since his arrival in the United States that he has used U.S. government facilities and the first time that the United States has assumed open responsibility for him.

December 3, 1979 — The Shah is moved from Wilford Hall to a suite of apartments adjoining Lackland Air Force Base in Texas.

December 4, 1979 — The United Nations Security Council unani-

259

mously adopts a strong resolution urging immediate release of the hostages.

Iranian Foreign Minister Sadegh Ghotbzadeh says the hostages will be tried as spies and judged by their student captors.

December 8, 1979 — Iran announces plans to form an international panel to "review the dossier of crimes by the United States Government in Iran" since the 1953 C.I.A.-backed coup which restored the Shah to power.

December 10, 1979 — The International Court of Justice holds a hearing on the hostage issue. Iran does not send a representative to the hearing, but sends a telegram saying that the Court has no jurisdiction in the case.

December 11, 1979 — Hamilton Jordan, White House Chief of Staff, flies secretly to Panama to ask Gen. Omar Torrijos to provide asylum for the former Shah. General Torrijos agrees to allow the former ruler to enter the country.

December 12, 1979 — The United States orders the expulsion of most Iranian diplomats in this country; the Iranian Embassy staff must be reduced from 60 to 15 persons, and staffs at four Iranian consulates around the country must also be cut down.

December 13, 1979 — President Carter says the national Christmas tree will remain dark until the hostages are free.

December 15, 1979 — Mohammed Riza Pahlevi leaves the United States for exile in Panama, following secret discussions between Hamilton Jordan and Gen. Omar Torrijos.

A spokesman for the students holding the U.S. Embassy in Teheran says that as a result of the former Shah's departure from the United States, spy trials for the hostages will "definitely begin."

December 18, 1979 — President Carter writes to Panama's President Aristedes Royo that he hopes the Shah's stay in Panama will facilitate a solution to the crisis.

December 21, 1979 — President Carter announces that the United States has decided to seek economic sanctions against Iran in the United Nations Security Council.

December 25-26, 1979 — The Soviet Union invades Afghanistan.

December 28, 1979 — The United States decides to defer its request for U.N.-sponsored sanctions against Iran, and instead to ask U.N. Secretary General Kurt Waldheim to travel to Iran to negotiate a release of the hostages.

December 30, 1979 — Kurt Waldheim announces that the Iranian Government has accepted a proposal for him to travel to Iran to attempt to negotiate a settlement of the crisis.

December 31, 1979 — The U.N. Security Council votes to give Iran one week to release the American hostages. If this deadline is not met, the Council says it will meet again to impose economic sanctions on Iran. Kurt Waldheim flies to Teheran.

January 3, 1980 — In his State of the Union address, President Carter says the United States is prepared to go to war if necessary to protect the oil supply routes of the Persian Gulf.

January 4, 1980 — Kurt Waldheim ends a troubled visit to Iran, and warns against any hope for a quick release of the hostages.

During this visit Mr. Waldheim had attended a meeting of the Iranian Revolutionary Council at which he had seriously misstated a previously agreed-upon American negotiating plan. He accepted the idea of establishing a United Nations Commission to investigate conditions in Iran under the Shah before the release of the hostages, rather than after.

January 13, 1980 — A U.N. Security Council vote to impose economic sanctions on Iran is vetoed by the Soviet Union.

January 19, 1980 — Hamilton Jordan meets secretly in London with French lawyer Christian Bourguet and businessman Hector Villalón. These men had been referred to Mr. Jordan by Panamanian leader Omar Torrijos as being close to the Iranian regime and therefore likely go-betweens for negotiations.

January 25, 1980 — Abolhassan Bani-Sadr, considered a moderate on the hostage issue, is elected to the presidency of Iran.

Christian Bourguet and Hector Villalón meet at the White House with Administration officials to present an Iranian proposal that the United States agree to an investigation by a U.N. Commission prior to release of the hostages. If this is done, they say, Iran would allow the commission to visit all the hostages.

January 29, 1980 — Canadian and American officials announce that six American diplomats had been hidden by Canadian Embassy officials in Teheran for two months and escaped the previous weekend (January 26-27), using Canadian passports.

February 6, 1980 — Iranian President Abolhassan Bani-Sadr condemns the students holding the American hostages as "children" who behave like "a government within a government."

February 7, 1980 — President Bani-Sadr demands, and receives, authority to deal officially with the militant students holding the hostages.

February 9, 1980 — Hamilton Jordan and Assistant Secretary of State Harold Saunders meet again with Christian Bourguet and Hector Villalón, this time in Bern, Switzerland. At this time, the four men work out a complete scenario for ending the hostage crisis. Mr. Bourguet confers by phone with Sadegh Ghotbzadeh and says the scenario is acceptable to the Iranian Government.

February 11, 1980 — Iran's Revolutionary Council asks Ayatollah Khomeini to approve a compromise plan that calls for the release of the hostages without a commitment by the United States to turn over the former Shah for trial. President Bani-Sadr tells a reporter that the hostages might be released soon, "perhaps even in the next few days" if the proposal is accepted by Ayatollah Khomeini.

February 12, 1980 — President Bani-Sadr says that the holding of the hostages and the return of the former Shah are two distinct issues which "must not be connected."

February 13, 1980 — President Carter announces that the United States has accepted a U.N. proposal for an international committee to investigate Iran's charges against the former Shah, and hopes that this will lead to the release of the hostages.

President Bani-Sadr says Ayatollah Khomeini has approved a secret plan for the release of the hostages.

February 14, 1980 — President Bani-Sadr says the hostages could be released within 48 hours if President Carter agrees to conditions approved by Ayatollah Khomeini.

February 16, 1980 — Hamilton Jordan meets with Sadegh Ghotbzadeh in Paris. The meeting had been arranged by Christian Bourguet and Hector Villalón. Mr. Ghotbzadeh says that the Iranian Government agrees to the release scenario worked out last week, and that Ayatollah Khomeini has approved it as well.

February 17, 1980 — Kurt Waldheim names a five-member U.N. Commission of Inquiry on Iran.

February 18, 1980 — U.N. officials say that the hostages must be released within a specific time frame or the newly formed Commission of Inquiry on Iran will abandon its work.

February 19, 1980 — Ayatollah Khomeini delegates supreme command of Iran's armed forces to President Bani-Sadr.

February 20, 1980 — Ayatollah Khomeini tells the Iranian people in a speech that they should not be satisfied until the former Shah is returned to Iran for trial.

February 23, 1980 — Ayatollah Khomeini announces that it will be left to the Iranian Parliament, not yet elected, to decide on the release of the hostages.

The U.N. Commission of Inquiry arrives in Teheran.

February 24, 1980 — Iran's leaders promise cooperation with the U.N. Commission of Inquiry, but begin to suggest that the commission can play no role in release of the hostages.

February 27, 1980 — Ayatollah Mahmoud Beheshti, a member of Iran's Revolutionary Council, says that President Bani-Sadr's attempts to speed release of the hostages are a "personal and private idea" and that the President has no authority on the matter. He suggests that the Iranian Parliament will not be ready to discuss the hostage issue until May.

March 3, 1980 — With a promised visit with the American hostages stalled by disagreements, the U.N. Commission of Inquiry says it will finish tomorrow with the first part of its mandate — its investigation into Iranian charges against the former Shah and the United States — and will be ready to go on with the second part — an attempted negotiation of the hostage issue.

March 6, 1980 — In a surprise announcement, the students holding the U.S. Embassy in Teheran say that "our responsibility is over for the hostages" and that they will turn the hostages over to the Revolutionary Council.

The U.N. Commission of Inquiry, which had been prepared to leave Iran without a visit to the hostages, stays on in hopes of a meeting.

March 10, 1980 — After several days of confusion over a possible transfer of custody of the hostages, Ayatollah Khomeini rules that the U.N. Commission of Inquiry not be permitted to see all the hostages unconditionally. He says the members of the commission should be allowed to see only those hostages said by the students to be linked to grievances against the former Shah, and adds that if the commission issues its report on the crimes of the former Shah while it is still in Teheran, it will be allowed a visit to all the hostages. This is unacceptable to the United States.

March 11, 1980 — The U.N. Commission of Inquiry leaves Iran without having visited the hostages.

March 12, 1980 — Ayatollah Beheshti says that the return of the former Shah and his wealth to Iran is still a necessary condition for release of the hostages.

March 14, 1980 — Two days of parliamentary elections in Iran begin.

March 20, 1980 — Christian Bourguet arrives in Panama with the final Iranian documentation necessary to persuade Panama to arrest the deposed Shah.

The Shah, who has become increasingly fearful of arrest by Panamanian authorities and disturbed by a medical disagreement over his treatment, finally agrees to accept President Sadat's longstanding offer of Egyptian asylum.

March 21, 1980 — Ashraf Pahlevi again writes to President Carter, this time urging him to permit the Shah to come back to the United States for an operation to remove his spleen. In response, the President writes to her that the Shah may have the operation in Houston if he desires.

In Panama, Lloyd Cutler tells the Shah that he may return to the United States but urges him to abdicate the throne before doing so. The Shah refuses.

March 23, 1980 — The Shah leaves Panama for Egypt, only 24 hours before the Iranian Government was to formally request his extradition. Sadegh Ghotbzadeh pleads with the Panamanian government to prevent him from leaving, but General Torrijos refuses.

April 1, 1980 — As part of a revised scenario for winning freedom for the hostages, worked out in the aftermath of the Shah's departure from Panama, Abolhassan Bani-Sadr says that the Revolutionary Council will take control of the hostages if the United States formally promises not to say or do anything hostile to Iran until after the Iranian Parliament decides what to do about the hostages. President Carter goes on national television early this morning (which is also the day of the Wisconsin Presidential primary) to announce this "positive step."

To follow up these announcements, a message is delivered to Washington that if President Carter agrees to recognize the right of the Iranian Parliament to decide the hostages' fates, they will be transferred to the control of the government. President Carter replies, acknowledging the competence of the Parliament to make the decision, through the Swiss Embassy, but this message does not arrive until the Swiss Embassy in Teheran has closed for the day. President Bani-Sadr, fearful that pursuing this plan will create problems with the Ayatollah Khomeini, vents his anger at the United States in an interview.

April 2, 1980 — President Bani-Sadr says President Carter has agreed to refrain from hostile statements and threats for the time being.

April 4, 1980 — Iran's government reportedly stops all discussion of the transfer of hostages to control of the Revolutionary Council, because of opposition from the hard-line Islamic Republican Party.

April 7, 1980 — Ayatollah Khomeini rules that the hostages must remain in the hands of their student captors until the Parliament decides their fate.

President Carter, in response, breaks diplomatic relations with Iran, orders all Iranian diplomats out of the United States within 24 hours and imposes a formal trade embargo. He says also that he will ask Congress to allow Americans to settle claims against Iran by drawing on Iran's frozen assets.

April 9, 1980 — Students holding the hostages vow to "destroy all the hostages immediately" if the United States begins "even the smallest military action against Iran."

April 10, 1980 — Foreign ministers of the European Common Market countries decline to impose economic sanctions on Iran, but issue a joint statement of condemnation of Iran for its continued holding of the hostages.

April 11, 1980 — President Carter secretly gives approval to a rescue mission for the hostages which has been discussed and planned for since November 1979.

April 17, 1980 — President Carter imposes a ban on travel by U.S. citizens to Iran. He also prohibits payments "to any person or entity in Iran" by anyone subject to U.S. jurisdiction, and asks for other sanctions. At his news conference he says that "some sort of military action" seems to be the only answer to the hostage situation.

April 18, 1980 — Barbara and Kenneth Timm, mother and stepfather of hostage Kevin Hermening, fly to Teheran in defiance of President Carter's travel ban.

April 21, 1980 — Barbara Timm is allowed to visit her son, Kevin Hermening, for 45 minutes. The United States says it will not prosecute Mr. and Mrs. Timm for going to Iran because they began their trip before the travel restrictions were printed officially, but the families of other hostages are urged to abide by the ban.

April 22, 1980 — Common Market foreign ministers, in reaction to President Carter's dissatisfaction with their previous actions, agree to impose phased economic and political sanctions on Iran between now and May 17 unless "decisive progress" is made toward release of the hostages.

April 23, 1980 — Japan announces it will join in the new Common Market moves, but urges President Carter not to take military action in Iran.

April 25, 1980 — At 1 A.M. the White House announces that a secret rescue mission had been canceled after equipment failure in the Iranian desert. During withdrawal from the area a helicopter collided with a C-130 transport plane and eight crew members were killed. Several others were injured.

April 26, 1980 — Students holding the American hostages say their captives have been removed from the U.S. Embassy compound and will be scattered throughout Iran in an attempt to prevent future rescue missions.

April 28, 1980 — Secretary of State Cyrus Vance, who opposed the secret rescue mission, resigns from his post.

April 29, 1980 — Senator Edmund S. Muskie is named to succeed Cyrus Vance as Secretary of State.

April 30, 1980 — Three armed men seize the Iranian Embassy in London, take its occupants as hostages and threaten to blow up the compound if 91 political prisoners in Iran are not released.

May 5, 1980 — British commandos storm the Iranian Embassy in London after two hostages are killed. The remaining 19 hostages are freed, but three of what is now said to be a group of five gunmen holding the embassy are killed.

May 6, 1980 — The bodies of the eight American servicemen killed in the aborted rescue mission are returned to the United States for burial. President Carter proclaims three days of national mourning.

May 9, 1980 — Iranians vote in run-off election for a Parliament.

May 16, 1980 — The foreign ministers of Britain, France and West Germany tell Edmund Muskie that they believe sanctions against Iran to be counterproductive, and that they will put only limited sanctions into effect as a show of support for the United States.

May 18, 1980 — The Common Market foreign ministers announce that limited sanctions against Iran will go into effect on May 22. Only trade which has been contracted since November 4, 1979, will be banned.

May 24, 1980 — The International Court of Justice orders the immediate release of the hostages from Iran and rules that Iran is liable for reparations to the hostages.

May 28, 1980 — Iran's Parliament convenes. Students holding the hostages send the body a message saying that a decision to release the hostages without the return of the former Shah and his wealth would have to be fully justified to the Iranian people.

May 31, 1980 — Iranian officials announce that more than 400 people, representing Third World countries and liberation movements, will arrive in Teheran tomorrow for a three-day international conference on the "crimes" of America. The officials refuse to name any of those who will attend, but say a delegation of Americans has been prevented from attending by the U.S. government.

June 2, 1980 — A 10-member American delegation led by former Attorney General Ramsey Clark arrives in Teheran, in defiance of President Carter's travel ban, to attend Iran's international conference on the "crimes" of America.

June 5, 1980 — Iran's so-called "Crimes of America" conference ends with a call for a speedy, peaceful resolution of the hostilities between Iran and the United States, but does not specifically mention the hostages.

June 29, 1980 — Barbara Timm ends an attempt to make a second visit to her hostage son. She had received State Department approval for the trip but was unable to enter Iran.

An Iranian Justice Ministry investigator says that one of the hostages, Michael Moeller, will be tried on charges of seducing and raping an Iranian woman who was later killed by her brother to protect their family's honor.

July 10, 1980 — Aytollah Khomeini orders the release of hostage Richard Queen, who is said to be very ill.

July 11, 1980 — Richard Queen is flown from Teheran to Zurich, Switzerland, and is hospitalized for observation of what is said to be a neurological disorder.

July 12, 1980 — Iran reportedly crushes a major coup plot, said to have been planned by supporters of former Prime Minister Shaphur Bakhtiar.

Richard Queen is taken to an Air Force hospital in Wiesbaden, West Germany.

July 14, 1980 — Firing squads execute 26 in Iran, including a general convicted of killing under the Shah.

July 15, 1980 — Richard Queen's ailment is diagnosed as multiple sclerosis.

Iran closes its borders for 48 hours in order to track down additional members of the coup conspiracy.

July 18, 1980 — Richard Queen returns to the United States.

An attempt to assassinate Shaphur Bakhtiar is made in Paris.

July 20, 1980 — Ayatollah Hashemi Rafsanjani is elected speaker of the Iranian Parliament. He is a conservative member of the Islamic Republican Party.

July 22, 1980 — Abolhassan Bani-Sadr is formally sworn in as President of Iran before the Parliament.

July 27, 1980 — Mohammed Riza Pahlevi, former Shah of Iran, dies in Egypt. Doctors attribute his death to collapse of the circulatory system, hemorrhaging, and dwindling blood pressure.

At least 175 Iranian nationals are arrested in Washington during a demonstration.

July 29, 1980 — The Iranian Foreign Ministry condemns the breakup of the demonstration in Washington as "one of the most shameful incidents in history."

CHRONOLOGY

July 30, 1980 — A letter signed by 187 members of the U.S. Congress, urging the Iranian Parliament to resolve the hostage crisis quickly, is read at today's session of the Parliament. Speaker of the Parliament Hojatolislam Hashemi Rafsanjani, presenting the letter to the assembly, accuses the United States of lying, not only about the causes of the crisis, but about U.S. attempts to defuse it.

Dr. Hassan Ayat, a member of Iran's Islamic Republican Party, says it may take a few weeks for the Parliament to resolve the impasse over the selection of a Prime Minister.

Eight people are killed and 36 wounded when a bomb explodes in the southwestern Iranian city of Ahwaz.

Eleven of the 12 U.S. Immigration agents charged with investigating the arrested Iranian demonstrators call in sick after being ordered by their superiors to drop a civil charge against one of the protesters. Two of the protesters have been released on grounds of insufficient evidence.

The arrested demonstrators are refusing to give their names to District of Columbia police.

August 3, 1980 — Ayatollah Khomeini charges that the Iranians under arrest in the United States are being "tortured" and otherwise mistreated.

August 4, 1980 — Iran's Parliament postpones any debate of the hostage crisis. Hashemi Rafsanjani says the Parliament has asked the Supreme Islamic Council to prepare for trials of the hostages. These steps are apparently taken because of the detention of demonstrators in the United States.

August 5, 1980 — All but one of the Iranian demonstrators are released after giving their names to immigration authorities. The one not released is returned to Washington to face charges of assaulting a policeman.

August 11, 1980 — Mohammed Ali Rajai, President Bani-Sadr's second choice for Prime Minister of Iran, is overwhelmingly approved by the Parliament.

September 1, 1980 — In a draft reply to the letter sent by 187 U. S. Congressmen to the Iranian Parliament, the Parliament's Foreign Affairs Commission outlines the first authoritative proposal for release of the hostages. The proposal calls for the United States to acknowledge its past role in Iran and to return the late Shah's wealth.

269

NO HIDING PLACE

The State Department announces that Edmund Muskie has sent a letter to Prime Minister Rajai urging release of the hostages. This is the first high-level contact between Iran and the United States since the failed rescue mission.

September 9, 1980 — Unexpectedly, the White House is contacted by the West German Government and given the information that an Iranian close to the seat of power would like to meet in Bonn with American officials to reopen discussion of the hostage situation.

September 10, 1980 — President Carter appoints Deputy Secretary of State Warren M. Christopher to head an unpublicized task force to prepare for the Bonn meeting.

September 11, 1980 — The United States asks the Iranian who requested the meeting — Sadegh Tabatabai, a brother-in-law of Ayatollah Khomeini's son — for some proof of his position in the power structure. In response, Mr. Tabatabai relays to the White House the information that Ayatollah Khomeini will deliver a speech the next day outlining conditions for the release of the hostages. The message also lists those conditions.

September 12, 1980 — In a broadcast speech to Moslems around the world, Ayatollah Khomeini lists four conditions for the release of the hostages: that the United States return the property of the late Shah to Iran, cancel its claims against Iran, unlock the assets frozen by President Carter, and promise not to intervene in Iranian affairs.

September 14, 1980 — Iran's Parliament hears a report from its Foreign Affairs Commission on the hostage situation.

September 16, 1980 — Warren Christopher and Sadegh Tabatabai meet at a West German Government guest house near Bonn to formulate a new scenario for the release of the hostages.

September 18, 1980 — President Carter says he will not apologize to Iran for past U.S. actions there. The matter of an apology has become a subject of much debate since Ayatollah Khomeini listed conditions for the hostages' release, which did not include a demand for such an apology.

Warren Christopher and Sadegh Tabatabai again meet to review the new scenario for release of the hostages.

Mr. Tabatabai says that the American conditions sound reasonable and that he will return to Iran on September 22 to get the approval of

Ayatollah Khomeini. But increasing hostilities between Iran and Iraq force this idea to be shelved.

September 19-21, 1980 — Border skirmishes between Iraq and Iran develop into full-scale war.

September 30, 1980 — The Iranian Parliament agrees to set up a special commission to study the hostage situation, but does not name members of the panel.

October 2, 1980 — Seven hard-line Islamic fundamentalists are named to the Iranian Parliament's panel to investigate the hostage situation.

October 6, 1980 — Hashemi Rafsanjani says that the Iranian Parliament might add conditions to those specified by Ayatollah Khomeini for release of the hostages.

October 17, 1980 — Prime Minister Rajai travels to New York to address the U.N. Security Council. He tells the body that Iran is the victim of U.S.-inspired aggression.

October 18, 1980 — Prime Minister Rajai says that he believes the United States, "in practice," has apologized for supporting the Shah.

October 20, 1980 — President Carter says that if the hostages are freed by Iran he will order the release of Iran's frozen assets and will seek normal relations with Iran.

October 22, 1980 — Prime Minister Rajai says he is "sure" the United States is ready to meet Ayatollah Khomeini's four conditions for release of the hostages. Of the hostage situation, he says, "We are in the process of resolving it."

October 25, 1980 — Carter Administration officials say that Iran has been told repeatedly that a partial release of the hostages is not in the national interests of either the United States or Iran.

Iran's special commission on the hostages is said to be circulating its proposals privately among members of the Majlis.

Former Foreign Minister Sadegh Ghotbzadeh tells a Japanese television reporter that he believes there "is no longer an essential gap between the attitudes of the United States and Iran toward the conditions for the release of the hostages." He adds that it is possible that the hostages will be released in stages.

Ali Reza Nobari says that one condition for release of the hostages is that Iran be given immediately at least some of the $8 billion in assets frozen by the United States last November.

Foreign Minister Saadun Hamadi of Iraq says his country is disturbed by efforts of the United States to achieve rapprochement with Iran. He says that any U.S. effort to support Iran could lead to a widening of the Iran-Iraq conflict.

October 26, 1980 — Iran's Parliament meets in closed session to hear the special commission report on the hostages, but adjourns without reaching a decision on the proposed conditions for release.

A high-ranking Iranian official at the United Nations tells a CBS News reporter that there is a "99 percent" chance that 40 of the 52 hostages will be released by October 30.

Thomas G. Shack Jr., an American lawyer for the Iranian Government, says that despite obstacles President Carter has legal options that might allow him to satisfy Iranian conditions for release of the hostages.

The Carter Administration says it has received no direct word from Iran about any possible release of the hostages, and would wait for the conclusion of the parliamentary debate on the issue.

Iran says that an Iraqi air attack on the city of Dizful has left more than 100 civilians dead.

European diplomats say Iraq has asked the Common Market nations to mediate in the Iran-Iraq war.

October 27, 1980 — Iran's Parliament meets twice to discuss the hostage issue, but defers any decision for at least two days. Members of Parliament will meet with Ayatollah Khomeini tomorrow.

Mohsen Rahahi, a hard-line member of the Parliament, says that the final decision on the hostages may not be made until after the election.

Ali Shams Ardakani, Iran's chief U.N. representative, says the U.S. media have "gone crazy" in their speculative reports on the release of the hostages.

Iraq, which has claimed several times to have captured the city of Abadan, Iran, is reported to be running into stiff opposition there.

October 28, 1980 — Ayatollah Khomeini speaks to the Iranian Parliament, but does not mention the hostage issue. His silence on the hostages is interpreted to be an attempt to let Parliament express its will freely.

A West German television report says that Iran might demand three hours of live television time in the United States to argue its case as a condition for release of the hostages.

Le Monde reports that Iran's political factions seem to be coming into alignment on the hostage issue; all but one small political faction is arguing for release of the hostages in the near future, if the United States agrees to the conditions set forth by Aytollah Khomeini.

Edmund Muskie says he has no reason to expect that the hostages will be released by Election Day, which coincides with the end of the first year of the hostages' confinement.

Fighting is heavy in Iran's oil regions.

King Hussein ends a two-day visit to Iraq, where he again expressed his full support for the Iraqi position in the conflict.

Saudi Arabia breaks diplomatic relations with Libya. Libya has supported Iran in the conflict with Iraq, while Saudi Arabia has grown closer to Iraq.

The Soviet Union is reported to be tilting toward Iran, while remaining officially neutral in the conflict.

President Carter, in a televised debate with Republican Presidential candidate Ronald Reagan, says the United States will "make delivery" on several hundred million dollars of spare parts to Iran if the hostages are released safely. Governor Reagan declines comment on what efforts he might make to end the crisis, but says that once the hostages are safely home there should be a Congressional investigation into why the crisis endured so long.

October 29, 1980 — Carter Administration officials repeat that about $240 million of military spare parts, purchased by Iran before the beginning of the hostage crisis, could be shipped to Iran as soon as the hostages are returned.

Iran's Parliament holds an inconclusive four-hour private debate on the hostages, then schedules a public debate for the next day. Ayatollah Sadegh Kalkhali tells reporters he is in favor of trading the hostages for military spare parts from the United States. He also says that a majority in Iran's Parliament wants to release the hostages before November 4.

Carter aide Frank Moore is quoted in the *Shreveport Journal* as saying that Ayatollah Khomeini has cancer of the colon and is not going "to last long." The White House reacts to this assertion by declaring that Mr. Moore is "not a spokesman" for the Administration on Iranian af-

273

fairs, and that the Administration has no information suggesting that the Ayatollah is terminally ill.

Iraq again launches artillery and air strikes against the Iranian city of Abadan.

October 30, 1980 — Iran's Parliament is forced to postpone its scheduled public debate on the hostages because of failure to assemble a quorum. A boycott of the debate by hard-liners is the reason for the failure. The Parliament will not meet again until November 2.

Members of an 18-person team responsible for insuring the health and welfare of the hostages upon their release fly to Wiesbaden, West Germany.

October 31, 1980 — Ayatollah Hussein Ali Montazeri, who is considered to be a possible successor to Ayatollah Khomeini, castigates the members of Parliament who boycotted yesterday's scheduled public debate, calling their actions "unacceptable to the Moslem and revolutionary people in Iran."

Carter Administration officials say there seems to be a growing consensus in Iran for freeing the hostages.

Reports from Stockholm say that a Scanair airliner has been chartered to airlift the hostages from Iran. U.S. officials say, however, that this was a private charter by an American businessman and not official U.S. action.

Heavy fighting is reported in Iraq's latest attempt to gain control of Abadan.

Reza Pahlevi, son of the former Shah, lays claim to the Iranian throne on his 20th birthday. The United States discounts his claim, saying it considers the current regime to be the legal government of Iran.

November 1, 1980 — Iran's hard-line Islamic Republican Party says in a newspaper editorial that it supports releasing the hostages before the U.S. Presidential election because the United States will be more conciliatory in the pre-election rush. The editorial warns, however, that if Iranian conditions are not met by the United States, the hostages will be kept and may be put on trial.

Militants occupying the U.S. Embassy in Teheran call for mass demonstrations on November 4, the first anniversary of the hostages' capture.

CHRONOLOGY

Families of the hostages prepare for ceremonies in the United States to mark the anniversary of the capture.

Anwar el-Sadat says he recognizes the current Iranian regime as its legal government, and will not change his position despite the fact that Reza Pahlevi, who resides in Egypt, has claimed the Iranian throne.

Heavy fighting is reported in the city of Abadan.

November 2, 1980 — Iran's Parliament agrees on conditions for the release of the hostages. The body adds no new conditions to those specified by Ayatollah Khomeini in September, but does say that the conditions will have to be not only accepted but met before all the hostages can be released. The possibility of a serial release of the hostages while conditions are being carried out is mentioned.

Militants holding the hostages say they will meet with Ayatollah Khomeini tomorrow to discuss the Parliament's decision.

President Carter calls the Parliament's conditions a "positive basis" for resolution of the hostage crisis.

Legal experts in the United States say that President Carter probably lacks the authority to meet immediately the demands of the Iranian Parliament, because of the private suits against Iran pending in the United States.

Vice President Mondale, in a campaign speech, says President Carter will do "everything humanly possible" to reach an end of the hostage crisis, but will not compromise American security to do so.

Kurt Waldheim says he is gratified by the Iranian Parliament's decision, and offers U.N. assistance to resolve the crisis.

Iraq says it has captured Iran's Minister of Petroleum, the Deputy Minister and four other Iranian oil officials.

Paris police force 120 Iranian students who have been staging a sit-in at Unesco headquarters to disperse.

November 3, 1980 — Militants holding the hostages meet with Ayatollah Khomeini, then announce that they have agreed to turn over the hostages to the Iranian Government.

The office of Prime Minister Rajai says later in the day that no decision has been made on whether or not to move the hostages, or on who will guard them in the future.

Algeria is named by Iran as its intermediary in any moves to release the hostages. The Iranian Government also sets up a special commission

275

to deal with details of the release. Algeria officially delivers the conditions of the United States.

Edmund Muskie says he is pleased with recent developments in Iran but cautions that these developments are only "initial steps in a process which will require time, patience, and diplomacy."

Hashemi Rafsanjani says at a news conference that if Iranian conditions are not met the hostages will be put on trial.

Penne Laingen, wife of hostage Bruce Laingen, says her husband has been seriously ill, having lost at least 15 pounds from a long bout with dysentery.

U.S. officials note that Iran has not asked for delivery of military spare parts as a condition for release of the hostages, but that if it does ask, only nonlethal items will be shipped.

State Department officials say that two other Americans being held in Iran, journalist Cynthia Dwyer and Mohi Sobhani, are prisoners, not hostages, and their release is not expected to be included in any release of the hostages.

Iraq is said to be making gains in its battle for control of Abadan.

November 4, 1980 — Day 367, first anniversary of the hostages' capture.

U.S. Presidential election. Ronald Reagan wins the Presidency, opening the possibility that unless the hostage crisis is resolved quickly, a second president will have to work on its resolution.

Iran calls on the United States to respond quickly "through the mass media" to the conditions set forth by the Iranian Parliament for release of the hostages. Prime Minister Rajai says it is up to the United States to make the next move to bring about the release. Ahmad Khomeini, the Ayatollah's son, says in an interview that no clear solution is in sight.

The Algerian ambassador to Iran meets with Prime Minister Rajai to discuss the situation.

The United States responds to the Iranian conditions by rejecting any quick action and by requesting clarification of many aspects of the conditions. Warren Christopher tells the Algerian ambassador to the United States that the United States wants to engage in negotiations on the terms with Iran to see if there might be any flexibility in them.

Reports say that the United States has prepared a bill to nationalize

276

Iranian assets in the United States to prevent private individuals or companies from suing Iran directly for damages.

President Saddam Hussein of Iraq says that Iraqi troops could be withdrawn from Iran "tomorrow" if Iran recognizes Iraqi territorial claims.

November 5, 1980 — State Department officials say that, although President-elect Ronald Reagan will be kept informed of all developments in the hostage situation, President Carter's efforts to secure release will continue on the same route as has been previously followed.

U.S. aides say President Carter can agree to Iran's conditions only if Iran agrees to a "narrow" interpretation of them. They say little progress is possible unless Iran agrees to some negotiation on the ambiguities in the conditions.

The U.N. Security Council asks Kurt Waldheim to send an envoy to the Middle East to try to negotiate a settlement of the Iran-Iraq conflict.

Ayatollah Khomeini vows to continue the war with Iraq "until the infidels are defeated."

November 6, 1980 — Hojatolislam Mohammed Ali Khameini, a member of Iran's special commission on the hostages, says it could still take months before the hostages are returned to the United States.

Hojatolislam Ashgar Mousavi Khoeiny, another member of the commission, and Prime Minister Rajai both say that the result of the Presidential election will not affect Iran's conditions for the release, although Hojatolislam Khoeiny says that resolution of the crisis would probably take less time if President Carter had been re-elected.

Ali Reza Nobari, head of Iran's Central Bank, says Iran intends to honor its financial obligations to the United States and other countries. He says the United States still owes Iran as much as $2 billion for unpaid oil debts.

Iraq elaborates on its capture of the Iranian Oil Minister, Mohammed Jawad Baqir Tunguyan, saying he was found wounded on a road near Abadan six days ago and is receiving medical treatment to "save his life."

November 7, 1980 — State Department spokesman John H. Trattner says the United States is "at the point of decision-making" in its response to the Iranian conditions. He adds that although the reply is almost ready, there remain problems which will have to be worked out with Iran.

Rumors about the whereabouts of the hostages include that they have all been reassembled in Teheran, possibly at the Evin Prison. An official at the prison denies this, but indicates that at least some of the hostages are still at the U.S. Embassy.

Iran charges that Iraq has tortured Iran's captured Oil Minister. Iraq dismisses these charges as ridiculous.

Former Iranian Foreign Minister Sadegh Ghotbzadeh is imprisoned in Teheran, after voicing criticism of the ruling Islamic Republican Party.

November 8, 1980 — U.S. officials say a reply to Iran containing specific proposals designed to meet the spirit, if not the letter, of the Iranian conditions is being prepared. They say President Carter is expected to approve the proposals within a few days.

A spokesman for Iran's prosecutor's office says charges have not been filed yet against Sadegh Ghotbzadeh, but that they may go beyond the accusation that he criticized the Islamic Republican Party.

Heavy fighting is reported between Iran and Iraq in several cities in the Iranian oil province of Khuzistan.

November 9, 1980 — Former Prime Minister Mehdi Bazargan asks Ayatollah Khomeini to intervene with authorities on behalf of Sadegh Ghotbzadeh. Angry exchanges in Iran's Parliament between moderate supporters and conservative opponents of Mr. Ghotbzadeh are heard.

Iraqi President Saddam Hussein calls his country's war with Iran a holy war, and calls on his countrymen to "defend the ideals" of the Prophet Mohammed.

November 10, 1980 — A delegation headed by Warren Christopher flies to Algeria to convey the formal response by the United States to the conditions set forth by Iran for release of the hostages. Although details of the response are not given, it is reported to include a pledge of noninterference in Iran's affairs, an agreement to unfreeze Iran's assets, and an explanation of legal problems involved in meeting the other demands.

President Bani-Sadr expresses hope that the crisis can be resolved soon. He specifically notes Iran's need for military spare parts.

Sadegh Ghotbzadeh is released from prison in Teheran. The release

278

is said to have been ordered by Ayatollah Khomeini.

General Motors files a $58 million suit against Iran, seeking damages from Iran for having made G.M.'s Iranian subsidiary "worthless."

Saddam Hussein again warns Iran that Iraq will continue to fight until Iran recognizes Iraq's territorial claims.

November 11, 1980 — Warren Christopher and his delegation return to the United States from Algeria after presenting the U.S. reply to Iran's conditions. Mr. Christopher reportedly spent four hours explaining to an Algerian delegation the problems the United States would have in meeting Iran's demands.

After learning the contents of the U.S. reply, Ali Riza Nobari says that it is "cool to us," that he now doubts a rapid resolution of the crisis but that it may still be resolved before Ronald Reagan takes office.

Japan's Mitsui & Company is said to be preparing to withdraw from an Iranian petrochemical project, taking a $711 million loss. The project has reportedly been bombed repeatedly by Iraq.

A high Iraqi official flies to Moscow, apparently to seek an uninterrupted flow of military supplies to Iraq.

Iranian officials say they hope the oncoming rainy season will slow down Iraq's advances in Iran's oil province.

Olof Palme of Sweden is asked by Kurt Waldheim to mediate the Iran-Iraq crisis.

November 12, 1980 — Iran officially receives the U.S. reply to its conditions. A spokesman for the Iranian Government says the reply will be made public soon.

Ayatollah Mohammed Beheshti says he is sure the United States could surmount any legal difficulties it might have in fulfilling Iran's conditions if it seriously wanted a solution to the crisis.

President Carter says it is now up to Teheran to make the next move on resolution of the crisis. He says of the U.S. reply: "I think our answers are adequate."

Hostage L. Bruce Laingen, in a telephone interview, counsels patience and calm in the current round of negotiations.

Syria seeks postponement of an Arab summit conference planned for this month because of the serious differences between Arab countries over the Iran-Iraq conflict.

Iraq steps up its shelling of Abadan.

NO HIDING PLACE

November 13, 1980 — Iran begins a detailed study of the U.S. reply, but makes no public comment on it it. Prime Minister Rajai confers with Ayatollah Khomeini. Iranian diplomats in Algiers say that the initial reaction of Iranian officials to the reply was not very positive, with some officials believing the United States is trying to stall.

Cuba's Foreign Minister arrives in Baghdad with a request from Iran ' for clarification of Iraq's cease-fire proposals.

District Court Judge Robert F. Peckham of San Francisco orders a stay of 90 days on all proceedings in his court which involve the frozen Iranian assets.

November 14, 1980 — Diplomats in Teheran say they believe the U.S. reply to Iran's conditions has led to disagreement and difficult decisions which Iran may need some time to resolve.

In Switzerland, lawyers for the Iranian Government obtain a court order freezing the proceeds from an auction of 15 jewels they claim belonged to former Empress Farah. The auctioneers claim that the jewels did not belong to her or to the Iranian Government.

Iraqi forces move on the Iranian city of Susangird from several directions.

November 15, 1980 — Iran announces it will allow American and British reporters to enter Iran in order to cover the war with Iraq.

Iraq claims to have killed 282 Iranian soldiers in various battles today, the largest number in a single day since the beginning of the war.

Kuwait and Morocco announce that they plan to attend the Arab summit conference scheduled to begin in Jordan on November 25.

November 16, 1980 — Hashemi Rafsanjani is quoted by Teheran radio as saying that the Parliament is "too busy" to continue discussion on the hostage issue.

Ayatollah Khomeini makes a plea for national unity in wartime, castigates the battling political factions in his country and ignores the hostage question completely.

Henry Kissinger predicts that the hostages will be released before President-elect Reagan is inaugurated January 20, because Iran will want to begin the Reagan era with a clean slate.

Iraq claims to have killed 500 Iranians in a battle for the city of Susangird.

CHRONOLOGY

Kuwait says Iranian warplanes have fired rockets at one of its border outposts twice in the last five days.

November 17, 1980 — Hashemi Rafsanjani says that the commission studying the U.S. reply to Iran's conditions for release of the hostages has not finished its deliberations. He says, however, that it is now up to the government, not the Parliament, to decide if the United States has fulfilled the Parliament's conditions.

A delegation led by Mr. Rafsanjani leaves for a trip to Libya, Syria, Algeria and Lebanon to explain the Iranian position in the conflict with Iraq.

Iran and Iraq issue contradictory statements about the day's developments in the area of Susangird. Both sides claim successes.

November 18, 1980 — A Manhattan judge grants a 90-day delay in action on Iran's $56.5 billion suit against the former Shah and Empress. The suit was filed shortly after the takeover of the U.S. Embassy in Teheran.

Ali Reza Nobari says that it will be a few more days before Iran makes a public statement on the U.S. response to the hostage release conditions. He adds that resolution of the crisis could still be a long way off.

Iraq says it is tightening its grip on pockets of resistance in the city of Susangird. Iran announces that Olof Palme, a special U.N. envoy, has arrived in Teheran to mediate in the war.

November 19, 1980 — Hashemi Rafsanjani, at a news conference in Algiers, says that the United States has agreed "in principle" to Iran's conditions, but that release of the hostages will be delayed until the conditions are actually met.

U.S. officials are pleased by the statement, but caution that it does not appear to be an official statement of the Iranian Government.

Dresser Industries and Control Data Corporation file multimillion dollar lawsuits against Iran.

November 20, 1980 — U.S. officials confirm that the United States has accepted "in principle" the Iranian conditions, but stress that they are willing to take only actions which are "in conformity with our Constitution and our laws and consistent with our national honor."

Prime Minister Rajai tells a news conference that Iran will seek some sort of clarification of the U.S. response to the conditions.

281

NO HIDING PLACE

November 21, 1980 — Iran bombs a major dam and several villages in the Kurdish region of Iraq. Olof Palme visits the battered Iranian cities of Dizful and Kermanshah.

November 22, 1980 — Prime Minister Rajai says he has sent to Algeria a request for a direct "positive or negative" response from the United States on the hostage conditions. He says the first U.S. reply was "neither explicit or clear."

Sadegh Khalkhali says that, while he would like to see a solution to the crisis, he does not believe it will happen before the inauguration of President-elect Reagan.

Iran denies having attacked Kuwait border posts. It says also that Iraq has attacked the town of Gilan with Soviet-made ground-to-ground missiles.

November 23, 1980 — Algerian diplomats fly from Iran to Algiers with Iran's request for an explicit reply to the Iranian conditions from the United States. Prime Minister Rajai's public relations director repeats Iran's request for a direct "positive or negative" reply. He says, "We cannot accept the responses with room for compromises or negotiations or anything like that."

United Press International reports that President Carter, asked if he had such a reply for the Iranians, answered, "No."

Iran reports that the refinery at Abadan has been set on fire by Iraqi artillery shellings.

November 24, 1980 — The State Department announces that an Algerian delegation will fly to the United States tomorrow with the Iranian message requesting an explicit acceptance or rejection of the Iranian terms. Edmund Muskie acknowledges that the U.S. reply to the Iranian conditions was not a clear acceptance, and tells reporters, "We are going to be holding for a while."

Olof Palme leaves the Middle East, saying that "we should not expect rapid results" in achieving an end to the Iran-Iraq war.

November 25, 1980 — The team of Algerian diplomats serving as intermediaries in the hostage crisis fly to the United States. They are scheduled to meet tomorrow with Edmund Muskie and other U.S. officials.

Hashemi Rafsanjani says that the hostages will not be released until

282

Iran's demands are met, and that Iran will not negotiate on its already-stated demands.

Iraq says it has turned back Iranian attempts to break its siege of Abadan.

Olof Palme flies to New York to consult with Kurt Waldheim about the Iran-Iraq conflict.

November 26, 1980 — Algerian diplomats convey to State Department officials assurances from Iran that the hostages "are in good health." The delegation spends most of the day conferring with U.S. officials.

Hashemi Rafsanjani says he had not expected the United States to be able to meet all of Iran's conditions on the hostages immediately, but says that some of the hostages can be released as soon as the United States begins to meet the conditions, and that he expects the United States to find a way to eventually fulfill them all. He says in an interview that Ronald Reagan will no more be able to launch a military rescue of the hostages than was President Carter.

Iranian bombers carry out several raids on Iraqi oilfields. Iraq says only limited damage results.

Olof Palme says that he has won an agreement "in principle" from Iraq and Iran to free 63 merchant ships caught in the Shatt al Arab waterway. He says he intends to return to Iran and Iraq again to work on a cease-fire.

November 27, 1980 — Militants who had been holding the American hostages say they have handed them over to the Iranian Government and no longer have anything to do with them. They say no hostages are currently being held in the U.S. Embassy.

The State Department says it has received no word of such a transfer of control, but that such a step would "be helpful."

The Algerian delegation leaves the United States after two days of discussions with State Department officials.

An Iranian delegation arrives in London to explain Teheran's position in the conflict with Iraq.

Iran announces it will attend an OPEC meeting scheduled for the next month in Indonesia.

November 28, 1980 — Transfer of the hostages cannot be confirmed.

The United States makes inquiries through diplomatic channels; transfer is denied by one of the militants.

John Trattner says it may take several days for the United States to formulate a response to the latest communication from Iran.

Iran says President Bani-Sadr visited the city of Abadan, which Iraq claims to be holding under seige, the day before.

November 29, 1980 — Iranian militants at the U.S. Embassy in Teheran state again that they have turned over control of the hostages to the government.

Hashemi Rafsanjani says again that Iran is in no hurry to see the hostages released, and that it is up to the United States to meet Iranian conditions as stated.

Iran and Iraq engage in a major naval battle in the Persian Gulf. Iraq claims to have destroyed three warships and three jets.

Syria deploys two divisions of troops along its border with Jordan and warns that it would defend "national security and interests by all available ways and means, even if they were unbrotherly."

November 30, 1980 — Iran claims to have captured Iraq's offshore oil-loading terminal of Mina al Bakr. Iraq says this claim is completely false.

Saudi Arabia sends a special envoy to Damascus in a bid to defuse tensions between Syria and Jordan.

Four people are injured when a bomb explodes in a car near the Foreign Ministry in Teheran.

December 1, 1980 — Warren Christopher flies to Algiers with a clarification of the U.S. response to Iranian conditions for freeing the hostages.

Prime Minister Rajai is reported by NBC News as confirming that the hostages have been taken into government control. But Bezhad Nabavi, who heads the commission set up to deal with the hostages, says they have "not been handed over completely by the students."

Iraq again suggests direct negotiations with Iran to end their war.

King Hussein asks the United States and other Western nations to speed the delivery of weapons already contracted by Jordan in light of the current threat from Syria.

December 2, 1980 — Warren Christopher gives Algerian diplomats the new U.S. response to Iran, and tells them that Iran cannot count on the Carter Administration's proposals being carried over by the Reagan Administration.

Iraq says it is in a position to take full control of Iran's oil province of Khuzistan. Iraq also charges that the United States is lending support to Iran.

Syria says tension with Jordan can end if Jordan accepts a list of 21 demands made by Syria. Reports say that Syria has begun removing some troops from its border with Jordan.

The National Park Service begins to decorate the national Christmas tree, which President Carter did not light last year in honor of the hostages.

December 3, 1980 — Edmund Muskie says the United States is trying to convince Iran that the United States cannot legally carry out all of Iran's conditions for release of the hostages but that President Carter is prepared to go far in meeting them.

The Iranian Government asks Parliament to vote more money to cover the rising costs of the war with Iraq.

King Hussein rejects the list of 21 Syrian demands necessary to ease tensions between the nations.

December 4, 1980 — Warren Christopher and his delegation return from Algiers without any prediction of when the hostages might be released. One U.S. official says the delegation asked that negotiations be speeded up to avoid the problem of having the new Administration take over the negotiations in January.

Saudi Arabia says Syria has agreed to pull back some troops from its border with Jordan. Syrian officials will not confirm this.

December 5, 1980 — Behzad Nabavi says the hostages are still being held in various places around the country. He says also that they will be turned over to "judicial authorities" unless the United States replies "on time" to Iran's conditions for their release.

The Algerian delegation arrives in Teheran with the U.S. clarification of its positions.

Iran says Iraq destroyed a major oil pipeline today.

December 6, 1980 — Iraq says Iranian warplanes have struck at targets in the Kurdish area of Iraq, apparently in an effort to cut supply routes to Kurdish rebels in Iran.

December 7, 1980 — Ayatollah Sadegh Khalkhali resigns as Iran's special narcotics prosecutor because of a controversy over whether torture is being used in revolutionary jails.

Iran and Iraq engage in attacks on the Shatt al Arab oil installations of both countries.

Behzad Nabavi says Iran expects to make "some practical suggestions" to help bring the hostage crisis to an end. He says that the latest U.S. message shows improvement over the earlier one and that "we are going to find easy ways to finish the job."

December 8, 1980 — Hashemi Rafsanjani says the hostage crisis "is now much closer to being solved." He says that "the United States has, to an extent, clarified its position" and that the United States has "almost made it clear that it is ready to meet these demands."

The State Department declines to comment on the latest statements from Iran, saying it will await Iran's official reply to its message.

Depositions given in a civil court case in Delaware attack the reliability of the type of warning system that grounded a helicopter used in the failed rescue attempt in Iran last April.

King Hussein of Jordan says Iraq has slowed the pace of its military campaign in Iran because it does not intend to take any more territory than it already has. Hussein also says that Syria and Jordan still have troop buildups along their common border, and Jordan will not withdraw its troops until Syria does the same.

A Beirut, Lebanon, newspaper reports that the hostages will be released on Christmas Day. Although Iranian officials deny this, speculation persists that some action is under way. (See December 11.)

December 9, 1980 — State Department and Pentagon analysts say a recently completed transit agreement between the Soviet Union and Iran may gradually increase Soviet influence in Iran, but that there is no sign yet that it will influence the Iranian economy or the course of the Iran-Iraq war.

December 10, 1980 — Testimony begins in the trial of an Iranian college student accused of murdering a Denver teenager.

Jordan says that Syria has begun to withdraw its troops from the border and that Jordan will begin to do the same tomorrow.

December 11, 1980 — A Beirut, Lebanon, newspaper reports that the hostages will be freed on Christmas Day, thanks to an American proposal for compromise on Iran's demand for return of the former Shah's assets. Iran's hostage commission denies the report, but speculation persists that some movement on the issue is under way.

An article in the newspaper of the Islamic Republican Party accuses Iran's centrists of having plotted to crush Iran's Islamic revolution.

Saadun Hamadi, Iraq's Foreign Minister, predicts that the war with Iran will continue for quite a long time; Iraq begins to ration gasoline.

December 12, 1980 — U.S. officials say they have received unofficial reports from Iran indicating that some progress is being made in the hostage issue. But they say that until they receive a formal report they cannot be sure how close an agreement is.

Iran executes six persons accused of collaborating with Iraq.

Four black American clergymen arrive in Teheran.

December 13, 1980 — Ahmad Azizi, director of hostage affairs in Prime Minister Rajai's office, says that the U.S. response to Iran's conditions for the release of the hostages has been "basically positive." Mr. Azizi says also that the four clergymen who arrived in Teheran the day before will not be able to obtain release of the hostages. The clergymen say their purpose is not to discuss the hostages but to "expand understanding between Moslems and Christians." They say, though, that if the Iranians want to discuss the hostages, they will respond.

Behzad Nabavi says that the next Iranian message on the hostages will contain the Iranian Government's proposals for implementing the terms of the release.

The families of the hostages are briefed by the State Department, and are told there is no way to predict when the release will come.

Iran takes a group of Western journalists to Abadan to show them that Iran now controls the embattled city.

December 14, 1980 — Ahmad Azizi says that the hostages might be released by Christmas if the United States acts quickly to meet Iranian demands. He repeats that the hostages might be released in stages if all the demands are not carried out to Iran's satisfaction.

A Kuwaiti newspaper says that President Hafez al-Assad of Syria has intervened in the hostage crisis to try to insure release by Christmas. Both President Assad and Ahmad Azizi deny the report.

President Bani-Sadr says, on *60 Minutes*, that President Carter no longer has the motivation to bring about the release of the hostages, now that he has lost the election.

Iranian and Iraqi delegates quarrel at a preconference OPEC dinner held in Bali, Indonesia.

December 15, 1980 — President Bani-Sadr says that the fate of the hostages now depends on a U.S. agreement to return Iran's assets frozen in the United States. He stresses that he is not referring to the Shah's assets.

Iran and Iraq ignore a cease-fire appeal from OPEC nations, and battle in Iran's western highlands and in the province of Khuzistan.

December 16, 1980 — Ayatollah Khomeini approves what he calls Iran's "final answer" to the United States on conditions for the release of the hostages. Prime Minister Rajai says, after meeting with the Ayatollah, that the hostages can be released by Christmas if the United States will provide certain "financial guarantees," which he does not specify.

U.S. officials, lacking details of the latest Iranian proposal, caution against excessive hope for return of the hostages by Christmas.

President Bani-Sadr says a proposal for a cease-fire between Iran and Iraq made by Third World countries has been rejected by Iran.

The Iranian student on trial for murder in Denver says he acted in self-defense in killing a Denver teenager.

December 17, 1980 — Algerian diplomats wait in Teheran to receive Iran's latest message to the United States. Details of the message are kept secret.

Ayatollah Mohammed Beheshti says at a news conference that the American position on the conditions "could be nearly an acceptable answer," but adds that "there were some necessary corrections." He again raises the possibility of spy trials for the hostages if Iranian demands are not met.

Iraq says it has begun to make use of American-made weapons captured from Iran in the war.

December 18, 1980 — Prime Minister Rajai says Iran's new conditions for release of the hostages have been delivered to Algerian diplomats and that the United States will receive them soon. He reiterates that the hostages could be released by Christmas Day if the United States will provide certain unspecified "financial guarantees."

An Israeli television report says that Simon Farzami, the Iranian

288

Jew who was editor of the English-language *Teheran Journal*, has been executed in Iran on charges of espionage for the United States.

Ayatollah Khomeini charges that Iran's universities, which have, for the most part, been closed since late 1979, were centers of communism and should therefore remain closed.

December 19, 1980 — Some details of Iran's new hostage conditions are made public as Algerian representatives leave Teheran to bring the new message to the United States. Included in the new conditions are stipulations that the United States must deposit in Algeria the assets frozen by the United States last year and must offer assurances of help for Iran in obtaining the former Shah's assets. The terms are said to include as well a "form of arbitration" proposal for the claims of U.S. companies and individuals against Iran.

U.S. officials say the new proposal raises new problems that rule out an early resolution of the crisis. It is not clear whether President Carter has the legal authority to transfer Iran's frozen assets to Algeria; an act of Congress may be needed.

Two earthquakes in Iran kill 26 people and damage the city of Qum.

December 20, 1980 — U.S. officials, angered by Iran's new demand that the United States deposit several billion dollars in Algeria as a condition for release of the hostages, say they are considering stopping substantive exchanges with Iran and leaving the hostage crisis resolution to the new Reagan Administration. The biggest problem with the new demands, according to U.S. officials, is one that calls for the United States to deposit between $5 billion and $10 billion to cover Iran's claims for the Shah's assets. A State Department official calls the demand "simple ransom."

Prime Minister Rajai says that the "main outstanding problem" blocking a solution to the crisis is the return of the Shah's wealth. He says that arbitration has been offered on private U.S. claims against Iran's frozen assets. Mr. Rajai says it is up to the United States to decide whether to accept the demands or "leave its Christmas tree unlighted next year, too."

The Iranian student on trial for murder in Denver is found not guilty.

December 21, 1980 — The text of Iran's latest message to the United States is made public. It calls for a deposit of $24 billion in Algeria to cover frozen assets and possible assets of the former Shah. Behzad Nabavi says in Teheran that "it is very easy for these conditions to be met by the United States."

Edmund Muskie calls the demand "unreasonable" and says it goes beyond the powers of the President. He holds out virtually no hope that the hostages can be released by January 20, when President Carter leaves office.

Behzad Nabavi says the hostages are staying in hotels in the Teheran area and will be interviewed on Teheran television on Christmas Day.

President-elect Reagan says he will not comment on the hostage issue until he takes office in January.

Petroleum Intelligence Weekly says the Iran-Iraq war has driven oil output to a ten-year low worldwide.

December 22, 1980 — The State Department charges that many of the hostages are not being kept in hotels but in prisons, and that some of them are not receiving needed medical attention.

The wife of one hostage says that six of the hostages have not been heard from since the failed rescue mission in April.

Hashemi Rafsanjani renews the threat that the hostages may be put on trial if Iranian demands are not met, saying, "It is a just and fair answer we have given."

Iraq says it has control of about one-third of Iran's oil province of Khuzistan.

Pope John Paul appeals for the release of hostages held for "political retaliation" or ransom.

December 23, 1980 — A Swiss diplomat says that Iran has refused requests to allow foreign clergymen to conduct Christmas services for the hostages, insisting instead that Iranian Christians will perform that service. The diplomat, Flavio Meroni, says he visited for about an hour with the three hostages still being held at the Foreign Ministry, and that they took the news of the latest stalemate in negotiations well.

Responding to a request from families of the hostages, the White House announces that the national Christmas tree will be lighted for 417 seconds on Christmas Eve, one second for each day of the hostages' captivity.

December 24, 1980 — Prime Minister Rajai lashes out at the United

States for rejecting the latest Iranian demands, saying, "Now, using the occasion of Christmas, America says to the people of the world that it is trying for release of the hostages, but that we are asking for money. But of course the conscious, free and independent people of the world will realize America's treacherous plan."

Ayatollah Beheshti, asked about plans for trial of the hostages, says that a decision on that cannot be made until Iran receives an official reply from the United States on Iran's demands.

President-elect Reagan breaks his silence on the situation and says the Iranians are "nothing better than criminals and kidnappers who have violated international law totally."

The United States asks Algeria to send its team of intermediaries to Washington to discuss what form a reply to Iran should take.

December 25, 1980 — Three Iranian Christian clergymen and the Papal Nuncio to Iran hold Christmas services for the hostages. The Papal Nuncio was taken blindfolded to the site where he met the hostages, and says the length of the ride indicated that it was in Teheran. The Nuncio says the hostages appeared to have good morale.

Film footage of the Christmas visit is shown on Iranian television, and spokesmen for the three U.S. television networks say they will show some of the footage soon. Some footage is shown in the United States late on Christmas night.

Iraq says 68 Iranians and 40 Iraqis were killed in the day's fighting.

December 26, 1980 — By tonight American television networks have received film showing 26 of the hostages; 21 of them make statements, the others remain silent.

Algeria's ambassador to Iran says he saw all 52 hostages on Christmas night and that all appeared to be well. The State Department welcomes this report, saying it has cleared up some doubt that all of the hostages are still alive and well.

Iraq invades Iran's Kurdistan province, thus extending the war front to the full extent of the Iran-Iraq border.

December 27, 1980 — Film and photographs of 15 more hostages are released by Iran. Officials in Iran tell CBS News that the 11 hostages not seen on any of the film chose not to appear. They say also that the eight who have been seen but did not speak made that decision for themselves.

NO HIDING PLACE

Prime Minister Rajai proposes a new plan for resolution of the crisis, in which the United States would be required to turn over about $9 billion in frozen assets to Iran immediately, and Iran would keep control of the hostages until all additional claims were settled. Several times in his presentation of his plan to diplomats and journalists he mentions evidence of espionage found in the U.S. Embassy in Teheran.

Edmund Muskie meets Algerian diplomats to discuss possibilities for further negotiations with Iran. The State Department refuses to comment on Prime Minister Rajai's latest statements.

Afghans living in Teheran storm the Soviet Embassy on the first anniversary of the Soviet Union's invasion of Afghanistan. At least one person is wounded by gunfire. Police and revolutionary guards disperse the demonstrators.

Iran reports fighting with Iraq in the Kurdistan province.

December 28, 1980 — Iran makes public the U.S. responses to its messages regarding terms of the release of the hostages. The documents contain a formal promise not to interfere in Iran's affairs, and a pledge to deliver to Algeria a signed Presidential order unblocking all the capital and assets of Iran under the jurisdiction of the United States.

The United States makes public its proposals over the last two months for resolution of the crisis. The United States had offered to return about $6 billion in frozen assets to Iran almost immediately, and to seek dismissal of court claims once an international commission was set up under binding arbitration to deal with private U.S. claims. Legal scholars question President Carter's authority to do some of this.

President-elect Reagan, asked for his reaction to Prime Minister Rajai's latest proposals, says, "I don't think you pay ransom for people that have been kidnapped by barbarians."

Edwin Meese 3d says that Iranians ought to know they should not expect to get a better deal from Mr. Reagan than from President Carter.

The Soviet Union delivers a formal protest to Iran over the storming of the Soviet Embassy in Teheran the day before.

The Algerian intermediaries in the hostage crisis meet with some of the hostage families, bringing letters from all but 10 of the hostages.

December 29, 1980 — The United States informs Iran it will not change its basic position on the conditions for the release of the hos-

292

tages, despite Iran's recent calls for financial guarantees. American officials and Algerian intermediaries are still discussing another formal message to Iran.

Another segment of film showing some of the hostages is released to the United States. It shows only one additional hostage not seen in earlier footage.

Hashemi Rafsanjani rejects President-elect Reagan's comments of the day before, saying, "If tyranny, swindling, military occupation and exploiting others is called civilization, then we are not used to such a thing." Ronald Reagan defends his remarks; U.S. officials say they do not believe the remarks will hurt negotiations, and may even speed them up because the Iranians might decide they do not want to have to deal with Mr. Reagan.

Ayatollah Khomeini calls on Iranians to be strong in the face of wartime shortages.

Reports from the United Nations say that a plan to free ships trapped in the Shatt al Arab waterway is stalled because Iran and Iraq will not agree on what flag the ships will fly for their departure.

December 30, 1980 — The United States gives Algerian intermediaries a "reformulation" of its proposals for release of the hostages. The latest plan offers to place $5 billion to $6 billion in Iran's frozen assets into an escrow fund in Algeria simultaneously with Iran turning the hostages over to Algeria. The escrow funds would then be released to Iran as soon as the hostages were on their way to the United States. The new proposal also sets a deadline for the week of January 11 for setting the proposals in action by the Carter Administration.

Heavy fighting is reported between Iran and Iraqi-backed Kurdish rebels.

December 31, 1980 — Algerian intermediaries leave Washington with the latest American proposal for ending the hostage crisis.

An Iranian radio broadcast threatens to put the hostages on trial and possibly execute them. The United States responds that it continues to hold the Iranian Government responsible for the safety of the hostages.

January 1, 1981 — Ayatollah Alemah Nouri, a leading Iranian cleric but not a member of the government, asks that the hostages be tried as spies. He says that "not putting spies on trial is wrong, whatever reason was given for it; they were caught on spying charges. We should not have indulged in bargaining." Mr. Nouri is generally considered a moderate cleric aligned with President Bani-Sadr rather than the hard-liners.

Ayatollah Khomeini appeals for cooperation between Iran's armed forces; the Parliament and the President control separate forces.

January 2, 1981 — Algerian intermediaries return to Teheran with the latest U.S. proposals. Iran makes no official comment on the new proposals.

January 3, 1981 — Algerian intermediaries discuss the new U.S. proposals with Iranian officials.

A Teheran radio broadcast says that it "seems completely unlikely" that the hostages will be released before the inauguration of Ronald Reagan as President, and it warns Mr. Reagan that Iran will not make any new concessions to him.

The New York Times reports that there seems to be renewed discussion of military rescue operations for the hostages among military planners.

Diplomatic sources report that Iranian air raids halted Iraqi oil exports for most of the last month, and that pumping has only partially resumed.

January 4, 1981 — Diplomatic sources report that Iran has transferred the three hostages being held in the Foreign Ministry to a new secret location, possibly with some of the other hostages.

Iran's Pars News Agency reports that the new U.S. proposals for settlement of the hostage dispute are under government study.

Iranian fundamentalist clerics denounce President Bani-Sadr's handling of the war with Iraq, saying he has failed to put the Iranian military on attack.

Iraq says that after four months of fighting it has won the war with Iran.

January 5, 1981 — The United States says it has received a report from the Swiss Embassy in Teheran confirming that the three hostages held at the Foreign Ministry have been moved to another location. It says it has been told that the move has been made in an effort to consolidate government control over the hostages. It says also that the three hostages successfully resisted such a transfer on December 23; there was a "pushing and shoving" incident that day, and the Iranians did not try to overpower the three Americans.

More than 30 of the companies who have filed suit against Iran file court papers opposing the Carter Administration's efforts to suspend the suits while the negotiations for the hostages are going on.

Iran announces that its troops have gone on a counteroffensive against Iraq.

January 6, 1981 — Ayatollah Khomeini gives his approval to Algerian assistance in efforts to resolve the hostage crisis. While details on the state of the negotiations are unclear, the remark seems to indicate that Algeria would act either as a go-between or a guarantor of American promises.

Carter Administration officials say Iran has asked for clarification of specific issues involved in the latest U.S. proposals. They say that responses to the Iranian questions will be expedited and sent tomorrow, but they again caution against assumptions that a breakthrough is imminent.

Iraq confirms that Iran has launched a counteroffensive but disputes Iranian claims of successes in the venture.

Algeria informs Washington that Iran is ready to complete a deal if it receives $9.5 billion in its frozen assets at once. (The United States replies that it could find only $7.3 billion that could be returned at an early stage.)

January 7, 1981 — Warren Christopher unexpectedly flies to Algiers to discuss the status of the current negotiations with Iran. He tells reporters that "nothing would please me more than to tell you that I thought we were on the verge of an imminent breakthrough, but I can't conscientiously say that."

Behzad Nabavi says that Algerian intermediaries have offered new suggestions for easing the resolution of the hostage crisis, and have offered to undertake the warrantees of both sides. Mr. Nabavi says the Algerian proposals have been agreed to in principle.

The Justice Department says it will not file criminal charges against Ramsey Clark, who defied an Administration ban on travel to Iran to attend a conference in Teheran in June 1980. No action will be taken against the nine other Americans who traveled with him, either.

Iran claims further victories in its counteroffensive against Iraq, but Iraq claims to have halted the counteroffensive.

Ronald Reagan expresses hope about the new developments in the Iranian situation.

January 8, 1981 — President-elect Reagan offers qualified support for the new negotiations for release of the hostages, but says he cannot sign a "blank check" for the Carter Administration's proposals if the crisis is not resolved by January 20. Asked if he would feel free to take a different negotiating stance should the crisis not be resolved by the beginning of his Administration, he says, "Yes. That's right."

Edmund Muskie says that the major difference between the American and Iranian positions at this point is how much money Iran will receive when the hostages are released. The Iranians want the totality of their frozen assets, while the United States says that several billion dollars of the assets cannot be released because they are subject to private suits in the United States.

Iraqi leaders ridicule the Iranian claims of success in their counteroffensive.

January 9, 1981 — Iran raises additional questions about the latest U.S. proposals, causing Warren Christopher to extend his stay in Algiers. But John Trattner, the State Department spokesman, reports that serious differences between the two countries' positions still exist.

President Bani-Sadr says that Iranian forces will continue to fight Iraq despite the high cost the war has imposed on Iran.

January 10, 1981 — Some details of the latest U.S. proposals on the hostage issue are released. Reportedly, the United States has told Iran that about $5.5 billion of the frozen assets could be released as soon as the hostages are freed. Another $1.5 billion could be made available as soon as arrangements are worked out with American banks abroad that hold loans on which Iran has defaulted. About $2.5 billion will have to be retained in the United States pending the resolution of private suits against Iran. The U.S. estimate of the total assets in the United States is $9.5 billion, considerably less than the $14 billion Iran claims or the $11 billion previously estimated by the United States.

Ahmad Azizi says that a reply — "most likely" an acceptance — to the new proposals will be given by Iran before January 16. He says the Algerian proposals are acceptable in principle.

Iraq claims to have crushed the Iranian counteroffensive; Iran claims to have broadened it.

January 11, 1981 — Ahmad Azizi says that Iran has accepted the Algerian suggestions, "which involve international guarantees given by the United States, instead of paying the money into Algerian banks. . . . Tomorrow or the next day, the final answer of Iran will be given to the Algerian delegation."

Warren Christopher remains in Algiers for a fourth day, in order to speed communications between Iran and the United States.

Ronald Reagan says in an interview with *U.S. News and World Report* that if the crisis is not resolved when he takes office he will "start with a clean slate" as far as negotiations are concerned.

January 12, 1981 — The Iranian Government introduces "emergency" legislation in the Parliament which would give cabinet ministers full power to reach agreement with the United States on release of the hostages. Two bills are involved; one authorizes arbitration behind closed doors and the other nationalizes the wealth of the late Shah and his family.

Hashemi Rafsanjani says he sees no reason why the Majlis would not approve the legislation.

President Carter says the possibility of resolving the crisis "looks better" but that he is still unable to predict success before his term ends.

Warren Christopher calls on President Chadli Benjedid of Algeria to express American gratitude for Algeria's role in the current negotiations. John Trattner says the visit was not intended to signal a breakthrough.

President Bani-Sadr says that Western sanctions against Iran have hampered his country in the war with Iraq. Iraq displays for journalists more than 30 tanks it says were captured in the process of turning back the Iranian offensive.

January 13, 1981 — Iran postpones the vote on emergency legislation designed to speed resolution of the hostage crisis after the Council of Guardians, which must approve the constitutionality and adherence to Moslem principles of all legislation, fails to attain a quorum. Officials say the vote will take place tomorrow.

Administration officials say they fear that chances of resolving the hostage issue by January 20 could be undercut by factionalism in Iran.

They say they believe that political opposition may be responsible for today's delay in the vote on emergency legislation.

Le Monde reports it has learned that a complete agreement between Iran and the United States has been reached; U.S. officials deny this.

Warren Christopher reports that progress is being made on the resolution of differences between Iran and the United States.

The Government of Iran files suit in New York against 65 persons, including members of the late Shah's family, who, it says, are guilty of "taking the money from the Iranian government and using it for themselves and their families."

The only surviving member of the group which seized the Iranian Embassy in London last May says that the seizure was planned and organized in Iraq with government help.

January 14, 1981 — Iran's Parliament passes the bill allowing arbitration of the hostage situation. Behzad Nabavi tells the members that "the hostages are like a fruit from which all the juice has been squeezed out. Let us let them all go."

Action on the bill to nationalize the late Shah's wealth will not be taken until at least Sunday, but negotiators say that the bill does not seem to be necessary for a resolution of the crisis.

U.S. officials express optimism while cautioning that a final agreement has not yet been reached.

At Iran's request, Swiss authorities move today to block the sale of the late Shah's villa there, pending a court ruling on who now owns it.

Olof Palme flies to Baghdad to begin a new U.N.-sponsored attempt to stop the war between Iran and Iraq.

Oil industry sources and the U.S. Government say Iran appears to have brought its oil export figures back to the level they were at before the beginning of the war with Iraq.

January 15, 1981 — Iran sends a formal response to the United States, reportedly saying that the current proposal involves "problems" but seems to be "workable."

Behzad Nabavi says Iran has accepted the proposal "in general" but that for it to work the United States must begin depositing the frozen assets in a third country, before the end of the day tomorrow.

U.S. officials are somewhat circumspect on the response, saying they need time to study it, but one official says that as a result of the response it now appears possible that the crisis will be resolved by January 20.

Officials of U.S. banks that have been negotiating secretly with lawyers for the Iranian Government say they have made their "last and best offer" for settling the financial disputes involved in resolving the crisis. One banking official says he believes the banks will accept any orders issued by President Carter concerning the frozen assets, and will sue the United States later for any damages they feel they have been caused.

January 16, 1981 — Iran sends a proposal that reduces its demand to $8.1 billion. The United States, by scraping together additional interest, comes up with $7.9 billion, to which Iran agrees. (Iran decides to use some of its unfrozen assets to pay off loans with overseas banks. This gives Iran somewhat less than $3 billion net. Iran proposes that the exact numbers involved be included in a document that would not be published immediately.)

A group of financial and legal experts from the United States and Britain is flown to Algiers in an attempt to work out a final agreement for release of the hostages. U.S. officials say there are still procedural problems involved in the transfer of frozen assets to Algeria. They insist that no final agreement exists, even in principle.

Behzad Nabavi says there is "no obstacle in resolving the issue. Only the real willingness of Washington can bring decisive results today." He says Iran seeks the return of its assets, minus money Iran owes on loans from U.S. banks.

January 17, 1981 — Iran and the United States continue to exchange messages in an effort to reach final resolution of the hostage crisis. The amount of frozen Iranian assets in the United States and the timing of their return appear to be the major outstanding issues.

January 18, 1981 — Behzad Nabavi, Iran's chief hostage negotiator, announces that agreement has been reached on the release of the hostages. Official announcement of the agreement by the governments of Iran and the United States is delayed, however, because of the need to translate and check the specifics of the financial terms.

The breakthrough in the negotiations reportedly comes because of an Iranian agreement to repay immediately almost all of its loans from American banks in return for unfreezing Iran's assets.

NO HIDING PLACE

President Carter makes plans to fly to Wiesbaden, West Germany, in the last hours of his Presidency to greet the freed hostages.

January 19, 1981 — An unexpected hitch delays announcement of a final agreement and forces President Carter to cancel his trip to West Germany. Iran blames American banks for the delay, saying bank officials filed an unexpected appendix to the agreement which would force Iran to drop its claims to certain of its assets which have not yet been located.

President-elect Reagan asks President Carter to serve as his special envoy to greet the hostages in West Germany when they are released.

Mr. Christopher signs three documents for the United States, two that are made public that set up a procedure for the return of the frozen assets upon release of the hostages, and one that is not made public. He also signs an "escrow agreement," which deals with the way unfrozen assets are to be moved to Iran.

January 20, 1981 — Agreement for release of the hostages is finalized and signed early today. An Algerian plane carrying the hostages leaves Teheran at 12:25 P.M. EST, minutes after President Reagan completes his inaugural address. The freed hostages fly first to Algiers, where they are met by the State Department team which negotiated their release. Then they go to Wiesbaden for several days of medical and psychiatric treatment before their return to the United States.

January 21, 1981 — Former President Carter greets the hostages in Wiesbaden. As the freed men and women begin to contact their families, stories of mistreatment while in captivity emerge. Hostages who had been freed earlier also begin to speak in stronger terms about brutalities they suffered.

Reagan Administration officials say they are reviewing the terms of the agreement with Iran, leading to speculation that the new Administration might decide not to meet some of the terms.

January 22, 1981 — As more stories about the treatment of the hostages appear, Iranian officials charge that the former captives are being brainwashed by the U.S. Government.

Reagan Administration officials say they fully intend to honor the agreement with Iran.

January 25, 1981 — The former hostages fly to the United States and are taken to the U.S. Military Academy at West Point for private reunions with their families.

January 27, 1981 — Forty-one of the former hostages hold a press conference at West Point. Afterward the freed men and women are flown to Washington for a formal reception at the White House.

January 30, 1981 — Twenty-one of the former hostages attend a ticker-tape parade held in New York City in their honor.

February 4, 1981 — Gregory A. Persinger, one of the freed hostages, files a $120,000 lawsuit against the Iranian Government, charging that his diplomatic privileges, immunities and civil rights were violated when the embassy was seized. The suit apparently challenges a part of the U.S. agreement with Iran which barred damage claims by the hostages.

February 18, 1981 — Cynthia Dwyer, an American free-lance journalist who had been jailed in Iran on espionage charges, is freed after being convicted of espionage and sentenced to the time already served since her arrest in May 1980.

Index

303

305

INDEX

INDEX

INDEX

INDEX